S0-DVC-441

Other parents have been there before you. They've felt intimidated by their own children . . . baffled when their grade-schoolers talk about RAMs, URLs, and ROMs . . . spent $50 on a software program their kids wouldn't touch. The PC Dads^SM came to their rescue. Now they can come to yours—with expert advice on getting started, going online, and becoming (almost) as skilled as your kids! Discover . . .

- The ABCs of taking control of and managing your home computer. Remember, you, not your kids, paid for it.

- How to make your home computer a family affair . . . great ideas, including tips for using the PC with your toddler, plus age-specific activities for older kids.

- The secrets of higher grades and improved self-esteem for your children . . . from math skills to researching online, it's all here!

- The danger of online stalkers and con men who come on to unsuspecting kids. Some great tips will keep this from happening to your children.

- How to steer your kids away from violent software . . . plus tips on protecting them from the seduction and risks of the pastime that's fast replacing TV: computer games.

PLUS . . . dozens of Web sites for education; special tips for home schooling families; wonderful software recommendations for toddlers, grade-schoolers, and teenagers . . . and more!

THE PC DADS^SM GUIDE TO BECOMING A COMPUTER-SMART PARENT

QUANTITY SALES

Most Dell books are available at special quantity discounts when purchased in bulk by corporations, organizations, or groups. Special imprints, messages, and excerpts can be produced to meet your needs. For more information, write to: Dell Publishing, 1540 Broadway, New York, NY 10036. Attention: Director, Special Markets.

INDIVIDUAL SALES

Are there any Dell books you want but cannot find in your local stores? If so, you can order them directly from us. You can get any Dell book currently in print. For a complete up-to-date listing of our books and information on how to order, write to: Dell Readers Service, Box DR, 1540 Broadway, New York, NY 10036.

The PC Dads^{SM} Guide

to Becoming a

Computer-Smart Parent

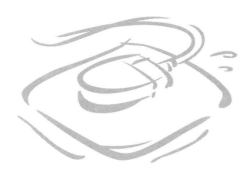

Mark Ivey and Ralph Bond

Chapter title artwork by Susan Williams

Computer illustrations and line art by Dan Mandish

A Dell Trade Paperback

A DELL TRADE PAPERBACK

Published by
Dell Publishing
a division of
Random House, Inc.
1540 Broadway
New York, New York 10036

Intel and the PC Dads are registered trademarks of Intel Corporation.

Please be advised that the ESRB rating icons "EC," "KA," "E," "T," "M," "AO," "ECI," "EI," "TI," "MI" and "AOI" are copyrighted works and certification marks owned by the Interactive Digital Software Association and the Entertainment Software Rating Board and may be used only with their permission and authority. Under no circumstances may the rating icons be self-applied to any product that has not been rated by the ESRB. For information regarding whether a product has been rated by the ESRB, please call the ESRB at 212-759-0700 or 1-800-771-3772.

Excite, Excite Search and Excite Logo are trademarks of Excite, Inc., and may be registered in various jurisdictions. Excite screen display copyright 1995–1998 Excite, Inc.

Portions Copyright Netscape Communications Corporation, 1998. All Rights Reserved. Netscape, Netscape Navigator and the Netscape N Logo, are registered trademarks of Netscape in the United States and other countries.

Purple Moon Place Web page printed with permission of Purple Moon.

The San Diego Zoo Internet home page courtesy and copyright of Zoological Society of San Diego.

Super Snooper main Web page reprinted courtesy of Super Snooper.

Text and artwork copyright © 1998 by Yahoo! Inc. All rights reserved. YAHOO! and the YAHOO! logo are trademarks of YAHOO! Inc.

Copyright © 1999 by Intel, A Delaware Company.

All rights reserved. No part of this book may be reproduced or transmitted in any form or by any means, electronic or mechanical, including photocopying, recording, or by any information storage and retrieval system, without the written permission of the Publisher, except where permitted by law.

The trademark Dell® is registered in the U.S. Patent and Trademark Office.

Library of Congress Cataloging in Publication Data
Ivey, Mark.
The PC Dads℠ guide to becoming a computer-smart parent /
by Mark Ivey and Ralph Bond.
p.   cm.
Includes index.
ISBN 0-440-50843-6
1. Computer literacy.   2. Computers and children.
I. Bond, Ralph.   II. Intel.   III. Title.
QA76.I94   1999
004.16—dc21   98-45672
CIP

Printed in the United States of America
Published simultaneously in Canada
February 1999
10   9   8   7   6   5   4   3   2   1

Acknowledgments

The PC Dads program would not be what it is today without the support of some very cool people, and the same is true of the book.

We'd like to thank everyone at Intel who has helped us along the way, but in particular Sandra Duncan, Dana Houghton, Tracy Koon and Pam Pollace. We'd also like to thank the folks who supported us on those long, sometimes grueling road trips, keeping the CyberSafari and PC Frontier workshops shows running on time: Charlotte Bryant, Bert Kinyon, Doug Guillot and the dozens of Intel volunteers at sites in Phoenix, Portland, DuPont, Washington, and San Jose, who jumped in to help, along with the thousands of parents we met along the way who provided comments that helped shape the book.

The book was truly a teamwork effort. Special thanks to our agent, Daniel Greenberg, who never tired of our calls and questions, our editors Mary Ellen O'Neill and Mitch Hoffman, who patiently pulled it all together never missing a beat, our crackerjack artist, Susan Williams, and to Portland photographer Michael McDermott—who makes us look almost as good as we do in real life—for the cover photo. We also owe a lot to the researchers, support staff and other Intel managers who have helped support our program and the book, such as Kristi Becker, Joanna Ellis, Charlotte Gibberman, Elizabeth Kemper, O. C. O'Connell and Jan Rowell.

We're truly glad to be part of a company with an environment that fosters creativity and risk taking, making it possible to develop a program like the PC Dads. We owe a lot to the original founders of Intel and the pioneers who built it into a global powerhouse. Their spirit is alive and well today in our program and thousands of others across the world.

Finally, we'd like to acknowledge our own families, who hung in there with us during the ups and downs that go with any book. Their experiences, feelings and frustrations dealing with computers provided the fuel for the book and their very presence provided inspiration that only a parent can appreciate.

Mark and Ralph

Contents

Contents

The PC Dads^{SM} Guide

to Becoming a

Computer-Smart Parent

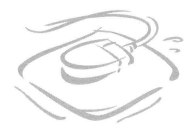

Introduction

Kids and computers are a lot alike; great when they work, maddening when they misbehave. Some days you might even wonder why you even brought the varmint home in the first place (the computer, not your kid). Yet you can't escape them: personal computers are everywhere, and combined with the Internet, their presence and impact is growing like wildfire. Listen to the language of the kids as they talk about "Web pages," "e-mail address" and "hypertext markup language."

What planet are we on anyhow?

This book is designed to help parents get a grip on computers and the Internet and, in a sense, level the playing field. Kids have a huge edge when it comes to computers. Many grew up with the things, they're not afraid of the keyboard and they probably have more *time* than you do to learn all this stuff. Watch a child play a video or computer game and you'll see a laserlike focus. When was the last chance you had hours to sit down and study a program, or anything? No wonder you can't understand what they're saying. It's as if they've been studying a foreign language.

We realize you may not have time to take classes or spend hours wading through computer encyclopedias that masquerade as guidebooks or, gasp, the actual computer manual. But with a little effort you can read this book and get a lot out of it—you may actually enjoy it. Rather than bitter medicine that you *must* take to feel better about that money you shelled out for that computer, think of this book like a good roadmap to a new world.

You need this book if:

- You want to become techno-hip so you can catch up with your kids and maybe impress the neighbors. Or you simply want to know more about buying, managing and enjoying the computer—and don't want to wade through a computer book.
- You've heard the horror stories about the Internet and you want to find out what's going on. You may have a preteen or teenage kid who's surfing the Net behind closed doors and you want to get on top of the situation before he or she gets into trouble.
- *You're* computer smart, but you want to help a friend, neighbor or spouse who needs advice and tips on computers and the Internet. Or maybe you're a geek and you want to know how to explain your vast knowledge in English.

The good news is we've written the book in simple concise English. As Intel's PC Dads (Mark Ivey and Ralph Bond), we've spent a lot of time distilling this material into something normal people can understand. We call a central processing unit the "brain" of the computer, the hard disk is the "filing cabinet" and memory is the "work bench": the bigger the work bench, the more work you can do, and so on (we're big on garage metaphors). We also restrained ourselves, editorially speaking. We're *not* going to tell you everything there is to know about computers, just the most important stuff. You won't read about managing memory or reformatting a hard drive. True, these are fascinating subjects, but not what most parents tell us they want to hear. We've based this on our road trips and workshops across North America and discussions with hundreds of parents, from Texas to New Brunswick. In other words, the book is designed from top to bottom for average humans—not geeks, engineers or Bill Gates wannabes, but nontechnical people. If that's you, keep reading.

We also bring a little different perspective to the subject than the usual computer experts. While we do know our way around the computer, we also have eclectic backgrounds—Mark's a former *Business Week* writer, Texan by birth and public speaker; Ralph grew up in southern California, was a computer technical writer and art history teacher for years, dabbled in writing and more recently worked in corporate marketing. We met back in 1995 and formed the PC Dads, which stands for "personal computer," not "politically correct." But our main claim to fame is we're computer-savvy parents. PC Dads, with an emphasis on Dads.

When you have survived a few years of parenthood (Ralph's daughter is fourteen, his son is ten; Mark's sons are nine and thirteen, his daughter is four), you wind up with a different perspective—slightly crazed maybe, but also broader in some sense. When we sit down to choose programs and work on the computer, we're not just looking to further our own goals. We've got to worry about our kids and our spouses, and each of them is unique. As you read this book, you'll see that our perspective is focused on parenting, child development and learning. The idea is to show you how to use the computer as a tool to help your children grow emotionally and intellectually, rather than just use technology for technology's sake. This is at the heart of our key concept—the computer-smart parent.

Last, we work for Intel Corp., one of the most powerful technology companies on earth. That's good because it means you're getting a lot of technical information from Intel. There are a lot of sharp engineers working around here, and we've been lucky enough to tap into some of that brainpower. Since 1996 with Intel's support, we've been on a personal and corporate mission: to help demystify the computer and the Internet for average folks. Our slogan all along has been we'll "go anywhere, do anything" to reach consumers. Our arsenal now includes articles, broadcast appearances, a Web site and our colorful, sometimes whacky, public workshops—the "PC Safari" and the "PC Frontier." We knew we were doing something right when Mark's mom in East Texas, who only recently updated her 1959-vintage rotary-dial telephone, saw us on CNN and commented that we "looked like we knew what we were talking about," although she didn't understand it all. We're getting there.

All of this definitely shaped this book, which is based on our personal experiences. The point is we're not going to try to impress you with fancy terms.

We just want to help you solve your problems, and learn enough about computers and the Internet to lead the way for your family.

The problems are more than just what kind of PC to buy or whether you should be on the Internet. They happen to be deeply seated in our attitudes toward computers. If you're a baby boomer like us, you didn't grow up with PCs and you may have an indifferent or even hostile view toward this Brave New World. You're not alone. We constantly hear the same concerns:

1. People are scared of technology. Computers are something foreign, something *unnatural*. Isn't this why we skipped those calculus classes in high school and college?

2. People are scared of their kids. Well, not literally, but many people are worried that their kids know more than they do about an important issue—much more. In his book, *Growing Up Digital*, author Don Tapscott calls this big knowledge gap a "generation lap" and extols the wonders of having kids lead the way into the new Digital Age. While it makes fascinating reading, this kind of trend worries a lot of folks who have been too busy earning a living to learn their way around a computer—or they just haven't been inclined. On the other hand, some parents worry their kids won't have the technology skills to thrive in the next century.

3. People are scared of change. Nothing seems stable anymore—jobs, families, the earth. And computers reflect the change as much as anything. They're always changing, advancing, getting more powerful—where is it all going? The Internet has further fueled fears by shattering boundaries of space and time and opening windows to a world that most of us oldsters could not have imagined. Who'd even heard of the Internet a generation ago? We strongly believe the changes the computer and Internet are unleashing will untimately lead to better productivity and more educational and personal growth possibilities, to name just a few benefits. But that's hard to see when you're in the middle of the storm. How people manage the computer and the Internet, to some degree, reflects how they're managing overall change in their lives.

This brings us to the core concept of the book, what we call "computer-smart parents." While these parents may have these fears, they're tackling them head-on. Most of them are not computer experts, but they're learning. They're also establishing home programs and approaches, using the computer as an educational tool, that will assure their family will move ahead into the Digital Age. We're encouraged and inspired by these efforts, and feel like they've been glossed over in the heated coverage of the Internet.

This book is designed to help you become a computer-smart parent—and, just maybe, catch up with your kids. We've looked back at the many parents we've met and the questions we've answered and carefully cherry-picked subjects of most interest to parents and average users:

- How do I know when to buy a computer when things are changing so fast? (Chapter 2)
- When should I start my daughter/son on the computer? (Chapter 7)
- How do I balance games and educational programs? (Chapter 4)
- How do I get started and go online? (Chapter 5)
- How do I keep my kids safe on the Internet? (Chapters 12 and 13)

You'll notice a few features of the book right off:

- Personal stories: we weave in personal anecdotes, when possible, to make our points. These will give you a "down in the trenches" view from our home front of some of the issues, such as buying nonviolent games for kids.

- Sidebars: these are usually key ideas we want to stress, or resources, such as Web sites or publications.

- Glossary and Appendix: you'll find a glossary in the back of the book featuring key terms, along with an appendix listing of the favorite software programs and Web sites mentioned in the book. Hang on to these for later reference.

- Focused questions: We felt like summaries were too easy, so we include "focused questions" at the end of each chapter. We want you to think about the matieral and use the questions to test your spouse or family. Think of them like pop quizzes.

A good tip is to mark key ideas or phrases while reading this book. You might want to keep a notepad handy to jot down ideas as you come across them. Then go back and focus on the chapters that pertain to your kids and family. Spend some time on them, maybe even go over them with your kids or spouse. This needs to be a family experience.

The book is mainly geared toward novices. It isn't a comprehensive tome on everything you wanted to know about computing. It's designed as a basic primer to help you get started and to tackle some of the basic issues. It's a starting point, not an end. So if you want to get computer hip, join us on our adventure.

Making Sense of Computers

Before you jump in, here's a five-minute history lesson. It'll show you where we came from and may spark some ideas if you're thinking of developing a computer literacy program. We've found that launching any kind of high-impact program like this requires creativity, perseverance and the guts to risk failure and look stupid at times. We speak from experience.

It all started with a single concept: making computers understandable—and fun. The name—PC Dads—would come later. But first we had to deal with making our subject matter halfway interesting, maybe even entertaining. That would take some doing.

Both of us had been at Intel a few years by the time we met in early 1995. While we worked in different departments, we were "cubicle mates" (if you don't know what a cubicle is, read the Dilbert cartoons) at Intel in Hillsboro, Oregon, just a stone's throw from Portland (if you have a strong arm). In our off hours, both of us were being bombarded with questions from neighbors and friends about the computer—after all, since we worked for Intel, we should know *everything* about computers, right? After comparing notes one day in the Intel cafeteria, we cooked up an idea of conducting an evening workshop for adults in a local elementary school. The focus would be on "how to buy a PC." The sixty-minute segment would cover all the basic issues and leave time for questions. To add a little color, we dressed up in jogging suits complete with ball caps and whistles and called ourselves the "PC Coaches."

The first show was an eye-opener. It was a May evening and eighteen weary parents piled into a cozy classroom at Oak Hills Elementary, in Beaverton, Oregon (between Portland and Hillsboro).

As we launched into our explanation of memory management, a tired-looking mom stood up and said, "Honestly, I don't care about RAMs and all that. I just want to buy something that works."

We were shocked—we always thought memory management was fascinating!

Then another mom chimed in with her perspective: "I'm not even sure where to start, and how to get to a point where I can start learning. All this jargon makes my head spin. Every time I sit down at the computer and open up a manual I feel like I'm lost in the jungle."

Ding!

A bell went off in our feeble brains. "This woman's on to something." "Jungle . . . jargon . . . lost . . ." It is a jungle out there! RAMs, ROMs, CPUs—what are we doing? Left to their own devices to deal with this jargon, people might as well be on another planet.

The next day we crafted a whole new presentation called the "PC Safari." The mission was to help people "cut through the jungle of jargon" and understand enough about computers to make good decisions buying, using and managing the beasts. To add color, we took a field trip down to the local army surplus store and bought green army shirts, camouflage trousers, boots and safari hats. We threw in machetes, rubber snakes and canteens to add some color. It was the beginning of what would become a new job, and a crusade, for us.

We did the school circuit for eight or nine months, putting on late-evening shows about every four to six weeks. Then in January 1996, we got our first big break: Intel's corporate marketing group needed some help with a traveling exhibition, the 150th America's Smithsonian, which Intel was helping sponsor. The company put us on a plane to Glendale, California, just outside Los Angeles, where we set up our show at a local mall. It would be our first show outside Portland—and the first of what would be dozens of cities across North America. The show was rolling.

More recently we've advanced to a show called the "PC Frontier," with a Western theme. With props like barbed wire, wagon wheels, rattlesnakes, it looks like a scene out of *Bonanza*—except for the computers and big-screen TVs. The idea is to show people the "frontier" of home computing, with the latest programs and gadgets. The *Rawhide* theme music appeals to aging Baby Boomers like us.

THE NAME

Coming up with a name wasn't easy. We wanted "PC Something" since our main focus was personal computers, but nothing seemed quite right. "PC Coaches" conjured up smelly locker rooms, and "PC Mentors" sounded stuffy. Then we hit on "Dads," which worked for both of us since Ralph has two kids and Mark has three. "Dads" sounded kind of old-fashioned and friendly, conjuring up those hokey 1950s shows like *Leave It to Beaver* and that old root beer brand.

Initially the name caused a stir at Intel and among colleagues;

they all wanted know what "D-A-D-S" stood for (everything in this business stands for something). We couldn't think of anything clever (Dads Against Doing Stuff . . . on the weekends), so we stuck with the truth: It's just dads, fathers, papas—nothing more, nothing less. The controversy eventually blew over.

Others, particularly TV hosts, would often ask us if "PC" stood for "politically correct." That was only good for one laugh and sound bite, then it was on to meatier subjects.

Then there was the legal issue. Intel decided to trademark the name, making PC Dads℠ Intel's first "human brand." The other trademarks—like Pentium processors—describe "things." Technically the SM in our case is trademarking a service, not Mark and Ralph, the people. We're still not quite sure how to take this— "human brand" sounds painful and being known as a "service" is an interesting spin . . . but it sounded like a compliment so we were glad to go along.

All along, from big cities to tiny towns, we worked hard to explain the technology in terms people could understand. We call our approach "down-home computing," and it's the basis for this book.

We've had our share of challenges along the road. We dodged a tornado at Disney World, a massive ice storm in Houston and a record heat wave in San Jose (is there a message here?). Because we often go into inner cities with our road shows, we deal with a wide range of computer users, from super-geeks aiming to take us on, to raw novices who are embarrassed to ask what a hard drive is. This creates special challenges and tremendous rewards.

Snapshot: Brooklyn Public Library, Brooklyn, New York, October 1997. We roll in with full PC Frontier gear, computers and all, and open the doors. There would be Open House all day for the public and a special workshop for teachers. When the curtain comes up, we're surprised to find that about half the

WHY THE PC DADS?
MARK:

It was a no-brainer when Intel offered me a chance to start the PC Dads as part of its educational outreach effort. I was passionate about public speaking and already speaking frequently before civic and school groups in Oregon, mainly focusing on technology and future trends. The PC Dads workshops allowed me to reach an audience far outside the state and expand my skills. It also gave me a chance to involve my three kids in my job, first my two sons and later my daughter. They could help out at the shows with me, try out the software, and work shoulder to shoulder with me. They thought it was cool. Most of their friends' parents go to work in suits and ties or normal casual clothes while I was wearing colorful costumes and conducting unusual cutting edge computer shows. All in all, it's been very rewarding for them and me. Who else has a dad who gets paid to speak and dress up like Indiana Jones and Jesse James?

RALPH:

In 1993 my family and I moved from our home in Irvine, California, and I left behind sixteen years of part-time teaching at a local community college to join Intel in Oregon. I loved everything about Oregon, but I really missed the rewards of teaching. When Mark and I cooked up the notion of doing live workshops, it represented an opportunity for me to keep my teaching skills alive. I couldn't resist. I could be a teacher again and work out all kinds of mid-life fantasies dressing up like a jungle explorer, and lately like a B-movie Western star. What a combination!

teachers have never been on the Internet. Words like "search engines" and "URLs" are Greek to them. About 10 percent of these teachers have never used a computer, and only a handful are up to date on the latest software programs. As hundreds of people shuffled through to try their hand at computing and the Internet and try out the latest gadgets, we're struck by the contrast between two worlds. There's our high-tech, digital dream stations, and there's the old library, a historical testament to learning with all its books and knowlege. We're also struck by the fact that our concept of literacy is expanding to include technological literacy as well as the ability to figure out what's on the printed page.

We like the kids, parents, teenagers, and senior citizens who pour through all day. Most seem sincerely interested in learning about computers. One little boy, about nine, seemed particularly impressed. Dressed in jeans, a Yankees baseball cap and blue-jean shirt, he hung on our every word and test-drove our computer programs and games for more than two hours. When we pulled him aside later we found that he and his (single) mom had just bought their first computer and he'd just sent his first electronic e-mail to an aunt in Florida. His eyes sparkled as he described his first day on the computer. It was like Christmas morning.

The book draws, in part, from that little boy and the thousands of other folks we've been lucky enough to come in contact with since the PC Dads were launched. Their questions, frustrations and experiences helped shape the book.

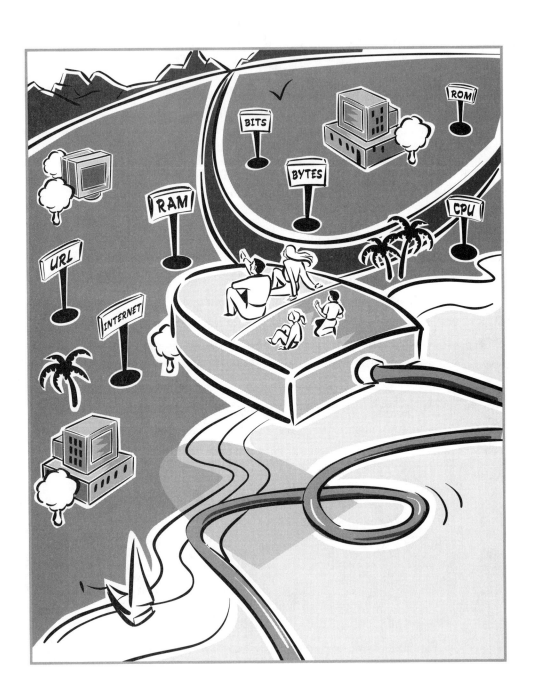

Taming the Mouse

DEVELOPING THE HABITS OF COMPUTER-SMART PARENTS

Are you using the computer, or is it using you?
—The PC Dads

New World

Imagine sitting down at your computer and beginning to install a new program, one you've been wanting to play for weeks. Suddenly, just seconds into the installation, the screen stops . . . freezes . . . locks up. You sit there staring at the blank screen for a while until it dawns on you: Nothing's happening. Nothing's going to happen.

What do you do? Do you:

a. Get help: Call your techie friend next door.
b. Get even: Get angry and throw something at the computer.
c. Get busy: Try to reload the program and/or reboot the computer.

If you answered "c," go to the head of the class—and keep reading. If you answered "a," you're still OK, but keep reading. If you answered "b," take an aspirin, sit down, and . . . yep, keep reading . . . fast.

This is just one example of how computer-smart parents manage these machines. It's easy to get mad at computers—who doesn't? But digitally savvy parents don't let it bog them down. They roll up their sleeves and attack the problem. If they can't solve it, they call on their geek friends. They learn from their mistakes.

As we've traveled the country, we've talked to parents of all stripes and flavors—rich, poor, black, white, and various shades of personalities. But they share a common determination to learn about the computer and manage it for their family.

These parents are a lot like you. When they first walked into a computer store and heard words like URLs, RAMs, ROMs, they may have felt like they'd landed on another planet or wondered if they were listening to chants from some ancient mystical religion. They might even have panicked when they heard those same "mystical chants" from their kids, and worried at the thought that their children knew more about an important subject (not football, baseball or music but technology!) than their parents.

But computer-smart parents have learned to take it in stride. They admit their fears up front (see sidebar, "The Seven Deadly Fears") and tackle them head-on. They take classes and talk to friends and teachers. They learn from their kids. And they're willing to ask themselves some soul-searching questions. What is my role in this new frontier? How much do I need to know? Where is

---

THINGS THAT GO BUZZ IN THE NIGHT

THE SEVEN DEADLY FEARS
(WHY PEOPLE DON'T COMPUTE)

Computing is a little like public speaking or ice skating; it looks so easy when someone else is doing it. Reality is a different matter. Here are some reasons people tell us they don't learn to compute:

1. Fear of looking stupid (in front of the kids). No one likes to be shown up by their kids, whether it's on the ski slopes or in front of a computer. Better not to try it at all.

2. Fear of the technical. Things that are technical are mysterious to many of us, and computers are no exception. Making it worse is that today's technology is pretty much invisible—you can't see inside that microprocessor. That makes it even scarier.

3. Fear of wasting money. No good parent thinks it is a good idea to waste money. To spend $1,800 for a computer today and see one twice as powerful for $1,000 a year later seems like a horrible waste. Many parents we talk to say, "I'll just wait and see what happens."

4. Fear of the unknown. When you were a kid did you ever dream of falling off a tall cliff or into a deep, purple sea? Some people have the same sinking feeling when they think about getting lost in a sea of computer jargon and programs. Just look at the computer ads. "64-bit AGP ATI RagePro 3D Graphics." Yikes! Where's your favorite blanky now that you really need it?

5. Fear that it's too late. Some folks think they're so far behind that it's hopeless. Better just sit on the sidelines and hope this computer thing passes.

6. Fear of being overwhelmed. So much information, so little time. The industry fans this fear by pouring out far too much information for the average human to comprehend. Check out the computer section in your local bookstore—it's filled with 500-page, twelve-pound books. It's enough to scare off the bravest among us.

7. Fear of turning into a geek. The ultimate fear. These folks see themselves turning into Bill Gates—minus the money. It ain't pretty.

Are any of these fears holding you back? Read on. You may not end up mastering public speaking or ice skating, but we're betting you'll feel a lot more confident at the keyboard by the end of the book.

the computer and technology taking us, as a society and as a family? How will my kids fare a year from now—ten years from now? Are we developing the necessary skills to stay ahead of the curve? Where is this all going?

In short, they do whatever it takes to get their arms around this beast, so they can move ahead personally and lead their families through this crazy, wonderful computer jungle.

Here's how they do it—and how you can too. Think of this section as the "Five Habits of Highly Effective *Computer-Smart* Parents."

1. They're not afraid to learn.

THEY CAN GET OUT
OF THEIR COMFORT ZONE

> *I am more and more sure that those who are in love*
> *with learning are in love with life.*
> —Charles Handy, *The Age of Unreason*

Unless you're a very young parent of very small children, you probably didn't grow up with computers. We didn't either. Color TVs and telephones were the big deal when we were kids. Then the 8-track tape came along and we were in heaven. Now kids take the computer and the Internet for granted. When Mark decided to go out car-shopping recently, his oldest son, Matthew, 13, looked at him like he was nuts. "Why are you going out to the car lots when you can go on the Internet?" he asked. While surfing the Internet for a car may seem strange to us, actually going out and kicking fenders seemed like a waste of time to Matthew. "I don't get it," he said (one of his favorite phrases).

Computers bring with them a new way of thinking, which means starting over in many ways. We have to learn new tricks and new approaches to how we communicate, learn and live with the computer and with all technology.

Much has been made about the "Net generation" kids. Several articles and books have glorified computer-savvy kids as the wave of the future, while inferring that parents are so far behind they'll never catch up—thus, the "generation lap" (*Growing up Digital*). While it's true that *most* kids do know more about computers than *most* of their parents, it's a stretch to generalize much beyond that or draw too many conclusions. The truth is that there are still many children who aren't computer literate and most kids are still learning their way around a computer. They're not designing Web pages or dabbling with digital imagery—just to take two examples. Millions of kids don't even have access to a computer more than a couple of hours a week at their school, and those may be old computers. And girls, in particular, still often lose interest by the time they get to be 12 or 13. So many kids are in the same boat as their parents: still learning.

We think that even computer-savvy kids need their parents involved. Just because they know technology terms and how to get on the Internet doesn't mean they're using the computer to learn, explore and get ahead in life. In most cases, that requires some adult help and direction. That's where Mom or Dad come in (of course this varies with age; a 10-year-old kid's going to need a lot more assistance, and a different approach, than a 15-year-old. In other words, you're not going to get too far treating a 15-year-old like their younger brother or sister—we've tried. It doesn't work).

Still, it is more of a partnership between kids and parents than when we were kids, and parents can learn a few things in terms of attitude from their kids. Many kids are natural explorers. They just keep poking around and experimenting until they find something that works, and many look at the computer and Internet as an exciting playground and resource, something to be mined for all it's worth.

Computer-smart parents take a similar approach. They're not afraid to explore until they figure something out. They're not afraid to start over and learn something new, whether it's a new software program or search engine on the Internet. They see it as an exciting challenge—not something to dread. But they go even further, setting up systems and approaches based on their years of experience in parenting.

Focus is the key. A smart parent learns just enough to stay ahead of the curve; they know how to find their way around the computer. They focus on programs that will help them and their family to move ahead, rather than aimlessly surfing the Web or dabbling in programs with little return. Less focused parents are all over the map. When they buy the computer they think they have to try out *every* new program. It's a bit like going to the library. Sure there are thousands of books on the shelves, but you don't have to read every one of them.

2. They value knowledge.

THEY KNOW THE COMPUTER CAN AID IN LEARNING

Knowledge is the fuel of the Information Age. With the constant turmoil in the job market, it's hard to imagine getting ahead nowadays without continuing to learn. Computer-smart parents understand this and make learning a high priority. TV takes a backseat to reading, computing and learning. Educational pursuits are highly prized; kids are rewarded at least as well for joining the chess club or mastering a tough subject as they are for scoring a goal or winning a popularity contest.

Of course, this is easier said than done. Kids gravitate toward what they like, not toward what you have in mind. But the computer gives you a new tool to help manage home activities and create a true learning environment. Part of the beauty of the PC is that, with younger children in particular, you're usually one-on-one with your child. This gives you a better shot at controlling computer activities and steering your kid in the right direction. Every hour that's spent on the PC, playing an educational program, is an hour the kid's not loitering on the street with buddies, watching TV or hanging out at the mall.

Another feature of computer-smart parents is that they approach computer time as "play." How they do this varies from family to family. Take typing, for instance. For months Mark worked with Matthew, 13, teaching him how to type using Mavis Beacon. He was doing OK and had learned the basic keys, but he lost interest after a while. One day Mark noticed him playing Age of Empires, a simulation game, with a buddy over the Internet (each at his own PC, playing on a single screen). He had to type secret codes and messages quickly to keep up with his friend, and his fingers were flying over the keys. As Matthew laughed along, Mark heard him say, "I'm getting pretty good at this typing." The moral for Dad: make learning fun (he still likes Mavis Beacon too).

A computer-smart parent looks for products that help children continue to learn, while engaging them on different levels (for more tips see Chapter 4: "Where the Rubber Hits the Road").

In her book, *Endangered Minds,* Jane Healy makes the case that everyday activities around the house are crucial in developing kids' minds. After reading Healy, even the ritual of sitting around the table having a dinner discussion takes on new meaning. The types of words parents use, the grammatical structure and their general level of intelligence in discussing issues all create a powerful framework for future learning. Healy claims (and a growing body of research supports her) that these ordinary activities help create physical connections in the brain that allow children to learn more quickly.

Computer-smart parents know the computer can aid this process of learning and maybe even brain development. It's a knowledge machine, waiting to be tapped.

3. They work together.

THEY SEE LEARNING AS A (FAMILY) PARTNERSHIP ACTIVITY

Here's a chilling story from an electronic mail message we received on AOL (America Online). We'd run a contest involving tips for protecting children online, and a thirteen-year-boy wrote in to say that he'd been in a battle of wits with his parents for control of the computer.

"My mom and dad don't have a clue what I'm doing on the computer. They may think they can manage what I'm doing on the Internet, but they're way behind," he wrote. "You can give them all the tips you want, but they don't have a chance."

Even if they turned off the power to his room or machine, he said, "I have a backup auxiliary system. I've got it all wired."

Clearly this was not a family in sync.

One of the best measures of a family, whether it's computers or anything else, is how they work together. With computer-smart parents and kids, information and knowledge flow both ways. Gone are the old days where Father (or Mother) knows best about everything. By the time the kid is eight or nine, a new type of relationship is emerging—a parent-child "partnership."

You can already see this in some classrooms. When we were in school, back in the Stone Age, the teacher was the almighty, single source of information. Now, slowly, it's starting to change. We saw this in our own backyard, after Century High, a local high school in Hillsboro, Oregon, was fully wired with Internet access. In some classes the teachers became more like guides or managers. They still drove the activities, of course, but much of the learning took place among small groups of students, learning from each other. This can be nerve-wracking for a teacher who is accustomed to full control. But it can be a blessing for one who's more flexible, since it opens up so many new opportunities.

Computer-smart parents are in the same boat. They teach, but they also learn. They lead, but also listen. Their role is more balanced than before, if somewhat less clear in some ways. It's a new model, with children and parents learning from each other.

The new partnership is a continuous balancing act. Sometimes, of course, you have to take control (as we tell our kids, this is a "guided democracy" and we're the guides). You also have to be willing to step back and let children fail sometimes. Computer-smart parents know their job isn't just to solve the kid's problems, it's to point them in the right direction so they can develop the answer. Giving a kid the freedom to explore, fail and finally solve a problem builds their mental muscles.

With a computer, a confident parent-partner will help guide a child through exercises, then pull back when the kid is trying to come up with the answer. Good parents have an intuitive knack for this.

4. They go with the flow.

THEY DON'T WASTE ENERGY RESISTING CHANGE

The computer and Internet are powerful new technologies that many of us don't fully understand, and it's difficult to compare them to older, mature technologies. Take your kitchen appliances. Refrigerators, toasters and other appliances are fixed; they're not going anywhere. They do one thing, or a few things, and that's it. The computer is different. It's organic, dynamic, changing. And when you use it right, you grow with it. In that respect, it's less like a gadget or appliance and more like an investment in a future stream of information, knowledge and entertainment.

Compare the computer to a car: A car gets you from point A to point B. Some cars go faster than others, some are bigger or more comfortable or operate more economically. But if you buy a car, you don't expect it to fly or travel under water. Its function is limited.

A computer's personality changes with whatever software you install—or software makers dream up. You may buy a computer thinking you'll use it for games, e-mail, keeping recipes or writing letters. The next thing you know you're using it to balance your checkbook, pay your bills, create a family photo album or compose music. When we bought our first computers years ago, we never dreamed that Mark's wife would wind up running a small business on it or that Ralph's wife would set up a sophisticated home financial management system on the PC—or that we'd be using it to write a book (including all the research on the Net).

Computer-smart families understand that the computer is unique and go with the flow. While others fuss over the rapid advances in the PC, and wait on the sidelines hoping that a perfect time will come to buy a PC, these parents jump right in and begin setting up systems that help them manage the computer and the changes that it will mean for their families.

The other big driver is the Internet and the growing trend of networked PCs. When you network or connect two computers and people you create a new phenomenon. No longer is the "personal computer" an isolated island; it's part of a

Moore's Law

What's behind this situation? The answer lies in the so-called microprocessor or "brain" of the computer (like the Pentium processors made by our company, Intel). Every eighteen months or so the speed of the microprocessor (actually, the number of transistors) doubles. (This phenomenon is known as "Moore's Law," named after our former chairman, Gordon Moore—a brilliant guy and nice man, by the way.) Moore's Law fuels an already intensely competitive industry. Every manufacturer of chips, computers and software is trying to outdo all the others in bringing more and better products to market cheaper and faster than the other guys. The only thing remotely close was the great horsepower race of the mid 1950s, and that was nothing compared to this.

All this competition leads to rapid advances in software and computers. This results in more powerful, lower-cost computers. And software makers push the potential of the new hardware with games and programs that are flashier, more realistic and more useful.

network, allowing people to exchange ideas like never before. This changes everything. Companies like Intel, where electronic mail allows employees to exchange ideas rapidly, operate much differently (and efficiently) than companies that don't use networks. The same will soon be true for families. Kids, parents, teachers and others who figure out how to communicate in this new electronic beehive will discover that it not only changes the way they receive and send information; it changes the way they live.

So where's it all going? No one knows exactly, and the possibilities are endless. But computer-smart parents will be prepared to ride the wave, wherever it goes. Even though keeping up with all the changes can be frustrating, smart parents don't blame the computer or technology for the way the world is. They understand that these tools aren't good or bad; they just *are*. Like other inventions before them, they can be used for good or bad.

Computer-smart parents look at the computer as an educational investment, more like a college education than a refrigerator. Their goal is to get the most out of their computer and help their family move ahead—nothing more, nothing less.

5. They're realistic.

THEY KNOW HOW TO BALANCE TECHNOLOGY WITH EVERYDAY LIFE

Once you're hooked on computing, it's tempting to think of it as an easy answer. Need to research? Go online. Need a date? Go into a chat room. Need a babysitter? Fire up the kid's favorite game.

But technology isn't an end in itself; it's a tool to get somewhere. Computer-smart parents never lose sight of the fact that computers have many limitations. A computer can never sing a toddler to sleep or replace a warm hug when times get tough. Computers also can't:

- Model or enforce a value system.
- Soothe a troubled child or make a scrape all better.
- Distinguish a mother's voice from everyone else's.
- Substitute for real-life experiences.
- Replace an absent parent.

Computers are best when they're reinforcing real-life experiences and learning. That's where computer-smart parents come in—they know knowledge doesn't happen in a vacuum or in a single sitting at the computer. They know that computer lessons must be tied into real life. After Mark's family visited a dinosaur exhibit at Oregon Museum of Industry and Science, they sat down at the computer and did some quick research on "dinosaurs" in Encarta, a multimedia encyclopedia. They looked up the history of dinosaurs, had the kids pick out their favorites and explore those, and studied various theories on why dinosaurs died off and became extinct. "Do you think it could happen to us?" Mark's son, Michael, asked. He was beginning to see a bigger picture.

Mark learned a little that day too. After he walked Nicole, then barely four years old, out of the exhibit, he stooped down and asked her how she felt about all those dinosaurs towering over her.

"Were you scared?" he asked.

She looked up at him, all blue-eyes, quizzically.

"Dad," she said. "They're dead."

So much for father knows best.

Looking Back, Looking Ahead

The computer and the Internet are ushering in a new era ripe with new promise and challenges. While all-electronic computers have been around since the 1940s, the real Information Age may really just be starting. Given this, it may help to think back to other times in history characterized by new technologies that ignited sweeping changes.

The printing press is a good example. When the movable metal type press emerged in the 15th century, it eventually generated a flood of books on everything from economics to farming to botany. Information could be transported almost anywhere. People went from communicating almost exclusively verbally to using the written word—a relatively complex, abstract code. Maps, legal documents and other paper-based forms of information emerged. Subjects like astronomy and history became available to the masses. Information could travel; education flourished.

Even today, five hundred years later, we're still figuring out how the printed word changes our way of communicating and thinking. Speech was and is heavily reliant on the senses. Both speaker and listener need to observe and feel. Emotion is inherent in the tone of speech and in the body language. (Think of the last time you yelled at your teenager.) In many ways, verbal communication is dynamic, open, free-flowing in a way that print is not.

That's because print is defined by the alphabet we use, the logical flow of information and the physical limitations of the page, just to name a few examples. Scholars like Marshall McLuhan have argued that the printed word forces us to think "in a linear, uniform, connected, continuous fashion," making us confine our communications to the new form, to adhere to new rules. He compared the book to a "hydrogen bomb" that created a new environment for communications, learning and living. The book and widespread use of printed material basically rewrote the rules of communications, forcing everyone to communicate and think in a different way.

A similar phenomenon may be taking place with the Internet, which is rewriting the rules of commerce and communications. The Internet—and networked computers—allow consumers to connect directly to merchants, parents to connect directly to teachers, kids to connect directly with other kids and so on. Space and time are evaporating as barriers, and mountains of information are now only a mouse click away. When children learn they have immediate access to information such as research material, or that they can communicate with friends across the globe, they look at the world differently. Never before have people been given so much information and potential power at their fingertips—and so little direction. It's not just a different way of doing business or research; it's a different way of communicating and dealing with the outside world. That means we need to begin *thinking* differently.

The short-term result is upheaval and confusion. But as the dust settles and as the old world of atoms gives way to a new one of bits and bytes, there'll be a clear separation between those who get it and those who don't. Computer-smart parents are already paving the way for their kids, creating environments that will help them to grow with the technology, to explore and learn and have fun. The idea isn't just to raise a computer-smart family, but to raise a smart family, using the computer and new technologies to get the job done.

FOCUSED QUESTIONS

- Are you eager to learn? What have you done to turn your home into a learning center? What are you doing to provide an educational role model for your kids? If you're not, what's holding you back?

- Do you value knowledge? What are you doing to make your home a center for learning? Are you focused on key learning programs and goals, or scattered?

- Are you working together as a family? What are you doing to learn from each other?

- Are you going with the flow? Are you flexible or do you fight change? What are you doing to master the new challenges and prepare for more change? Are you enjoying the ride?

- Are you realistic? Are you looking at the big picture or mired in details and the grind of daily life? Do you understand the limitations of the computer and technology? Have you articulated this to your kids?

2.

Buying a PC

UNDERSTANDING THE LINGO,
BEING A SMART PC SHOPPER

RAMs, ROMs, CPUs, what is all this stuff!
Every time I sit down in front of my computer I feel lost in the jungle.
—Parent attending a PC Dads workshop at the
Oak Hills Elementary School, Beaverton, Oregon

Public Service Warning: This chapter contains material that may not be fit for adult
consumption, and worse, could put you to sleep. Then again, it may
help you save tons of money, get the computer that's right for your family and
communicate with techno-crazed friends and kids.

The first thing you notice when you walk into a computer store as a new-comer are all the signs with alien terms, like "random access memory." How could anything "random" be good for your computer? Just how much memory is enough? And what does memory have to do with computing any-way?

Computer stores are fascinating places if you know the lingo. If you don't, you might as well be in another country. And if you want to buy a computer (let alone bring it into your home and make it an almost-member of the family), you need to know a few basic terms.

When we were growing up, teenagers talked about eight-cylinder hot rods and engine torque and used other car-related vocabulary. Now your kids and even once-normal neighbors throw around terms like "32-bit bus" and "24X CD-ROM" as if they were talking about the weather or sports.

Well, take heart. What follows are a few tips and pointers that will help you wade through the worst of the techno-gobbledygook. You won't become an expert or a nerd, but you will learn enough to hold your own the next time you go to the computer store or just want to talk to one of your kid's teenage buddies.

Note: The material that follows is geared to the novice. Even if you're already an expert this chapter may help you explain basic PC terms and concepts in plain English.

This chapter will help you:

- Understand the basics of the PC "landscape."
- Have the basic language skills needed to communicate with computer people and your kids.
- Be a smart PC shopper.
- Understand the ins and outs of buying a PC via mail order.
- Know if leasing or renting a PC makes sense for you.
- Figure out if buying new or used is the right path to take.

Looking Under the Hood

Don't run off and grab a screwdriver. We're not asking you to pop off the hood of a PC. What we'll do here is show you around the PC neighborhood, introduce you to the key players and explain why you need to know them. This exercise will help you work up the courage to bring one of these beasts into your home and the knowledge to feel a little friendlier toward it if it's already there.

Who's Who in the PC Neighborhood

Think of your personal computer as a complex city with energy and information surging around from one component to another. Essentially, all PCs take in information (or data, as computer nerds say), do something with it and produce a result—an image on the screen, the answer to a math problem, a text file you can print or send as electronic mail and so on. Making it all happen requires a team consisting of a brain chip (or microprocessor), memory, storage, and a cast of support hardware and software players to display pictures, make sounds, allow you to enter data and do other important stuff like surf the Internet.

What follows is a general view of the main characters in the PC neighborhood.

Hardware Versus Software

Before we move another muscle, let's make sure you get the difference between "hardware" and "software." "Hardware" refers to the "iron" in your PC. It covers everything from the box, keyboard, monitor, printers and all the components inside like the microprocessor (the brain chip) and the circuit boards. "Software" refers to the computer programs clever people create to do stuff like word processing, financial management and games.

The PC Dads List of Seven "Must-Know" PC Terms

1. Power Supply
2. CD ROM
3. Hard Disk
4. Floppy Drive
5. Fan
6. Sound Card
7. Modem Card
8. Graphics Card
9. Intel Pentium® II Processor
10. Motherboard
11. Memory Modules

Desktop PC (Tower Version)

• **The Brain or "Microprocessor."** This is a fancy term that stands for the chip or set of chips that execute all the instructions coming from the software. Executing a program simply means to take all of your information and requests (input via the keyboard and mouse), plus instructions from the computer program you're running, and make the decisions needed to run the program correctly. By itself, the microprocessor is like a super air traffic controller running a busy airport. It's also known as a CPU or Central Processing Unit.

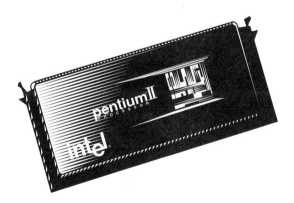

Microprocessors

• **The Operating System.** This is the master software control program that kicks into action before you run any other programs. These special programs (Microsoft's Windows for most PCs, and Apple's Mac OS 8 for the Macintosh crowd) work hand-in-hand with the brain chip to coordinate how each program will operate and in what form (pictures, sounds or printouts) the results of the program will be delivered to the user (that's you).

• **The Hard Disk.** Also fondly known as the "hard drive." This is your system's data file cabinet, the place where information is stored for later use. That includes material you and your kids create, programs you install and all the operating system and program information. The bigger the cabinet, the more it can hold, just like a regular file or tool cabinet. You measure the size of a PC hard drive in terms of millions (mega) or billions (giga) of bytes of storage capacity.

Hard Disk Drive

• **Bits and Bytes.** No, this isn't the bit you stick in a power drill. It's the basic unit of a code system that computers use to represent text characters or numbers, kind of like the genetic code for computers. In this code system (called the "binary system" because it uses only two digits) each bit can represent "yes" or "no," "on" or "off." It takes eight bits to represent a number or letter of the alphabet. A group of eight bits is called a "byte" of information.

• **Random Access Memory (RAM).** This one only sounds scary (random what?). It's actually a set of memory chips that serve as temporary storage for information from computer programs that the brain chip acts upon. This is where the operating system and the programs store information that's ready to be fed to the brain or shipped out to your monitor, printer or speakers. Turn off the computer and—*whoosh*—you lose the information in RAM (in contrast to the permanent information stored on a hard disk). Think of your PC's RAM as being a workbench. The bigger the bench, the more tools you can hold and the more work you can do. Get as much RAM as you can to run your programs smoothly.

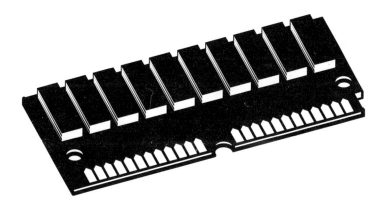

RAM / Memory Chips

• **Modem.** Computers used to be shy, now you can't shut them up. Like a teenager, PCs spend a lot of time on the phone these days, only these days most PCs are squawking to each other via the Internet. When your PC uses a regular telephone line to call up a service like America On-line, it's using a special computer "telephone" called a modem.

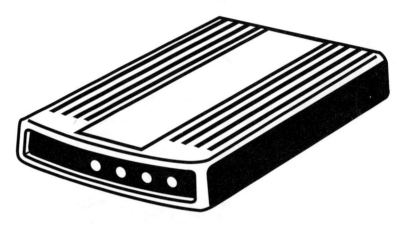

External Modem
(outside the PC)

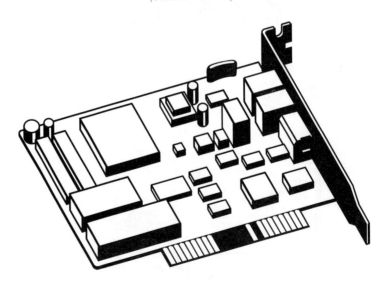

Internal Modem
(inside the PC)

• **CD-ROM Drive.** This is a piece of equipment that pops out a tray designed to hold disks that look just like music CDs. PC CDs hold huge amounts of information like text, images, videos, sounds, and software. Just like a music CD player, you place a PC CD on the tray, press a button and it slides into the player. Your PC system brain chip can "read" the information on the CD. (Trivia time: CD-ROM stands for "compact disk, read-only memory.")

Tip: Don't try using the CD-ROM tray to hold beverages. We ran across a guy who tried this and told us it doesn't work very well.

What's in a Name?
Fascinating Modem Tidbit

"Modem" is the contraction of two words—modulate and demodulate. In English, that means the modem takes the digital bits and bytes PCs understand and turns them into analog waves that the regular telephone line coming into your house can handle (that's the modulation part). A modem in the computer receiving your transmission translates the analog waves back into digital bits and bytes (demodulated). By translating all those bits and bytes, a modem helps users send and receive words and pictures over the phone line using your computer.

CD-ROM Drive

What Makes Computer Salespeople Tick

Computer salespeople have to eat too, so it makes sense that they want to move the products that offer them the best commission. That may not necessarily match up with your needs. The more you know about what you want to do and what kind of horsepower you need for the jobs you want to do, the better your chances are of finding the right PC.

Tip: Ask the salesperson if he/she is paid a commission before you buy. Not all computer stores have commissioned salespeople.

The PC Dads Five Golden Tips for Becoming a Smart PC Buyer

If you waded through the material so far, you should feel a little better. Okay, maybe it gave you a headache, but at least you're a lot more knowledgeable now. You're still not quite ready to hit the stores, though. Personal computers aren't like other appliances. You never have to worry about, say, a toaster becoming obsolete or wonder if the bread you buy two years from now will still be compatible with the slots. That's what makes computers interesting (and maddening). Buying a PC is an adventure. You're the guide, and along with cutting through the jungle of jargon, you have to learn the pitfalls so you can have a safe journey. Here are some tips to get you started:

TIP #1: START OFF ON THE RIGHT FOOT

So many people make the mistake of running down to the computer store with no pre-planning. You don't buy a car, boat or even power tool without figuring out why you need it. Why not apply the same common sense to a computer? The more you can articulate your needs, the better you can *manage* the computer salesperson and find the right solution.

TIP #2: PLAY THE FAMILY PC QUIZ GAME

Sit the whole family down and give a sheet of paper and a pencil to each "player." For the little ones too young to write, have an older brother or sister lend a hand. Ask each member of the family to respond to the following home PC quiz:

- What's the most important thing you want a PC to do—games, educational programs, exploring the Internet, home financial management, help with homework, word processing, all of the above?

- Are multimedia features such as realistic graphics, video and sound effects important to you?

- What about the Internet? How many minutes or hours each day do you plan to go "online."

- Are you planning to use a PC to edit, store digital pictures and/or movies?

- How much time do you plan to be on the computer?

- Who do you think is going to use the PC most of the time?

Now gather all of the answer sheets and read them out loud. Take notes and look for patterns. Tip: If entertainment, multimedia and doing anything with digital images appears consistently, you're going to need a powerful PC with lots of that RAM memory stuff and a big filing cabinet (i.e., a monster hard disk with lots of gigabytes). Think of it like buying a car. If rugged off-road driving is your passion, are you going to buy one of those hotsy-totsy convertible sports cars? Establish firm answers to your quiz so you can determine what kind of system you need *before* you go in the store.

P.S. Did you catch our trick question? We tossed in the last quiz question just for fun. The answers to it won't help you size up what you need, but it will give you some early warning on which family member thinks he or she "owns" the PC.

TIP #3: FIND OUT WHAT YOUR SOFTWARE WANTS

Check out the kind of software you'll be running. Software boxes display what the nerds call "system requirements." Look on the side or bottom of the box and you'll find a list of the components needed to run the program. Here are two samples representing the extremes of the home software spectrum: a demanding 3D game and a mainstream home activity program:

1. Hasbro Interactive's *Small Soldiers* action game system requirements are: "Pentium 100 MHz CPU; Windows 95; 16 MB of RAM,

4X CD-ROM drive; 3DFX card recommended; 25 MB free hard drive space; 1 MB SVGA card; 28.8 baud modem (for Internet play); Sound-Blaster compatible; mouse, DirectX version 5.0 required (included on CD-ROM). Supports Microsoft Sidewinder Gamepad."

2. Palladium Interactive *Ultimate Family Tree* program (which helps you research, design and display a family tree) requires these components: "IBM PC compatible 486DX/33 or higher (Pentium recommended), Color VGA monitor 256 colors minimum, thousands of colors capable video card recommended when using color photographs, double-speed CD-ROM drive, sound card. Win 95: 16 MB RAM min, 70 MB hard disk space. Windows 3.1: 8 MB RAM min, 49 MB of hard disk space. . . ."

Caution: If you see the words "minimum requirements" in a system requirements statement it means the bare bones equipment you need to operate the program. Look at the "recommended system" features list. This tells you what you *really* need to make the program run smoothly.

Make a list of the software you'll want to run and the recommended system requirements for each package. When you're done, find the program with the most demanding recommended memory, hard disk storage and microprocessor requirements. Use this data to determine *your* rock-bottom minimum system baseline.

So far, so good. Here's a sample chart we created to inspire you. Yep, it's dry and looks like a tax form, but it's designed to do a serious job. Copy it or make your own version and take it to the software department of your local computer store.

Software Requirements List

SOFTWARE TITLE	MEMORY Requirements (Recommended RAM)	HARD DISK (Megabytes) Recommended Amount	OPERATING SYSTEM	MICROPROCESSOR Recommended
Highest/Total				

Just for kicks Ralph did a quick audit of his home software collection at the time this chapter was being written. Microsoft's *Monster Truck Madness II* was the big hit game around his fort at that time. According to the box you need a minimum of a "multimedia PC" with a Pentium processor (133 megahertz speed minimum), 16 megabytes of RAM, and at least 30 megabytes of hard disk storage space. Unfortunately, system requirements statements like this don't tell you what kind of experience the minimum system will deliver. Ralph's business laptop, as it turns out, fits this minimum model. He loaded *Monster Truck Madness II* on it to see what would happen. It was quite a shock. He could play the game, but the images were crude and jerky and everything moved slowly. In contrast, his Pentium II processor–based home PC with 64 megabytes of RAM and a giant hard disk put him right in the thick of the race. He got full-screen, full-motion video, beautiful 3D graphics and super sound effects. The big lesson: Always buy ahead of the power curve if you can afford it.

Take the easy way out: If you're not up to all this homework or just feel lazy, make a copy of our "PC Dads Handy Buyer's Checklist" and take it with you to the store. Note, however, that things change fast in the computer world, so be sure to come to the PC Dads Web site and look at our latest recommendations (Go to www.intel.com/go/pcdads).

PC DADS HANDY BUYER'S CHECKLIST

Warning: Technology moves fast. Use the checklist below as a *general guide* to target the features to look for in a PC. As you'll see, the key elements to look for are a powerful brain, lots of memory and a big hard disk.

- **A Powerful Microprocessor.** The brain inside your computer is the most important component no matter what kind or brand of computer you buy. For general computing, a system with an Intel Celeron processor delivers good performance. For the best experience running games and other programs with demanding multimedia, opt for as much power as you can afford. In the world of PCs running the Windows operating system, Intel's Pentium II processor was the top-of-the-line at the time of this writing. Tip: Find out if the brain chip can be easily pulled out and "upgraded" later with a more powerful, newer model.

- **Hard Drive.** Permanent storage or "filing cabinet" for your computer, which stores all your main programs. Prices on hard drives continue to plummet. Go for one that can store 6 to 8 "gigabytes" (6 to 8 billion bytes).

- **RAM (memory).** These days you need 64 megabytes of memory. Make sure you get a computer with empty memory expansion slots designed to allow you to add memory modules as your needs grow. Memory modules are tiny boards or "cards" with memory chips on them that can be inserted into expansion slots. Also make sure you have free expansion slots to at least double the memory size.

- **CD-ROM.** Speed is the key in CD-ROM players (the thing in a PC that looks like a music CD player). The faster the "spin" rate, the faster all the information from the CD can get into your PC for processing. Spin rates on computer CD-ROM players are indicated by a number followed by a lowercase "x." The higher the number the better. CD-ROMs are available in a wide range of speeds, from 8, 16, 24, 32x and up. Don't settle for anything slower than a 24x CD-ROM. Tip: If the system offers a DVD drive (Digital Versatile Disk) instead of a traditional CD-ROM player *go for it!* DVD drives can play disks with capacities great enough to hold entire feature-length movies. They can also run your existing PC and music CDs.

• **Monitor.** This is the TV thing. To avoid grainy pictures and headaches insist on a monitor with .28 dp (the "dp" stands for "dot pitch"—that's the space between each of the tiny "pixels," or red, green and blue combination picture elements that make up the images on the monitor sceen). The lower the dot pitch number, the sharper the image. If you can afford it, go for a monitor that measures at least seventeen inches diagonally.

• **Graphics Adapter.** This is the system inside the PC that helps display pictures and video. A Super VGA (SVGA) type graphics card with at least two megabytes of video memory is the rock bottom minimum needed for today's computing. If you're a gamer, or do anything with digital pictures or video, opt for a graphics board with 3D acceleration, support for Microsoft's DirectX technology and at least four megabytes (MB) of video memory. Today's entertainment and even home productivity programs (such as desktop publishing or Web page design software) increasingly employ sophisticated 3D images. Microsoft's DirectX technology for its Windows operating system helps speed the process of generating and displaying 3D images. Tip: If you're buying a new system powered by an Intel Pentium II processor, chances are good it can support an AGP technology–based graphics card. AGP (accelerated graphics port) technology gives 3D and graphics in general a real shot in the arm. If your new system can support an AGP graphics card, make sure to take advantage of it.

• **Universal Serial Bus (USB) Connector(s).** These babies can often be found on the back of new PCs alongside those funny looking "holes" where you plug in a printer, mouse and keyboard. The computer crowd calls these holes or plug-in places "connectors." USB connectors look something like telephone wall jacks and they're designed to make it super easy to hook up stuff like scanners, printers, monitors, keyboards and joysticks via a uniform plug. The idea is eventually to eliminate separate connectors for each thing you plug into a PC. Having a USB connector is a good investment for the future. In any case, make sure you have a full set of connectors to accommodate external add-on goodies (printers, scanners, external modems, digital cameras and so on).

• **Sound System.** Educational and entertainment software today demands sound. A must have in the PC audio department is a sound card that's 100 percent compatible with the defacto industry Sound Blaster and/or Windows sound "standard." Sixteen-bit sound is the minimum; 32-bit or 64-bit delivers higher fidelity.

• **Internal Expansion Slots.** One of the great things about PCs is their ability to be customized to meet a huge array of tasks. Want to record digital video or watch TV on your PC? No problem. You can buy what computer people call an "add-on" card (a circuit board) to do the job. Add-on cards for this and hundreds of other nifty things can be plugged into the inside of a computer via internal expansion slots (receptacles). Tip: make sure your PC has at least 3 free internal add-on card expansion slots.

• **Speakers.** Test drive the speakers. You decide. Tip: for gut rattling effects, try out a speaker system with a sub-woofer for super bass.

• **Modem.** When it comes to modems designed to work on your good old standard telephone line don't settle for anything slower than a

56kbps (or 56,000 bits-per-second) model. Right now that's the fastest standard speed possible using regular phone lines. Note: due to telecommunications regulations, the maximum speed a 56kbps modem can support is 53,000 bits-per-second.

• **A Big Box or a Laptop.** There are two types of PC boxes—horizontal and "tower" versions. A tower box generally gives you more room to grow but requires more desktop space.

Laptops are attractive for obvious reasons, but they might not be the right choice for your main home system. To cram all the technology of a PC into a portable package takes a lot of engineering—and that translates into stiff price tags from $2,000 at the bottom end all the way up to $5,000 and more. Laptops aren't easy to upgrade. Because they're so small, you can't easily open up the box and add goodies at a later date, like a bigger hard disk. Most laptops are slower than their desktop counterparts. Limited space and costs often make it hard for laptop designers to pop in the latest super microprocessor brain. We think traditional desktop PCs are generally the best bet for family computing. You get a full-size keyboard (important for the kiddies), a large screen and, most important, the option to easily add things and upgrade components.

Desktop PCs

Tower-Style PC (monitor stands beside the box)

Horizontal-Style PC (monitor sits on top of the PC)

Bottom line: Buying a PC today can be very challenging and confusing. There's so much out there at every price range, from modestly priced models for under $1,000 to deluxe machines costing anywhere from $2,000 and up. The big lesson we're trying to drive home is don't buy based on price alone! Get as much power, memory and hard-disk storage as you can afford, and make sure it's easily upgradable. The same is true with a modem—speed is king, and faster is better. (See a pattern here?) Mortgage the house, borrow from the kinfolk, but try to get as much system as you can (OK, that's a stretch—but you get the idea).

Don't forget the bonus items. If you're into sounds, you can't beat a good PC sound system and some great speakers. If you do a lot of graphics work (digital pictures and desktop publishing), or even if you don't, consider a large 17- or 20-inch monitor. The more software that comes bundled with and pre-installed on the system (that means pre-installed and sold with the PC as part of the package), the less monkeying around you'll have to do to get the system set up. Most PCs come with the Windows operating system software pre-installed as well as a software bundle offered by the PC maker. You may have a choice between software bundle packages that emphasize gaming or are geared more for education or home office use.

Don't neglect service, either. In the next chapter we'll walk you through all the issues to consider *before* you sign on the dotted line.

We're big on upgrading, which we'll cover in detail in the next chapter. Remember, be sure you can add more memory and can easily upgrade your brain chip, and have plenty of internal expansion slots to add special function cards (for fun stuff like adding a TV tuner to your PC or for connecting two or more computers together to share files and printers). We also like a "tower"—the stand-up box with lots of available spare add-on card slots and space to add more hard drives and other goodies. Make sure you also get plenty of connectors for external devices like printers, scanners—who knows, maybe even a digital camera. Tell the dealer you want room to grow. And tell him or her the PC Dads sent you (say it with enough authority and they *may* be impressed).

TIP #4: FIND A KNOWLEDGEABLE CO-PILOT

Now that you've got the results of your family PC quiz at hand along with your software system requirements figured out, you're ready for the next step: finding a computer-savvy mentor to act as your PC-purchasing agent. Computer nuts are all around, and many would probably be glad to help you. If you work for a reasonably sized company, talk to the folks who install and maintain your PCs and networks. See if your town has a computer users club. If you have access to the Internet through a techno-hip friend, ask them for help in searching the Web for helpful resources and buying-advice articles.

Other possibilities: Contact your local high school or community college job placement office. See if they have any students looking for part-time computer "consultant" work. In major metropolitan areas fun places called cyber cafés are popping up like weeds. These are coffee shops or restaurants filled with PCs linked to the Internet. The idea is to come in, have some refreshment, surf the Web and meet people with similar interests. These can be great places to network and find some free advice and help. Another option is to go to your local computer store and buttonhole a service technician (the folks who repair PCs). Give them your homework lists and start grilling them (okay, nicely ask them questions). There's almost always *someone* around who is willing to give you a hand.

TIP #5: FIGURE OUT A BUDGET
BEFORE YOU GO TO THE STORE

Starting out with a clear idea of how much horsepower you need and the size of your wallet will greatly reduce your PC-buying headaches. One of our friendly techies at Intel likes to say that "choices equal stress." That's the dilemma facing today's PC buyers who have to make some hard decisions and ask equally tough questions: Should I go with a $1,000 or under PC? How much do I really gain by buying one of the $1,500 or $2,000 hot-rod systems? Do I really need all that power? Is having more RAM and a bigger monitor going to make that much difference?

To tackle these questions you need to understand how the PC business has changed in the past few years. Not long ago PCs with last year's "latest" technology were marketed as budget systems. Today the situation is totally differ-ent. The PC industry now builds systems with modern technology to address all budgets. The key to determining if the $1,000 or under PC is right for you, or if you need a $1,500 to $2,000 powerhouse, lies in what you want to do. The latest crop of $1,000 and under PCs do a darn good job running today's busi-ness, entertainment and educational software. However, if heavy-duty desktop publishing, digital image editing or state-of-the-art gaming is your bag, or you want to make sure you're ready for tomorrow's software, the path is clear—you should consider a high-performance system. In the end, your best bet is to make sure the system you buy more than covers your needs today but, if pos-sible, buy added features to give you the best return on your investment.

Now that you're empowered with some key lingo and insider buying tips you can wheel and deal with the best of them. Go for it!

To Mail Order or Not to Mail Order, That Is the Question

Okay, maybe Hamlet didn't say this, but it's still a profound question for us. Not too many years ago our answer to this question was easy: buy from a store. Mail order meant hassling with returning bad merchandise and other headaches nat-urally associated with remote purchases.

That's all changed. Direct-mail PC makers like Dell Computers and Gate-way 2000 now offer excellent on-site service and support packages for a mod-est additional annual fee. Some even have a Web site where you can specify just what you want and order your PC online.

Nowadays, it's a personal preference issue. Some people feel more com-fortable knowing they can run down to the store where they bought a PC and talk directly to a service tech.

It's up to you. Compare prices and service packages. Talk to friends and neighbors who bought PCs in the last year or two. Draw a line down the mid-dle of a piece of paper. Put a "Pros" and "Cons" list together, then match that up with your own preferences.

Mark bought an early Pentium II processor–based system (233 MHz) from Gateway 2000 back in the summer of 1997, after configuring the system on their Web page. There were several problems early on with the video graphics card, and then the CD-ROM drive. Later, he had problems with the sound card. With Gateway's "gold service" hotline, he was usually able to get help quickly. When he couldn't get the video graphics card fixed after two tries, Gateway sent a technician out to his home who fixed it. It wasn't exactly a joy ride. Still, no matter when he called (24 hours/day) or how weird his computer problem, the technical people were always patient and polite. After a while, he began thinking, "These are the kind of people who enjoy this." It almost made wrestling with computer problems fun. Almost.

The Lease or Rent Alternative

If always staying ahead of the technology curve is important to you then renting or leasing a PC might be an alternative to buying new or used. Exploring this path is easy. Here's a snapshot of your options:

Lease a new PC. Several of the major PC manufacturers, such as Dell Computers (www.dell.com/dfs/leasing), offer flexible twenty-four or thirty-six-month leasing packages for desktop and laptop products. Under the Dell leasing program, leasing a brand-new $2,000 PC for twenty-four months would cost approximately $98 per month, with a payment of $75 per month for the thirty-six-month package (at the time of this writing). As with car leasing, most PC leasing deals allow you to return the system for a newer, more powerful system, or purchase the system you're leasing for a fixed percentage of the original purchase price.

Rent a new or used PC from a local dealer. Based on calls to several Portland, Oregon, PC rental outfits, we found monthly rental fees for a high-performance, Pentium II processor–based PC with a 3 gigabyte or more hard drive, 64 megabytes of RAM, a fast CD-ROM and a 15-inch monitor ran about $300+ per month. And for a modest entry level PC (with a Pentium 200 megahertz processor, 32 megabytes of RAM, a 2.5 gigabyte hard drive and a 15-inch monitor) the charges came in on average at $250 per month. The bottom line: This is an option we recommend only for short-term quick fixes.

Buying New or Used

Buying a computer is different from buying a car in some ways, such as when it comes time to consider the question of new or used. Older cars can still get you down the road—it's not like they're obsolete or can't meet minimum highway speed limits. For a PC, though, these are real concerns. Whether you want to buy a new or used PC depends on several factors, including your own preferences. Consider the questions below as you try to decide:

- **What will you use the PC for?** You need to decide this before you do anything else. If you have no use for any functions other than word processing, e-mail and browsing the Net, then a used computer with a fast modem may work for you.

- **What kind of deal can you get?** Bargain for the best deal you can (spell that *cheap*). Find a source of used computer prices so you have a benchmark standard. We recommend spending a little time in a used computer store, or calling ACE (the American Computer Exchange) at 1-800-786-0717. You can find them at www.amcoex.com. Or check out your local newspaper classified ads.

- **How does the used computer price compare with a new one?** All you have to do is open your newspaper or pick up a magazine. Computer ads are everywhere. Look in the classifieds and chances are good you'll find listings for used computers. We've seen three-year-old PCs going for as little as $300. However, with brand-new systems going for $1,000 and under you'll be much better off going all the way and buying new. Tip: Don't rule out buying a new PC by assuming you must spend $2,000 or more. Good performing new home PCs may be less expensive than you think. At this writing, units are available for less than

$1,000 with solid performing microprocessors, modems, memory and hard disks that can easily handle the majority of today's general purpose software. These bargain basement new PCs won't deliver the most exciting experience, especially in the games department, but they'll at least get you going with a system built around modern components and technology.

• **How much risk are you willing to take?** Used computers may come with a lot of wear and tear. You don't know what the hard drives and other moving parts have endured. There's a trade-off here. What happens if the monitor or hard drive goes out? If you're risk inclined or don't mind popping the hood and working on your PC—or if you just want a PC for a year or so—a used system may be the way to go.

• **Will you be able to upgrade?** If you buy something that meets your needs today, can you upgrade the CPU, add more memory or change other components later on to make it more powerful? Sometimes the reason a computer is on the market is that it cannot be updated.

• **Are you broke?** If you have only a few hundred dollars to spend, forget our other advice. An older computer is better than no computer.

Final Notes

If you plowed through this chapter and found it absolutely captivating, give us your name and number; we may have a job for you at Intel. Just kidding!

Even if you weren't fascinated by this material, if you've read this far, you're well on your way to understanding the basics of a computer, and that's an important step forward. You now know enough about your PC to get around and conduct a simple conversation with PC people. You have a leg up on the millions of consumers who are still intimidated by the whole subject. And if you want to buy your first PC, you'll be far more knowledgeable than many folks when they set out for their first trip to the computer store.

It's time to celebrate. Make a copy of the Firm Grip Award certificate that follows, frame it and proudly display it along with your family pictures (your kids will undoubtedly be bowled over by this achievement). You're ready for the rest of this book.

Still feel a bit overwhelmed? Don't fret. Come back to this chapter in a couple days and try it again.

FOCUSED QUESTIONS

- Is the difference between hardware and software clear to you?
- Can you outline the key hardware and software elements that make up a PC?
- Do you have a grasp of the basic lingo of the PC world? If someone uses terms like microprocessor, hard disk, modem, CD-ROM, mem-

ory or add-on card do you have a general idea of what in the heck they're talking about?

- Do you feel like you now have enough knowledge to keep up with to-day's PC technology (not to mention your kids)?

- Can you read an ad for a PC and understand the importance of the features highlighted?

- Do you understand how to determine clearly what kind of PC horse-power your family needs?

- Can you outline the pros and cons of a laptop vs. a desktop PC?

- Do you fully understand the ups and downs of buying, leasing or rent-ing a PC?

3.

Upgrade or Move On?

WHAT TO DO WITH AN OLD PC

I just bought a brand new PC to replace my old system. It still works,
and I hate to see it gathering dust in the garage. What do I do with it?
—Fellow dad attending a PC Dads workshop
in Scottsdale, Arizona

Today's games and educational programs—and even a growing number of Web sites—feature flashy graphics, dazzling videos and realistic sound if you have the power to drive them. Otherwise, lacking power, you can be stuck with jerky video and lapses in sound quality, or maybe not be able to run the programs at all. New software features just keep coming with no end in sight. Next year you'll need even more power to keep up.

There's no hard and fast rule to tell you exactly when to throw out the old computer and buy another one. It all depends on your needs and the system. Generally, today, if you have a two- or three-year-old computer, upgrading with a newer processor may be a viable option. Anything older than that is questionable. Many of the key ingredients, such as the way data is transported inside the system, the graphics display cards and even the memory chips, have dramatically improved in the past few years. Even if you pop in a new processor (or "brain chip"), you might not get the full performance benefit a brand-new system offers. It's like putting a new fuel injection system in an older engine—it'll run a little faster, but it's not the same as a new engine.

In this chapter you'll:

- Understand if upgrading your old PC makes sense or not.
- Learn how to protect your PC investment.
- Find out what to do with your PC when it's time to put it out to pasture.

Computers are like cars in some ways: Often you get so accustomed to one, you don't want to let it go. There are several ways to upgrade your old PC and get some more mileage out of it. Here are some examples:

   1. Swap Out Your Brain. Not *your* brain, your computer's brain. Your system's microprocessor is the key element in gaining adequate power and speed. If you're poking along with an older Intel386 or Intel486 microprocessor and want to play the current hits, you'll need a more powerful brain right away. In fact, your best bet would be to move up to a new system altogether. However, if you're not ready to give up your old friend, then ask your computer dealer about microprocessor upgrading options for your particular system. Popping in a new processor can give you a boost of up to 50 percent or more. If you're leery of doing any kind of surgery yourself, hire it out. Around our area there are dozens of Mom and Pop shops that can do the job cheaply. In terms of cost, upgrading your system with a more powerful chip will set you back from $200 to around $300.

   2. Add Memory Chips (that RAM stuff). This is always a good move no matter what microprocessor you have. At this writing 32 megabytes is considered standard, with 64 MB being better to handle Windows and today's increasingly power-hungry programs. As with processing power, the bar will continue to rise every year. Your best bet is to read the "system requirements" statements on the boxes of software you want to run and see how much memory is recommended for optimal performance. Tip: as you know with your own mind (if you can remember) you can never have too much memory—buy as much as you can afford.

Warning: Installing new memory chips or pulling out old ones is not a task for the novice. Have this done by a qualified technician or experienced techno-nerd friend. In general, don't monkey around inside your PC unless you know what you're doing or have a certified PC geek at your side.

3. "Defrag" Your Hard Disk. This only sounds painful. When writing data to a hard disk, the operating system plops information into open areas anywhere it can find them. As a result, pieces of programs and the files you create with them are fragmented; that is, they're scattered all over different physical locations on the disk. When you start a program, the operating system has to find all these pieces and stitch them together. This takes time. Check your operating system documentation for instructions for running the defrag utility. The handy defrag utility will gather up all related data fragments from the hard disk and then lay them back down in a contiguous "line." Here's the cool part: Once everything is lined up and pieced back together, the operating system and brain chip can find everything they need a whole bunch faster. Retrieving files from your hard disk and running your programs becomes turbo charged.

Neat, huh?

4. Upgrade Your Graphics Card. Inside most PCs you'll find a special circuit card called a "graphics adapter" by the computer crowd. Its job is to run the monitor and make all the images on the screen come to life. As the processor manages running a program (a game, word processor, anything), it sends special instructions to the graphics card to make the pretty pictures. The graphics card is a mini "system" unto itself that takes these instructions and does the magic that transforms them into program screens, menus or pretty pictures.

Here's the rub: graphics cards made only a few years ago often are overwhelmed by the intense graphics of modern business, education and especially game software. The latest graphics cards come with lots of special graphics turbo-boosting features to project complex, 3D and photo-real images on the screen. If your PC is three years old or older, and you've noticed you're not getting the kind of flashy graphics you see running on the systems at your local computer store, then a graphics card upgrade may be a good idea.

The first step is to make sure an upgrade is really needed. See if the owner's manual that came with your PC has a chapter describing the technical capabilities of your graphics system. Show this chapter to a computer nut friend or service technician and ask if the card can handle today's Windows (like Windows 95 or Windows 98) operating system and program needs.

If an upgrade is needed, insist on a graphics card with 3D acceleration, that supports Microsoft's DirectX technology, and has at least four megabytes of video memory (more if you can afford it). Don't worry about what all this techno-babble means. Just show this paragraph to the salesperson. To really target what kind of card is right for you, check the graphics recommendations on the software you want to run to get a quick snapshot of the graphics horsepower or other graphics features you may need. In terms of price, graphics cards with the kinds of features we recommend will cost from $100 to $250.

5. Leapfrog to the Future. Take a blank sheet of paper, list all the items you need to upgrade your old PC, write down the prices and add it all up. For what it costs to implement one or more of the previous steps, you might be better off moving up to a new PC; this makes a lot of sense with prices constantly falling. Refer to the PC Dads Handy Buyer's Checklist in Chapter 2 for info on what features to look for. Better yet, get the most up-to-date information by visiting us on the World Wide Web at www.intel.com/go/pcdads.

RALPH LEAVES THE COMFORT ZONE AND ENTERS TWILIGHT ZONE

While technically it may not be considered an upgrade, "networking" home computers will definitely help you get more bang for your buck. Networking, or connecting your home computers, will allow everyone in your home to collaborate—you can share files, play games and so on. To date, networking PCs has been a task only computer buffs knew how to do. It's still not easy, but if you're willing to invest some time, it can be done. Below is Ralph's saga.

"I figured I knew my way around a computer. I knew how to install software and hardware parts, how to work my way out of most problems, and how to ask questions to get help. Then I tackled something new: the Networking Monster. I decided to connect my family's three home PCs together so we could all share files and printers.

"It was alien territory, a sailing venture into the dark unknown. There were strange terms like 'Network Interface Cards,' 'twisted pair,' and 'coax cable'—not to mention 'network protocol software settings' in Windows 95. Yikes! My strategy: act stupid, ask for directions—and pray. I pored over the documentation that came with Windows 95. It had pieces of the puzzle sprinkled all over, but no clear step-by-step instructions for connecting PCs together.

"Next I went to several bookstores and Web sites hoping to find the magic formulas. No luck. I started tapping the brains of my tech friends who assured me it was a breeze. Right.

"Finally, I hit the local computer super store and spent some quality time with the salesperson who specializes in network products. I wound up buying a start-up kit, with all the hardware, cables and instructions needed.

"Time for the happy ending, right? Not.

> "The documentation in the start-up kit also assumed everyone knows what to do. I spent hours working different solutions, banging away, until I finally got everything installed and running. The research and persistence finally paid off. My computers are all on one network, meaning they can talk to each other.
>
> "The moral of the story: don't be afraid to try new things, keep asking questions and don't give up. I came out of the process with a home network that's humming along just fine, and two kids who learned a good lesson in risk taking and perseverance."

How to Protect Your PC Investment

Don't ignore service and support issues when buying a PC. Something will undoubtedly break or go wrong the first year or so of your computer. Then what? Unless you're weird like us and enjoy messing with computers, you need someone to call on, preferably the company that made the computer. Consider these tips when you start looking into service issues:

- **Investigate the warranty.** Ask the salesperson about the service issue before you buy a computer. Ask questions like:

  - Within how many days can you return the unit for a full refund if you are not happy? Is it a no-questions-asked policy?
  - Is there a one-year parts and labor policy covering all components?
  - Is there an option for an extended warranty? If yes, does it cover all parts?
  - Does adding a component yourself void your warranty? Some policies only cover a PC if all service is performed by the company offering the warranty.

• What is the turnaround time if they send a technician to your house?

• **Find a service that suits you.** Some companies still offer lifetime technical support for their products. Some will come to your house. Others offer thirty to forty-five days of free technical support, then you start paying. One service gives you a direct line to technical help for a $90 one-time fee; someone's available to help you twenty-four hours a day. We've heard enough bad stories about folks calling up a technical support phone line and waiting for an hour or more to know it's a burning issue with consumers. On the other hand we've had good experiences with companies like Gateway, Hewlett Packard and Dell, with their hand-holding technical services. If you want on-site home service, be sure to ask what the guaranteed turnaround time is to send a technician to your house. Is it one day? Two days? A week?

One promising trend is the appearance of new pay-per-call or monthly subscription hardware and software support services designed to provide total care packages. Intel, for example, launched its Answer-Express monthly subscription service in 1998 that gives users e-mail and phone access to an army of technical gurus (call 1-888-795-7357 or visit www.answerexpress.com for more information). The PC Crisis Line service charges a per-minute fee for support calls (call 1-800-828-4358 or go to www.pccrisis.com).

• **Compare prices.** How much does the company charge for the service? Some companies charge by the half-hour, others a flat fee per call.

• **Consider convenience.** If your PC has to go into the shop, where will the service be performed? Do you have to bring the machine back to the same store, lug it to an independent contractor across town or ship it off? How quickly will you have the machine back?

• **Test drive the support team.** Try this experiment (before you buy the PC). Get on the company's technical help line and see how long you have to hold. Try it on different days and at different times. This will give you a glimpse of what you may face down the road.

Although they don't replace professional support arrangements, there's plenty of help on the Internet and from the major online services if you know where to look. Online service providers like America Online, Prodigy, CompuServe and Microsoft Network have bulletin boards and people you can ask for help. The Internet also has a wealth of help resources. If you run into something you can't handle, you can find a good bulletin board or newsgroup and post your problem via an e-mail message. If you're lucky, someone will help you. Many companies have their own online bulletin boards with technical help areas. Or you can e-mail your questions to the support staff of the company that made your PC. Of course, response time varies dramatically, so do your homework *before* you buy. And whether you're sending an e-mail or calling a support hot-line, remember the Boy Scout motto and be prepared: Think through the problem and get as much information together as you can.

In the end, you'll come out ahead if you can increase your basic PC knowledge and learn how to do some basic troubleshooting for yourself.

FIVE WAYS TO LEARN MORE ABOUT YOUR PC

1. **Read this book and others.** When you've mastered this book start checking out from your library or buying other books written for PC novices. If you're inspired and want to get a little more techie, look for the "Dummies" series of books from IDG Books Worldwide. These large paperback books cover everything under the sun, from how to run the Windows operating system and individual programs, to understanding the Internet and do-it-yourself repair.

2. **Read magazines.** Buy at the supermarket or subscribe to magazines like *FamilyPC, Easy Computing,* and *Smart Computing.* These monthly publications offer tutorials on PC basics, reviews of family software and loads of tips.

3. **Take some classes.** Take an introduction to PCs class at your local high school (Adult Education), community college or public library. Many colleges offer night or weekend classes designed for rock-bottom beginners. You'll not only learn a lot in a nonthreatening environment, you'll meet fellow novices. Hey, why not start a home PC support group? Tip: Make sure the class you take uses the hardware and software you own. A class with machines running Windows operating system is not going to be much help to an Apple Macintosh owner, and vice versa.

4. **Use the Internet to learn more.** Some of the best information about computers is online. Some great sites include:

• *FamilyPC* magazine: www.zdnet.com/familypc

• *Smart Computing* magazine: www.pcnovice.com

Giving Your Old PC an Active Retirement

If you're ready to retire your old computer, the choices may seem limited: Either use it for a boat anchor or unload it at the next garage sale. But you actually have more possibilities if you look around.

Schools, libraries and vocational training centers will often accept a PC if it's not too ancient. If the school in question is building a computer lab to support the latest software, they may not want an older PC. But if their goal is to teach keyboarding and basic computer skills such as file management, an older PC might do the trick (and you may be eligible for a tax deduction). An older PC, combined with a good modem, can also be used to give students basic, text-oriented access to the Internet. Or it can be put to work collecting and processing print jobs from multiple computers hooked up to it via a network.

For that matter, you can keep the older PC around the house and use it as an extra system, much like you would with an older (but still functioning) TV after you come home with a new big-screen extravaganza. Put the old PC in a corner of the kitchen or one of the kids' bedrooms and use it for basic keyboarding, word processing, e-mail or text-based research on the Web. Heck, if you're really feeling macho and weren't scared off by Ralph's adventures (see sidebar, "Ralph Leaves the Comfort Zone and Enters Twilight Zone," pages 61–62), you can even try networking your computers together!

If you do want to find a new home for your PC, however, start by contacting your local schools or libraries and asking if they accept donations. Or call your favorite charity and see if they need an extra PC to run basic office applications. Here's a very small sampling of the many national and regional groups that specialize in collecting and distributing donated PCs and related equipment:

- **Computer Bank Charity** (206) 365-4657. Donates computers and related equipment to nonprofit organizations and individuals primarily in the Seattle area, giving priorities to people with disabilities. They will consider applications elsewhere in Washington State if transportation can be arranged.
- **The Detwiler Foundation** (619) 456-9045. Refurbishes and supplies used computers to elementary and high schools in California.
- **Nonprofit Computing, Inc., New York** (212) 759-2368. Donates computers and related equipment to nonprofit organizations, schools and government agencies primarily in New York City. Will also work with other groups in the U.S. if they provide transportation.

On the Net, you can find a comprehensive list of organizations dedicated to distributing used computers to schools and nonprofit organizations at this web address: www.wco.com/~dale/list.html.

If you'd prefer donating to a neighborhood group start by contacting the reference librarian in your public library or calling the headquarters for your local public school district. There may be a vocational training center that needs PCs, or classrooms where your system could be put to work. And don't forget that you can always donate your old PC and equipment to Goodwill or the Salvation Army.

FOCUSED QUESTIONS

- If you own a PC, what shape is it in? When do you bump up against its limits? Have you put off buying new software because your current machine can't do it justice? Have you had a service technician or techno-nerd friend look at your system's upgrade options?

- How comfortable are you working through technical questions and problems when they come up? Do you want round-the-clock hand-holding, or do you enjoy digging into manuals and figuring things out on your own?

- Do you understand all the warranty and ongoing support options available? Do you know what questions to ask to find the right service package for you?

- If your PC is ready to ride off into the sunset, how would you like to see it used?

4.

Where the Rubber Hits the Road

BUYING SOFTWARE THAT MAKES
SENSE FOR YOUR FAMILY

Software is like shoes—try it on for size before
you take it home. It may not fit.
—The PC Dads

When it comes to computers, few things are worse than seeing your child's eyes glaze over after you load a new software program on your personal computer. You were sure it was going to be a big hit. (Why else did you shell out $40?) Now it's attracting dust on the shelf. Ouch.

This happened to Ralph when he picked up *Mario Teaches Typing* from Interplay. Mario is a clever typing program for kids, featuring the famous Mario character from Nintendo, funny music and an arcadelike game format to make typing drills fun. That's the theory anyhow and many kids love it. But after about an hour, his son Jeff tired of the repetitious format. Soon he could see it wasn't Jeff's idea of a fun game. His cost: $35, and another lesson.

There's some consolation knowing we're not the only ones who screw up buying software. Many people pick up software that doesn't fit their needs or their kids' needs. Maybe it's too demanding for their PC or extremely out of date.

In this chapter we'll show you how to avoid some of the most common mistakes in buying software. We'll also teach you some of the tricks of being a family software buyer, including what to do when you get the program home. We'll use educational software as an example, but many of these ideas apply to buying and using almost any kind of program.

After completing this chapter, you'll know how to:

- Do a family survey that will help you target software that's right for your family and individual members.
- Develop a balanced home educational software library.
- Judge and pick out strong titles.
- Keep your kids from gorging on "junk food" software.
- Find software bargains.

Educational Goals

Parents everywhere make the same common mistakes when it comes to buying educational software:

- They buy programs on a whim, based on flashy packages with cute characters.
- They're not clear on the educational problem they're trying to solve or the skill they're trying to improve.
- They haven't done their homework (like talking to the child's teacher, reading software reviews).

How do you get smart when it comes to buying educational software? First, think about where you're trying to go and what type of (educational) skills you're trying to develop. Ponder these questions for starters:

- In what area(s) does your child need to augment their schoolwork?
- What skills in the area(s) in question need to be improved? Does Johnny or Susie need help in reading or writing? Are they falling behind in math or science?
- If you could choose only three skills to improve, what would they be?

- What other mental skills outside of "the basics" are you trying to sharpen? Critical thinking, creative thinking, problem solving, etc.
- Are you looking for a program that focuses on repetitive drills to build skill strength, or more "creative" activities designed to develop critical or logical thinking?

What follows is a snapshot chart to help jumpstart your thinking. We know that "audit" conjures up images of the IRS and accountants in green eye-shades, but this chart will help you develop a list of educational goals. Talk to your child's teacher. Identify weaknesses and areas where they need improvement. Get them on paper.

Educational Goals Audit

Current Skills Snapshot:

	Strong	Average	Low
Reading	☐	☐	☐
Math	☐	☐	☐
Writing	☐	☐	☐
Science	☐	☐	☐

Specific Skills to Work on by subject

Reading _____

Math _____

Writing _____

Science _____

Software used in your child's school

_____

_____

_____

_____

Understand Your Child's Personality

The second step is lining up your educational goals with your child's personality and personal tastes. Kids have an inclination toward certain types of programs, depending on their personalities and learning styles. Look at how your kids play different programs. What features keep them coming back to play? Which ones turn them off?

Here are some other questions to consider *before* you buy that software program:

• Would you describe your child as an analytical and logical thinker? Do they enjoy taking a problem apart and figuring out how to solve puzzles? If not, are these skills you want an educational software program to exercise?

• Does your kid like to read? Or do they respond primarily to visual material? Your answers here will help you seek out or avoid programs that emphasize the reading of passages of text as part of the activity.

• Do you have a little Pablo Picasso at home? Does your child like to draw, make up stories and create their own toys? If yes, then feel free to buy one of the many great kid art software packages. If not, and your child is intimidated by artistic activities, look for creative software that combines "clip art" elements (that is, pre-created art objects) with tools that allow a child to draw or build their own images.

• Is the prospect of practicing scales on the piano something that sends your child screaming out of the room, or do they see it as an interesting challenge? The answer here will give you a clue as to how your child will react to an educational program that uses repetitive drills to build skills.

• When it comes to story time, does your child favor simple or complex story plots? Some educational software involves complex and long story lines (such as *Oregon Trail*). If this presents a challenge then start with simpler offerings such as the *Living Books* series of software.

• Does your child like visual action, multimedia bells and whistles? Some kids like heavy computer graphics, others are distracted by them.

• What are your child's favorite game and educational software programs? What are the "style" qualities of these programs that appeal to them? Do they respond to highly detailed and colorful images, musical tracks and sound effects?

Computer Skills

As you're figuring out your educational goals and child's personal style and preferences, don't neglect their computer skills. How well they can navigate a computer will determine if they're content with one program over another. Give a kid who isn't comfortable on the PC a program that requires higher-level computer skills and you've got a sure-fire prescription for frustration. Some questions to consider:

• Can your child turn on a computer and run his/her own programs?

• Can they hunt and peck their way around a keyboard?

• Are they comfortable using a mouse to "point and click" or a joystick?

Compare your answers here with the descriptions on the software box regarding how the program is operated. The good news is that most entertainment and educational software allows you to choose the way you operate—mouse, keyboard or joystick (or a combination).

Wow! That's a lot to cover, but the rewards are worth it. Now you can march into a software store and tell the salesman what *you* want—not accept what he or she has in mind. Chances are, by thinking all of this through carefully, you'll increase your odds of finding programs your child will actually enjoy. Now the fun part: checking out the software.

MARK:

All my kids like programs that carefully use colorful graphics, sounds and other multimedia touches. But each child is different. My oldest son Matthew, thirteen, has never met an action-thriller program he didn't love; he thrives on nonstop action and arcadelike games (examples: *Need for Speed* from Electronic Arts and *Monster Truck Madness* from Microsoft). Strangely enough, though, he does like chess games, which require a lot of patience. Maybe it's because they're mentally stimulating, or he just enjoys whipping me. *Chessmaster 5500* from Mindscape is one of his favorites. Another title he has always liked is *Oregon Trail II*; but as you might expect, he often spends too much time hunting and trying to blast his way across the trail.

My middle son Michael, nine, likes action-thrillers too, but also likes to work through mysteries and thought-provoking science programs like Microsoft's *Magic Bus* series and *Thinkin' Things* from Edmark. Davidson's *JumpStart* series was also on his favorites list. He liked the wide range of exercises and quizzes.

Their younger sister Nicole, four, likes a wide range of software, from art programs like *Kid Pix* to playful programs like *Putt-Putt* and even the Purple Moon *Rockett* series (we have to help her on these programs, as they're geared for older girls). Her favorites are reading programs like Dr. Seuss and Broderbund's *Living Books* series (*Just Grandma and Me*), which she can play over and over and over and over.

Analyzing Software

Not all programs are created equal. They vary dramatically in educational value, quality and multimedia bells and whistles, just to name a few features. There's too much to pick from, and it's not like you have a full Saturday to waltz around the computer stores. Filling in the chart on page 76 can help you wade through the morass of titles you are inspecting. The chart can be modified to cover other programs beyond educational programs.

RALPH:

Math programs provide a good test. The majority of the math skills building software for grade school kids breaks out into two types: electronic versions of the good old flash-card repetition exercises and more innovative programs. The second category of programs attempts to make learning addition, subtraction, multiplication and division more fun, while providing some learning. Right off the bat I learned that repetition and drill software titles left Jeff cold. I shouldn't have been surprised. From day one he's lived in a house loaded with computer gadgets and lots of game software (my addiction). What grabs and keeps Jeff's attention are programs with colorful graphics, funny characters, animation and interactive questions.

With this revelation in mind I set out to find programs that would look and smell like the games he loves but deliver the educational goods. Before running off to the store to buy what I *thought* he'd like, I decided to ask *him* (what a concept). I found out that at school he liked the *Math Blaster* series from Davidson Software, which weaves together math exercises, wacky adventure stories, goofy characters, sound effects and arcade game action. Now I was ready to shop.

After trying out about ten programs, he hit on a favorite math program: *Major League Math, Second Edition* from Sanctuary Woods. This program fit Jeff's personal profile like a glove. Using baseball as the backdrop (Jeff's favorite sport) the child has to mange a team and decide how to execute each play. To make things happen, such as throwing a pitch, you have to answer one of 2,000 math questions cleverly composed to relate to baseball history or statistics. A typical quiz question shows a list of three teams displaying the number of wins each achieved for the 1995 season. Above the list is the question "Which team had the even number of wins?" Answer correctly and you see the play via lifelike 3D animations spiced up with an audio track of roaring crowds. Seeing the plays come to life motivated Jeff to plow through the questions. *Major League Math* hit the mark with its combination of entertainment and learning and, most important of all, it tapped Jeff's personal interests.

Software Audit				
Title:				
Type of Program:				
Educational:				
Entertainment:				
Productivity:				
Specialty:				
Age Recommendation:				
Program Style:				
Ease of Use (rate from 1 to 5):				
Level of passive or active involvement:				
Puzzle or mystery solving:				
Story based concept (program follows a story path):				
Level-based game (you conquer a level before going on):				
Good use of graphics, animation and/or video:				
Educational Value:				
Targets key goals set for the user:				
Has won awards:				
Recommended by teacher:				
Lasting Value:				
Contains multiple levels to ensure growth path:				
Rating if any:				
System Recommended (Horsepower):				
Processor:				
Memory:				
Graphics:				
CD-ROM:				
Joystick:				
Mouse:				
Sound System:				

With educational software you have two basic choices: single-subject programs, such as math packages that focus on one skill, and so-called "edutainment" programs that cover many subjects. Some of these programs focus on one grade level; they provide a slew of activities, from reading to problem solving, for a specific grade level rather than a single subject. These can be great starter programs. For example, the *My Personal Tutor* series from Microsoft is a comprehensive program for preschool, kindergarten, first and second graders.

While covering a wide range of subjects, it also has a strong and entertaining tutorial feature that keeps kids going. The *JumpStart* series from Davidson is also highly regarded.

One caveat: don't expect these programs to really cover everything you need for one grade. They generally do fine on reading, writing and math, but are often thin on history, music and other non-basic subjects. Use them to supplement your current school and home educational programs.

Once you decide the general type of software you're buying, you still need to decide on specific titles. Consider these tips:

- Find programs that reinforce the important ideas and skills your kids are learning at school, while also paving the way for them to explore new creative ideas.

- Look for programs designed to keep children interested over time. Some programs fizzle out after a couple of weeks. Good programs will include story lines, content and multimedia bells and whistles that keep kids coming back.

- Don't concentrate exclusively on the 3R's. If you do, you might end up overlooking software that offers your kids the opportunity to expand their creative potential by drawing, painting, going from story screen to story screen and so forth.

- Look for programs that provide immediate positive feedback.

- Look for programs with activities that can be changed quickly so children don't feel trapped or get frustrated.

- Shop around for the best price. Most of these programs range from $25 to $50, but the same program that cost $50 in one store could be $35 or $40 in another store.

If your child needs help in one area, consider the specific subject programs, like *The Magic School Bus* for science or *Math Blaster* for math; otherwise, start with the general programs. If you do opt for a program for a specific subject, beware of software that focuses on drills and repetitive procedures. Parents get sucked into purchasing these programs because they feature the kind of learning we grew up with. However, there are plenty of single-subject programs that offer much more creative and interesting approaches to the material. These programs really help your child learn and understand the concepts instead of drilling them. If your kids are struggling with a subject, the last thing they need is a trip to "computer boot camp."

Look for programs that entertain as they teach. One good example for very young kids is Edmark's *Millie's Math House*, which introduces youngsters to shapes, patterns, problem solving, numbers and other concepts in a fun way. The six exercises are arranged in different rooms of Millie's house. (Get this—Millie is a talking cow.) For instance, in a segment called "Little, Middle and Big," kids are asked to help three cartoon characters try on shoes, matching the smallest character with the smallest shoes and so on. The characters request their shoes, and a cat's around to mix them up. In the cookie factory, kids are asked to decorate cookies with jellybeans. They have to use different gadgets and count jellybeans to pull this off. All the exercises are easy to use and engaging.

Choose programs that have entertaining graphics and sounds. They should be easy to use, but offer enough challenge to keep kids coming back. They should also be interactive in a way that provides positive feedback. Kids get yelled at enough in the real world. Give them a break with programs like *Millie* that offer friendly, patient feedback.

Classic examples of educational programs that embody these qualities and have been enduring hits in our homes include *Oregon Trail* (MECC software), *Super Solvers Gizmos & Gadgets!* (a science program by The Learning Company), the *Magic School Bus* series published by Microsoft, and thoughtful "edutainment" games like *SimCity* from Maxis.

Talk to Local Experts

Like marriage and kids, everyone seems to be an expert when it comes to software. Our advice: pick experts you can trust. You want to find people who share your perspective on education, really know the programs and understand how kids respond to them. And keep in mind that no expert can possibly know your kid as well as you.

For now, forget all the national big shots and keyboard thumping experts (except us, of course). Start in your own backyard, at your kid's school. Begin by interviewing your son's or daughter's teachers, librarians or school computer lab manager. Play reporter—get a pad of paper and pen, and prepare to go after your "story." Might as well have a little fun at it; involve your kids if it helps.

What questions do you ask? Try these to get things going:

- What software is most popular with the kids?
- What features do kids respond to?
- Are you using specific titles to reinforce skills being emphasized in class? If yes, what programs?
- What types of programs tend to turn kids off? Are there any that clash with what's going on in class?

Next Stop: The Magazine Stand

Start with consumer publications which review software (see sidebar). These magazines do a great job. *FamilyPC*, for example, regularly runs features based on research of parents, showing what programs are best fitted for different age groups, and their software reviews are easy to understand. Later, check out the books cited in the "Finding Software Reviews" sidebar. Avoid the monstrous encyclopedia books that try to describe everything, unless you want a good doorstop. Many of these weigh in at five pounds or more and give you far more than you need.

FACTS—AND LOTS MORE—AT YOUR FINGERTIPS

You want educational software? You got it. There's a program out there for every conceivable interest—more than 20,000 titles as of this writing, and more hitting the stands every week. But no matter how many specialty packages you get, there's still a place for basic reference material. And boy, are these a lot more fun than the musty encyclopedias and atlases we all grew up with.

Two of our favorite encyclopedias are the *Grolier Multimedia Encyclopedia* series and *Microsoft Encarta Encyclopedia Deluxe* series. Unlike the encyclopedia gathering dust on your bookshelf, these encyclopedias present information with more than text and static pictures. There are graphics, moving images, sounds and more. Instead of just reading a famous speech, kids can actually hear it, including the character of the voice, the inflections, and the emotions behind the words. Instead of just reading about a panther, kids can hear its hiss, see it move, watch it attack its prey— the next best thing to a trip to the zoo. And kids can go online with these encyclopedias, using hypertext links to find limitless documents of related information via the Internet.

For geographic information, these three sources are at the top of our list:

- *Microsoft Encarta Virtual Globe.* This atlas lets kids glide over 3-D representations of the continents or get a multimedia overview of topics like plate tectonics or how to read a map. There are 6,000 articles, plus 9,000 Internet links. Kids can search in a variety of ways, including by country, world music and videos.

- *3D Atlas 98* from Creative Wonders and ABC World Reference. Of all the atlases, this one offers frequent updates. It features 3-D rotating globes, surveillance satellite images, and 3-D fly-through, not to mention statistics and printable charts, video documentaries and research links for every topic and country. Go online with it and you get "map pins" to locate lost civilizations, monuments and recreation.

• The *Complete National Geographic* from Mindscape. This 30-CD set (also available in DVD format) has 108 years of *National Geographic*—every article, every photo. The photos are stunning. No more digging through boxes of musty magazines in your garage. The access is clean and immediate.

With reference sources like these, you'll have to kick the kids off the computer so you can get your turn!

Test Drive Before You Buy

Nothing takes the place of first-hand experience. Put your kid in the driver's seat. Sit back and listen to their comments; it may save you some money—and headaches. Here are seven test-drive steps you can try:

1. Look for stores that provide lots of PCs loaded with demos of software.

2. Rent PC CD-ROMs from your local video store.

3. Check out PC CD-ROMs from your local library.

4. See if your school computer lab manager will loan you titles.

5. Borrow software from parents you know from the office, the neighborhood or the soccer sidelines.

6. See if your local computer store sells "demo" CD-ROMs of programs (these often include the first level of a game or activity program

Finding Software Reviews

Check out these sources of family software reviews (most have Web sites too):

BOOKS, MAGAZINES AND NEWSLETTERS

FamilyPC magazine

Smart Computing magazine

EasyComputing magazine

Great Software for Kids & Parents, published by IDG Books

The Computer Museum's Guide to the Best Software for Kids, published by HarperCollins Perennial

The FamilyPC, Guide to Homework, co-published by Hyperion and *Family PC*

Children's Software, a quarterly newsletter jointly created by the Department of Communication, Technology and Computing in Education at Teachers College, Columbia University

ON THE INTERNET

SuperKids Educational Software Review: www.superkids.com

The Review Zone: www.TheReviewZone.com

The Games Domain: www.gamesdomain.com

FamilyPC magazine: www.zdnet.com/familypc

designed to give you a taste of what the full program can do).

7. "Download" free trial versions of programs from the Web sites of software manufacturers.

Finally, Chaaaaarge—Hit the Stores!

You've done your homework. Now organize all your research, including your personality profiles and software title checklists, into file folders and take it with you to the store. Walk in, whip it out and smile confidently. The salesperson will either think you're the smartest buyer on the planet or completely out of your mind. In either case, be sure to tell them we sent you!

For the first few trips to the computer store, we recommend you go alone or with your spouse rather than bringing the kids along. It's hard enough to review the huge selection and think clearly in a computer store with all the techno-babble, and it's nearly impossible when you have kids around.

Look for Software Bargains

We spend a lot of time in computer stores—just ask our wives. This has given us ample time to find bargain deals on software. The strategy is pretty simple: when you first come into the store, avoid the crowds around the latest games and other "pricey" stuff and head to the clearance bins. They're usually located in the back, out of the way of the main traffic.

Software changes fast. Last year's $50 game is now fetching $20. As manufacturers introduce new revisions to software ("revs" as the geeks call them), the dealers and mail order houses need to clear out the inventory to make room for the latest stuff.

Bargains are everywhere. Check out the big computer retail stores and office supply houses. Both run sales frequently on selective programs. We've found winners like the first generation of *Baseball Math* by Sanctuary Woods (a wonderful math exercise program that originally sold for about $30) for $5.95. We've also found titles under the *Dr. Seuss* and *Putt-Putt* series in the bargain bins, all for under $20. Other bargain hunters have found even better deals.

One more tip: check out the bundled programs like the *Sim* series and *Thinkin Things*, from Edmark. These packages often include three "classic" programs for the price of one. Not bad.

How to Feed Your Family a Balanced Software Diet

When it comes to software, perhaps the biggest challenge for parents is finding balance. You wouldn't let your kids eat junk food every day, so why should you let them play games every day?

Much of this is just common sense. First, make sure you have a balanced software library. Your library should include:

- Word processing programs
- Desktop publishing programs (example: *Microsoft Publisher*. These programs allow you to create fancy, home-made newsletters, forms and other business documents.)
- Software to build specific skills, such as typing, math and science
- Creativity packages such as card- and banner-makers

- Special programs like "family tree" makers or software designed for hobbies

Another good tip: set up a usage management system.

Take Control of the Home PC

You paid for it, right? Try this: make a photocopy of the check you wrote to pay for the PC, frame it and display it on the wall next to the computer. Whenever you have a dispute over how to use the PC, quit talking (you can't out-talk a kid anyhow) and quietly point to the framed check. Any complaints—just point to the framed check. Your kids will finally get so sick of this tactic, they'll either go along with you or try something else.

When all else fails, turn the PC off. It works wonders.

Rotate the Soil

Obsessive Burnout Syndrome (OBS) may not be on the government's list of leading contagious diseases, but in computer-hip families it can be a problem. It's a malady we identified after talking to thousands of parents and watching our own kids at home. We're talking about the copy of Disney's *101 Dalmatians* video that's been played at least 101 times in the last month. On the PC side, it's the game or storybook program your kid has been playing nonstop for weeks.

To keep young minds fresh and stimulated, try a technique millions of parents have used with toys—rotate the soil. Keep a few favorites in reserve. When interest starts to flag (or even before), rotate some of the current stuff out and put your "reserves" on the shelf. The key is to manage exposure, while assuring a steady series of challenges from new programs.

The most important thing to avoid is having a kid burn out on using a PC altogether because they've become bored with a limited set of software stimulation. So rotate the soil.

R A L P H :

My 10-year-old son and I have an understanding that when he and I sit down to-gether in front of the PC, it's not going to be all fun and games. My wife and I had figured out long ago that he needed the same thing that he was getting at the kitchen table each day—a balanced diet. In his case this translated into a balanced mix of games, surfing the Internet, and educational programs. Here are three "deals" we hammered out with Jeff that may work for you:

- Before playing a game, you need to spend thirty minutes playing one or more of your educational programs.

- Before playing a game, search the Internet or use one of our PC encyclopedia CD-ROMs for thirty minutes and find three interesting facts about an animal (he gets to pick). We've nicknamed this the "treasure hunt." The sky is the limit. You can pick any subject under the sun and the child gets a mini-taste of what research and re-porting are all about. To add to the experience, teach your child to use a word processor or spreadsheet program to document and present their discoveries.

- Before playing a game, flex your creative muscles. Use our digital camera, one of the drawing and/or photographic editing software packages on our PC, or the scan-ner (or a combination of all of these tools) to create an original piece of computer art. Granted, many families may not have the scanner or digital camera, but you get the picture (sorry for the bad pun). Nearly all PCs use the Windows operating system and it includes a simple drawing program.

The system has worked pretty well. Jeff gets to play his games, but he also gets a dose of educational programs. Try it out.

FOCUSED QUESTIONS

- What are your child's academic strengths and weaknesses? How can you use the computer to help them build on their strengths and overcome their weaknesses? Have you surveyed your family to figure out what kinds of programs would work best?

• What sort of programs do your children prefer—mysteries, puzzles, action games? Why do they like the programs, and how can you leverage that information to find programs that appeal to them?

• What programs do you prefer? What hobbies and interests do you have that you might use the computer to explore further?

• Have you done your homework? Have you read reviews of software. What "local experts" have you interviewed?

• How do you plan to avoid software burnout?

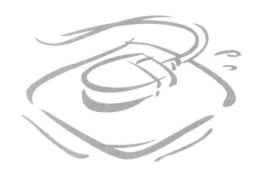

5.

Driver's Ed on the Internet, Part I

LEARNING BASIC CONCEPTS AND LINGO

I finally felt like I had a handle on all this PC stuff, when my teenage son starts
hitting me up for an e-mail account and an on-line subscription so he can
make his own Web site. I feel like I'm starting all over again.
—Parent attending a PC Dads workshop
at the Liberty Science Center, New Jersey

A few years back all you needed to be a digitally hip family was a desktop computer and a printer. Those are already starting to look like the good old days. Now there's all this "WWW" and "dot com" this and "dot com" that stuff. Along with RAMs, ROMs, microprocessors and gigabytes, now you've got to deal with URLs, browsers, electronic mail and Web pages.

What's a parent to do?

Think about it like a journey or a trail ride across a new frontier. There are treasures, opportunities and plenty of fascinating side trips. And, yep, there are also varmints—plenty of them. We've talked to hundreds of parents in various stages of this journey and have a pretty good handle on the issues, so we've put together a set of simple guidelines to help you get started.

Okay, the easy part's over. It's now time to start learning the ropes. Here's what we're going to do in this chapter:

- Explain why you should care about the Internet and the World Wide Web.
- Give you a taste for what going online can do for you and your family.

- Help you become hip to the lingo of cyberspace, including such terms as the Internet, World Wide Web, Web pages, browsers, search engines, modems, you name it—all that stuff you've been hearing coming out of the mouths of your kids and your cyber-savvy friends.
- Throw in some handy information that will enlighten you immensely about the Internet and the World Wide Web.

Audience Check

This chapter is geared for "newbies," folks who are just getting online. Experienced cyber-surfers who need a hand explaining the world of the Internet to normal people should read this chapter for tips on translating all the techno-talk into human speak.

Why Bother?

Lots of folks still ask us, "Is the Internet really worth it?" The answer is, yes! We could cite all kinds of studies from eggheads, but that would be too easy. Instead we cooked up two real-life stories from our home fronts to show you what's happened in our families thanks to the Internet. We call them "A Tale of Two Dads."

A TALE OF TWO DADS

 RALPH'S FAMILY GOES CYBER

My family discovered the Internet about two years ago. Now I can't get them off it. My wife's on the Web multiple times a week, monitoring our online bank accounts, or e-mailing her investment-club friends and PTA partners. My 14-year-old daughter surfs rock band Web sites and exchanges e-mail and pictures with her friends—or, if nothing else, scours Web sites for homework help. My 10-year-old son, the game nut, is up there checking out the latest game sites and downloading trial software demos. Clearly, my family's gone cyber.

My latest adventure in cyberspace involves connecting with my cousin in Connecticut. In early 1998 my cousin got online, found my e-mail address and started sending me notes. I responded with messages and pictures of the kids. Through the Internet our relationship has grown from an annual Christmas card exchange to a fun and rewarding family reunion (albeit electronic!) several times a year.

Even my son sees the benefits now. In fourth grade his teacher asked each kid to become an "expert" on a subject of their choice and prepare a class presentation. Being fascinated with airplanes, and knowing that his grandfather had been a gunner on a B-17 bomber during WWII, he decided to do his report on the venerable aircraft.

Rather than slog down to the library, he hit the Internet. Online, all we had to do was fire up the PC and search the Internet for Web sites on B-17s. We hit a gold mine—loads of sites dedicated to the subject, including Boeing Corporation's history pages packed with photos and information about the venerable B-17. Through the miracle of electronic "copy and paste" we were able to grab passages of text and photos, which we transferred to our PC and printed out. Soon we had the raw material to make a really cool poster. Best of all, we did it together right in our den.

MARK'S TRIP TO BEANIE BABY LAND

I've noticed a pattern over the years. The more I try to get my kids or wife to do something, the more they resist. So I didn't push it when my kids showed little interest in the Internet a couple of years ago. Then two things happened: Matthew, the oldest, discovered cars and Michael fell in love with Beanie Babies, those lovable little character dolls that have turned into collector items.

Both were driven there by peer pressure. Whether you're 9 (like Mike) or 13 (Matt) you simply can't risk being uncool. Matthew loves to check out the car sitesnot station wagons and vans, of course, but dragsters, sports cars and muscle cars. He checks out the "specs" of these cars, reports them back to me or his buddies in detail—illustrating the RPMs, how fast this or that car will go, and other performance lingo that makes no sense to me. His other interest is in games. He checks out all the online games and even plays with his buddies, using the modem. Strangely (to me), he'll play a modem-to-modem game with his neighborhood friends, while talking to them by way of his walkie-talkie radio. Go figure.

Michael's interests are more practical. It's not enough for him to collect Beanie Babies—he has forty or so. He has to keep up with them. Why? Because the company is constantly "retiring" some babies, and that drives the value up. Mike's friends have seen some of their dolls skyrocket from $7 or so to over $100 (some fetch over $1,000). This is one of the shrewdest marketing ploys since Pet Rocks. To be "in the know," Mike had to get on the Web and check out the dozen or so Beanie Baby Web pages. These sites are filled with Beanie Baby facts and rumors as people try to guess which of the dolls is going to be retired next. I can't say that he's made a killing on any of these rumors, but there's always hope. For now, at least, it's piqued his interest in the Internet and kept him off the streets. Next mission: Mike's personal Beanie Baby Web page.

Learning the Lingo: Gophers, Usenet Groups and Other Varmints

Not long ago, when people came to us complaining they didn't understand the Internet lingo, we took them to heart. We spent hours in our first "Cyber Safari" workshops in various cities with sophisticated technical explanations. This made our geek-friends back home happy and worked wonders for insomnia cases, but it didn't do a lot for our audiences; the most common response was still "huh?"

So after massive research (several conversations at the office cafeteria) and experimentation, we boiled it down to a simple glossary of Internet terms. The following pages give the "must-know" terms, the essentials of the Internet. Read through them several times and maybe even chant them around the house for good measure. It'll help you remember them and impress the teenage kids, who'll wonder what you're up to.

PC DADS DOWN-HOME INTERNET GUIDE

• **Internet:** Bunch of computers connected together through the global, sprawling telecommunications network that talk to each other using an internationally accepted lingo. When you connect to the Internet (we'll explain how in a bit) your PC and you become a part of the Internet. If you want to be cool, call it "the Net." The key is that all of these computers—from the one in your home or office, to giant systems in major corporations and colleges—can share and pass along messages, images, sounds and even video.

• **Cyberspace:** Fancy term meant to describe the online world of the Internet.

• **Information ("Info") Highway:** City slicker word for the Internet that's been milked unmercifully by reporters, keyboard-thumping experts and shameless self-promoters.

• **World Wide Web:** The World Wide Web and Internet are often confused, but they are different beasts. The Internet, as you now know, is a bunch of computers strapped together via the worldwide telecommunications system. The World Wide Web is the graphical presentation part of the Internet that you see displayed on your screen when you use a browser to visit a Web site (hang in there, you're moments away from an explanation of "browser" and "Web site").

Let's take a short trip to the supermarket to explain the difference between the Internet and the World Wide Web. The aisles and carts give you a transportation and delivery system for moving around the store and finding the products you want. Think of that as being the Internet. Now think of each product in the market as being a Web site containing pictures and text to help you understand what's inside. The internationally recognized method for creating, addressing and delivering Web pages with pictures, text and the ability to link (connect) to other Web sites is called the World Wide Web. The engine that makes the World Wide Web tick is the vast network of Internet computers that deliver Web pages created with an internationally accepted programming language called HTML (Hyper Text Markup Language). The Web, with its Web sites created with HTML, gives us the Internet in a friendly, easy to operate graphical "shell" (kind of like what the geeks call a Graphical User Interface, or GUI) that "sits" on top of the Internet communications infrastructure.

The World Wide Web was invented in 1989 and launched the explosive growth of the Internet in the '90s. Suddenly anyone who could use a mouse and keyboard could easily look at or retrieve information from Web sites, send messages or even listen to audio files or view video.

• **Browser:** A point-and-click software program designed to make it super easy to travel or "browse" throughout the World Wide Web. The most famous browsers today are Netscape and Microsoft's Internet Explorer. Once your PC is connected to the Internet (you'll learn how to do that later in this chapter) all you have to do is run the browser of your choice, type in the World Wide Web address (example: www.parentsoup.com) and press the "enter" key on your keyboard. The browser then takes advantage of the World Wide Web and the Internet to help fetch the requested Web site and display it on your screen. Don't know the address of a Web site? No sweat. That's the job of the search engine—more on that in a moment.

Netscape Browser and PC Dads Web Page

Note: The browser is represented by the frame at the top with all the buttons. The PC Dads Web page below the gray frame is the Web page.

A browser and the HTML code used to create Web sites makes it easy to "window shop" the pages within a single Web site or move from one Web site to another (that's where the nickname "browser" comes from). Earlier in the definition of the World Wide Web we mentioned in passing that Web sites can have links to other Web sites. When you look at a Web site often you'll find underlined, highlighted text or graphical buttons. These elements of a Web page are made possible by the HTML code and are called Hyperlinks. Take your mouse, move your cursor over the underlined text and more often than not double clicking on it will cause your browser to call up another Web site (a linked Web site) or a page within the Web site linked to the home page.

• **Web Sites and Home Pages:** This is where the information lives on the World Wide Web. Companies, schools, nonprofit organizations or individuals can create Web sites. Most Web sites are stored on, and delivered by, big powerful computers called servers. The home page is actually the front door or starting point to a Web site. Make it friendly enough and folks might come on in and stay awhile. You don't have to be a big shot to build a Web site and beam your mug out to millions of people or share your favorite recipe for meat loaf or cornbread.

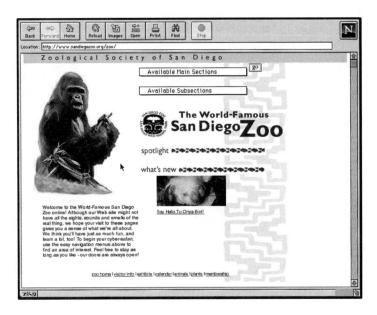

Sample Web page. This shows the typical elements of a Web page including pictures and boxes (links) you can activate with your mouse pointer to get additional information or to travel to another related Web site.

• **Web Site Address or URL:** Often fondly known as the "Uniform Resource Locator" (URL is pronounced "earl" or spoken out as U, R, L). URLs, or Web addresses if you prefer, are entered (via keyboard) into a special address box found at the top of a browser. Most Web site addresses start with http:// (which stands for Hypertext Transport Protocol—this is the technical name for the communications protocol standard of the World Wide Web scheme). Nearly all of the Web sites you'll encounter will follow the http:// part with the letters www for World Wide Web. The one thing about Web site addresses that is interesting is the tail end. An address with .com at the end, such as http://www.intel.com means it's a commercial business Web site (with com being shorthand for commercial). An .org ending generally means the Web site is from a nonprofit group, .edu represents an educational institution and .gov stands for government agencies. As you branch out and become a global Web surfer you'll encounter URLs for foreign sites. A .uk in a Web address, for example, means the site is from the United Kingdom.

• **Search Engine:** Search engines are special Web sites that will help you locate other Web sites by subject. They act as super reference librarians of the Web and go by creative names like Yahoo, WebCrawler, Infoseek, Excite, HotBot, Dogpile and Lycos. Most browsers have a search button that will take you to a search engine Web site. Another way to think of the search engine site is as being like the long distance telephone operator or an automated Yellow Pages service.

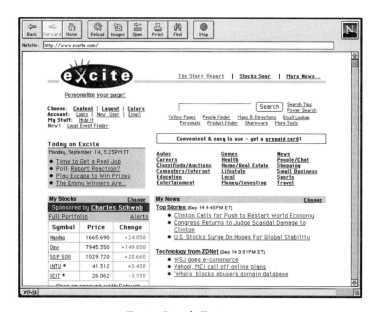

Excite Search Engine

Let's say you want to find Web sites on RV parks or snakeskin boots (or whatever). You type in a keyword or words, like RV park, press the enter key and the service uses the World Wide Web and the Internet to search for all the Web addresses in its database that match your subject request. In a few seconds your screen fills with a list of Web sites and their Web address. Click on an address and the browser swings into action navigating cyberspace to find and deliver the Web site to your screen. Search engine Web sites are generally free as most are supported by advertisements displayed on the site's pages.

• **Going Online:** You'd think someone was weird if they said they were "going online" to make a telephone call, or "going on the asphalt" to describe driving down to the hardware store. In the world of the Internet, however, the words "going online" refer to the act of connecting your computer to the Internet or a commercial online service (don't worry, you'll learn how to get connected in the next chapter).

• **Modem:** When your PC uses a regular telephone line to call up a service like America Online, it's using a special computer "telephone" in the PC called a modem. In the next chapter you'll discover what modems do and how to buy one.

• **E-mail:** Short for electronic mail. Just like the old fashioned letters you write except you compose them on your PC and mail them over the Internet. While electronic mail is sent over the Internet, you can actually subscribe to a pure e-mail service like Juno that doesn't include the browser and surfing privileges (some of these are free). It's fast, fun and you spare a lot of trees in the process (Oregon readers take note).

With these basic terms under your belt, you're ready to master some the ultra-hip Internet and World Wide Web slang terms. Watch your kids light up when you start tossing these around:

• **Surfing:** Once mainly a guy thing, now a gal thing too, meant to describe exploring the Internet, often randomly, in search of pure knowledge (okay, it's goofing off). Like channel surfing with a TV remote control, but instead of forty or fifty channels, it's millions of Web pages.

• **Download:** Bringing information or pictures into your computer from another distant computer. "Upload" is when you send the information the other way, say if you want to post a picture of your favorite hunting dog to your personal Web page or send it to your significant other as a file that rides along with an e-mail greeting.

• **Bandwidth:** We like milkshakes as much as the next guy, but just try to sip one through one of those wimpy little cocktail straws. That's what it's like sometimes trying to download information over a phone line. Like watching paint dry in the rain, kind of slow. Bandwidth is all about how fat your straw is. Speedy modems help, but fatter, higher-capacity digital phone lines are even better. You'll hear communications junkies use the words "Integrated Services Digital Network," or just ISDN in reference to one of the more common high-capacity lines.

• **Chat Rooms:** Virtual "places" where you join a few or hundreds of fellow Internet surfers for text exchange conversations. Chat rooms can be hosted by the owners of individual Web sites and/or special sections of an online service for subscribing members only. (More on chat rooms awaits you later in Chapters 12 and 13 on Cyber Safety.)

• **Bulletin Boards:** In the 1970s, most people going online used so-called Bulletin Board Services (BBS) to send e-mail, exchanged messages in discussion groups and downloaded (copied) files from a remote computer. In the early days bulletin board systems were typically run by independent local services hosted by companies, clubs, special interest groups or individuals. Often they were set up to share information on specific subjects. Today many provide Internet services including e-mail.

• **Gopher:** Little critter (actually an Internet system employing programs comprised of simple menus and text commands) used a lot before the invention of the World Wide Web, browsers and search engines to find information by subject. These services would "go for" the information you wanted. You can still find gopher services if you're willing to dig deep (pardon the bad pun), but do this only if you're working on a homework assignment on the history of the Internet. Stick with search engines.

• **Hyperlink:** When you're looking at a Web page and see a word or phrase that's underlined, try clicking on it—a whole new document or Web page pops up on your screen. That's because there's a hyperlink that lets you zoom from one document to another, even if the first one is from a Web site stored on a computer in Akron and the second one is on a computer in Zanzibar.

• **Snail Mail:** U.S. postal service, still used in many parts of the country, known for its lack of speed. Mules and jets come to mind when comparing it to electronic mail.

• **Usenet Groups:** Closely related cousins to bulletin boards. Through Usenet groups, you can get together online to share all kinds of ideas and information from the latest Elvis sightings, new computer contraptions and the latest fashion statements from the PC Dads.

• **Virtual:** A fancy term to describe something simulated on a computer, or something that is . . . but it isn't (virtual reality). Get it?

So far so good. You're getting closer to taking the plunge. Go over the terms and concepts in this chapter until you master them. Then move to the next chapter where you'll roll up your sleeves and learn the steps and gear needed to go online.

FOCUSED QUESTIONS

- Are you "Internet ready"?
- Do you know the basic lingo? Do techno-savvy kids intimidate you (or just annoy you)?

- Do you know the difference between a browser and the World Wide Web?

- What would it take (knowledge, courage, time) to make it possible for you to go online?

- In other words, if you have a PC but aren't online yet, what's holding you back?

6.

Driver's Ed on the Internet, Part II

HOW TO GO ONLINE, GET AROUND AND COMMUNICATE WITH FRIENDS AND STRANGERS

Everybody at work spouts off words like Internet, World Wide Web, browsers and search engines like everyone knows what they're talking about. I've watched them surf the Net but there's so much I don't follow. I don't get it.
—Cyberspace "newbie" parent attending a PC Dads workshop in Moncton, New Brunswick, Canada

With the cyberspace lingo and basic concepts you gained in the last chapter it's time to get serious and down to work. Here's what we'll do in this chapter:

- Learn what equipment and software you need to go online.

- Learn, step-by-step, how to set up an online subscription account.

- Understand how to drive a browser.

- Understand how to use a search engine.

- Find out about some of the fun things to do on the World Wide Web.

- Discover why people are so high on e-mail, and what e-mail options you have.

- How to express your deepest emotions in text e-mail using "emoticons."

- Find out where you can learn more about the Internet and the World Wide Web.

Equipment Check

Any journey, of course, requires a certain type of gear. This is true of going on-line as well.

STEP ONE: GET A PC.

This is a no-brainer. If you're reading this book, you probably already own a computer. Or you've read the "Buying a PC" chapter so you know everything you always wanted to know about how to buy one. While the modem (see Step Two) dictates much of your experience on the Internet, you still need a computer fast enough to handle all the fancy multimedia sounds and videos you'll be downloading or playing on-the-fly. If you need a refresher go back to Chapter 2.

STEP TWO: GET A GOOD MODEM.

A modem is a little box that sits outside your PC or it can be a special card that goes inside your system. Its job is to be your PC's telephone to reach the Internet and communicate with the millions of computers in cyberspace.

Speed is king when it comes to modems. The speed at which a modem can send and receive all the bits and bytes that make up the text, pictures, sounds and video is measured in kilo-bits-per-second (1,000 bits-per-second). Remember that it takes eight bits to make up one letter or number in the language of computers. Currently 56,000 bits-per-second modems are the standard. Speed is key not just for the sake of going fast, but to cut down on the time you have to stare at the monitor as you wait for files to reach your computer. Let's put this into perspective: A one-million-byte word processing or image file will take about nine to ten minutes to get to your PC if you're using an older 14,400 bits-per-second modem. With a 28,000 bps model, that time comes down to approximately five minutes. Zoom up in speed to 56,000 bps and you'll get results in about three minutes. Warning: these speed estimates are for a perfect environment. Your results will vary depending on Internet traffic, the quality of your phone line connection, etc.

Special tip: we like external box modems with the pretty green and red flashing lights that let you know something is happening.

STEP THREE: FIND A SPARE TELEPHONE JACK IN YOUR HOUSE.

The modem needs to connect to a spare phone outlet just like a regular phone (it's the phone for your PC, remember?). Your modem will come with a regular telephone line to connect it to the wall jack. This part is real easy.

By the way, as you enter the ranks of the Internet-hip, you may be hearing about ultra-high-speed alternatives to regular phone lines, such as digital phone service, cable modems, satellites and even microwave alternatives. Keep your eyes open on these; they could change the whole Internet experience. More about this in Chapter 15.

STEP FOUR: SUBSCRIBE TO AN INTERNET ACCESS SERVICE PROVIDER.

Bonus: Free PC Dads Marriage Salvation Tip

Get a second phone line for your computer and modem so you and your family can surf the Web without competing with each other's telephone time. Surfing the Net is a whole lot of fun, if not downright addictive. Before you know it, you'll be fighting with your spouse and the kids, who may actually want to use the phone line to make a *phone call* (imagine that!). If you value your marriage, get a second phone line.

Also try to go into your modem program or documentation and see if you can turn the squawker (ahem, the speaker) down; it can grate on the nerves. We know a radio DJ in Long Island, NY, who would sneak out of bed at night and go online, but the squealing of the modem would jolt his wife out of bed. His answer: cover the modem with pillows. Why go to all this trouble if you can simply turn it down? By the way, the weird hissing and squawking sounds your modem makes when it connects with an online service's modem is actually a code. The coded exchange between the two modems is designed to determine the maximum speed each can support and other communications control features.

You can't just dial up into the Internet directly. That would be like installing a phone in your home and trying to dial out before you sign up with a local phone company. To go online, you need, in the lingo of cyberspace, an Internet Service Provider (ISP).

Luckily, you have lots of options. Most folks take the easy route and sign up with one of the giant national providers like America Online, Prodigy or Microsoft MSN. Each of these services gives you access to the Internet and a bunch of other features specific to that service and sections (like departments in a magazine). Go to the bookstore or grocery store magazine rack and buy a publication like *FamilyPC;* more often than not it'll contain a free diskette with start-up software you can install on your PC to get the ball rolling. America On-line and other service companies put free start-up disks in magazines to seed the market with potential subscribers.

Shopper's Tip: The major national services like America Online, Microsoft Network and CompuServe do more than just provide access to the Internet. They also offer proprietary special interest features and services for members only. If surfing the Internet and looking at Web pages is *all* you want to do, try signing up with a local service provider based in your community. Check out the business section of your newspaper or the yellow pages under "Internet Service." Call the provider you select and ask for a "start-up" software kit. Monthly subscription fees for local services generally stay in the $20 range, and sometimes less.

Whether you choose a big national service or small local access provider, chances are good you'll start with a diskette with software you need to load before you can venture out into cyberspace. To give you a taste of what that process is like, here are the eight steps it takes to load up America Online's diskette:

1. Turn on your PC and put the diskette in the floppy disk drive.

2. Follow the written instructions on the floppy diskette label to be-gin running the set-up program.

3. The set-up program will install all the magic control software and Net surfing essentials like a browser on your PC.

4. Once the basic software is installed you'll get step-by-step in-structions for setting up your modem to work with the service and for making your initial new subscriber call-in.

5. Turn on your modem (only need to do this if it's an external box type that is outside of your PC's case), make sure there is a phone line (just like the one used for your regular phone) connected from the mo-dem to a phone wall outlet.

6. Follow the set-up program instructions for dialing up the service to register (should be an 800 free call).

7. Enjoy the weird noises your modem makes as it starts talking to the service's modem.

8. Once you're connected to the service (like Aunt Sue picking up the phone and saying "hello") a menu will appear asking some questions to determine how you'll be billed (expect to pay an average of $20 per month), what password you want, etc. In about five to ten minutes you'll be up and running.

The downside of some of the big national services is that you might get busy signals when you try to dial them up.

Tip: see if you can set up the dialing portion of the service program to repeatedly auto-dial until you connect. While you wait, pick up a book and sit back and relax. If you are unhappy with repeated delays, find a different provider. Better yet, ask around to see which ones have the best local connect track records.

STEP FIVE: LEARN HOW TO USE A WEB BROWSER.

Right now the most popular browsers are Netscape and Microsoft's Internet Explorer. The good news for you is that browsers are typically provided free of charge as part of the software included with your subscription to an Internet access service. It doesn't really matter that much which one you choose, give or take a few features. They'll both work on most of the local provider services out there and the national services as well. Starting up a browser via a national online service is easy. The opening menu screen for most greets you with a menu of options, one of which will be the Internet. Click on the Internet option and the service's browser comes up.

At the top of most browsers (see the following illustration) is a place to enter the "address" of the Web page you want. The whole browser deal works something like the good old postal service. If you know Aunt Sue's address, you write it on an envelope and mail it.

To go to a Web site, you can enter its Internet address in the space at the top of the browser and press the enter key. In a few seconds, or minutes, the web page pops up on the computer screen.

Browser Example: Note the rectangular box where
you key in the URL and the toolbar running across the top of the screen. This is
where the features of the browser can be requested.

Wait! What if you don't know the address, or even what Web sites are out there on the subject you're trying to locate? No sweat, that's the job of the search engine.

STEP SIX: LEARN HOW TO USE A SEARCH ENGINE.

Let's go back to our phone analogy. If you don't know the phone number for a business or person, you can go to the phone book or call the operator and get the number. In cyberspace you do the same thing by calling up a special service Web site called a search engine. Look closely at your browser's buttons. One of them should be labeled "Search." Click on it and you'll open one of the many search engines available free of charge on the World Wide Web. You can click on the main subject categories to see suggested Web sites by topic, or you can key in search words or phrases.

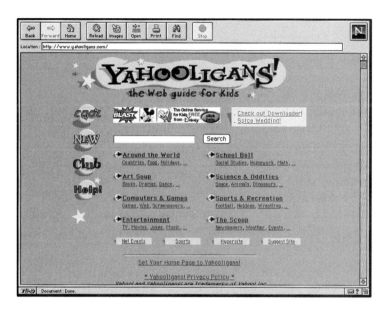

Children's Web Guide

Remember Ralph's son's B-17 research project? They found a bunch of airplane Web sites by using the Yahooligans (www.yahooligans.com) search engine. In a few seconds up came a long list of kid-safe Web sites dedicated to this subject. When you click on the highlighted portion of a listed site, your browser calls up the site and delivers it.

Browsers and search engines are *easy* to use. Just type in words and point and click. But they have one problem: they can swamp you with information—sometimes thousands of citations. Luckily, some smart folks are designing new programs that will help do some of the filtering work for you. Many search engine companies use sophisticated technology to scour the Net looking for the best sites in various categories (e.g., "The Mining Company" at www.miningco.com). Other sites allow you to create personal pro-

Our Top Search Engine Picks

Our favorite search engines include Yahoo (www.yahoo.com), Infoseek (www.infoseek.com), and Excite (www.excite.com). There are several search engines designed for kids (such as Yahooligans). And if you want to do some *really* heavy-duty research, try a search engine like Dogpile (www.dogpile.com), which uses more than a dozen of the main search engines, including those mentioned earlier. It's a super search engine.

Online Auctions

Why not go shopping? You can buy almost anything online: blue jeans, cowboy boots, camping gear, power tools, all the life essentials so to speak. Music is a big seller. Go to Amazon.com and you can find CDs to fit almost any taste—and even listen to some of the songs before you buy.

But here's something even cooler: online auctions. These sites allow you to bid on items from stereos and TVs to collectibles and antiques. You just set up an account and you're ready to jump in. Some of these are just like real actions, just online. First Auction (www.firstauction.com), for instance, offers thirty-minute bidding events, with prices starting as low as $1. You can see if you're winning by clicking on your "personal page." Competition is fierce so don't expect to walk away with a steal. Another one is eBay (www. ebay.com), which puts 20,000 items a day up for sale—comic books, Beanie Babies, videos, etc. And here's a different twist: you don't have to hang around to see your bid through. Pick a maximum amount, and eBay will bid for you until you reach your maximum. The auction here is done over three to seven days, so you have time to come in and out and boost your bid. Best of all, you can sell items too—the auction is open to anyone.

files geared to your own tastes. Search engines like Yahoo and Excite are doing this as well as big name news sites like CNN interactive and *The Wall Street Journal*. While this may not help you when you're researching a subject, they can be useful on a day-to-day basis. You can set up a profile for news topics that interest you—sports, local weather, and so on. Then, whenever you go on, you see a personally tailored news page.

The Check's in the Mail: e-mail

We never cease to be amazed at the power of e-mail. When we're on the road we can fire up our laptop PCs, plug the modem into the hotel phone jack and check for mail messages on our America Online account. Mark's son is a big e-mailer; he constantly sends Mark e-mails to keep him up to date on the latest happenings around the house—so and so just bought a new bike, the dog just dug up the garden and so on. He gets a kick out of it when Mark updates him on his daily activities.

E-mail breaks down barriers of space and time. Recently Mark received a "letter" from a cousin he hadn't seen in fifteen years. She was living in South America and had somehow gotten his e-mail address and was writing to say "hi" and catch up. He may not have ever heard from this woman again if not for e-mail.

Of course, there's always the flip side: what happens if e-mail goes down? Back at Intel, we live on e-mail, spewing out thousands of messages a day.

Once when the electronic mail system went down, there was near panic as people scrambled to figure out what was going on, dialing colleagues, yelling across the aisles. Heads popped up over cubicles like prairie dogs. Luckily the system was revived in less than an hour and the panic subsided. But it was scary.

Here's what a typical e-mail looks like (using America Online as an example):

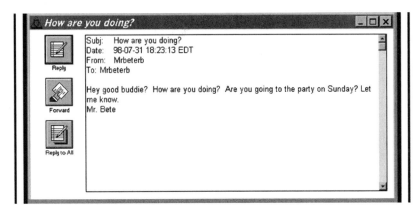

Note: The top band of the screen display gives the title of the e-mail as created by the sender. All the usual to, from and date information is also provided. On the side are handy buttons to make sending a reply or forwarding the message to another person easy.

Even for many normal humans, e-mail is critical; it's often the main reason for going online in the first place. And no wonder. Unlike "snail mail" (envelopes, paper, stamps and the Postal Service) or fax machines, e-mail lets you create messages and send them to anyone in the world with an Internet e-mail address—and they receive the message just seconds or minutes after you hit the send button. They can print your message, store it on their hard disk for later review or pass it along to friends or business associates.

Sending text messages is great, but it's far from the limit of what e-mail can do today. You can send files along for the ride with your text messages (the geeks call it "attaching" a file to a text message). These files can be word processing, spreadsheet or even digital artwork, pictures or sound files.

Basically there are three kinds of e-mail, with some flavors in between:

Express Yourself with "Emoticons"

When you communicate on the Web—either in chat rooms, bulletin boards or e-mail—you don't just use text words to express your emotions. That's boring. You use what are known as "emoticons." Below are a few examples. Guess what they mean?

1) :-x

2) : -(

3) =:-o

4) >:-<

5) ;-)

6) :-D

7) >:->

8) d:-o

9) :-()

10) :-y

11) :->

12) :-I

13) :-#

14) *<: -)

Answers: 1) Blowing a kiss 2) Unhappy 3) Surprised 4) Very Angry 5) Winking, flirting 6) Laughing 7) Devilish remark 8) Tipping your hat 9) User has a moustache 10) Saying it with a smile 11) Sarcastic 12) Indifferent 13) User wears braces 14) User is wearing a Santa Claus hat

• Web-based services: you get e-mail services, along with the rest of the package, when you subscribe to one of the services like AOL or Earthlink.

• Independent, "free" Web-based services:. These aren't really free because you have to pay something for a service like America Online to get online in the first place, but they're still cool. An example is Yahoo e-mail, found on the Yahoo search engine Web site as an additional service. (One good feature of both of these services is that you can check your e-mail wherever you are, just as long as you can access the Web with your browser.)

• Pure e-mail: If all you want is e-mail—no surfing, no Web browsing—you can subscribe to a pure e-mail service. Some of these are free, like Juno (www.juno.com). Services like Juno and Yahoo e-mail embed display screens with paid advertising to cover the cost of offering the service free of charge.

The point is to find a service that works for you. Some have better "interfaces" or features that allow for easy navigation; others may have easier installation or better dial-up services. Do your homework and you'll learn what millions of e-mail fanatics already know: electronic mail is cool (or as Mark's oldest son says, making fun of his dad's '60s upbringing, "groovy").

RALPH: STAYING IN TOUCH WITH E-MAIL

In 1998 my wife took a week-long trip to Long Island on family business. It was the first time my kids had been separated from her for that amount of time. In addition to the good old telephone we decided to have some digital fun and send Mom sound greetings and digital pictures. As luck would have it, she had access to a laptop that could connect to the Internet. Each night we used a microphone connected to our PC's sound card to record short one- or two-minute greetings. For photos we used our trusty digital camera to create and then store the photos on the PC. My son or daughter would write an e-mail message and with a click of a button (we used America Online's e-mail), we "attached" the files to the message and clicked the send button. When my wife logged on, she could download the recorded message file and listen to it, see the photos and read the e-mail message. She loved it.

Anatomy of an Internet
E-Mail Address

Most newbies to the Internet first dive into the water of the World Wide Web to surf Web sites and see what's out there in the boundless realm of cyberspace. Close on the heels of this favorite sport is sending and getting e-mail. To do that, as you've seen, your Internet access provider will give you an e-mail address. In a way, your address will look a bit like a Web site address. Here's what it may look like: joe.blank@gogosurf.com. In this case Joe's first and last name comprise the initial part of the address with "dots" (to be hip you must call them dots, not periods) separating the first and last name. The @ symbol part of the address comes before the name of Joe's Internet Service Provider's computer (or company, school or organization server). Finally, the ".com" means that Joe's e-mail is handled by a commercial service provider or he works for a

Where to Learn More About the Internet and the World Wide Web

To learn more about the Internet, check out:

The Internet for Dummies, IDG World Books

Good directories of family web sites:

www.yahooligans.com

family.disney.com

www.edmark.com

commercial business. E-mail addresses will vary a lot, but now you can at least decode the basics.

FOCUSED QUESTIONS

• Do you understand what equipment, software and services you need to go online?

• Do you have a feel for the bare essentials of browser and search engine operation?

• Have you researched Internet Service Providers?

• Have you talked to a friend or neighbor with Internet access who could give you a guided tour and tell you who the good local Internet Service Providers are?

• Have you determined if a local or national Internet provider is right for you?

• What topics would you or your kids like to research on the World Wide Web?

• Are you ready to cyber surf?

7.

Jump-starting Your Child into the Digital Age

TIPS, STRATEGIES AND SUGGESTIONS FOR BUSY PARENTS

Teach your kids about computers while you can;
it won't be very many years before they're teaching you.
—The PC Dads

Parents frequently ask us if there's a perfect time to start their kid on the computer. A mom in Portland, Oregon, with a 2-year-old daughter was typical. "She seems so young, but she likes the bright colors. Is it too early?" Another set of parents in Minneapolis, who have an eight-year-old boy and are buying their first computer, wondered if they were "too late." The answer in both cases is: nope. There is no magical age to start a child computing, and there's no proof that starting them out before age two is much of an advantage. So, if you're feeling guilty because your child has already started school and isn't a keyboard whiz, get over it. There's plenty of time.

In this chapter we'll take a look at how you can get your child computing happily at any age. You'll see how to kid-proof your investment while also making the PC kid-friendly. We've included some special tips for dealing with those crazy toddlers, along with info about how you can use the PC to promote independence, develop solid decision-making skills, even help with homework or home schooling.

So, take a deep breath and begin thinking about how you're going to enter the Digital Age with your kid, to assure it's a win/win deal. The time to start your child computing is when:

• **You're ready!** It's critical that you know your way around the computer. You don't try to show your kid how to drive a car until you can drive, and the same is true with a computer. You should at least be able to navigate around the screen and operate the basic programs. You don't need to be a complete computer geek, you just need to be able to get around.

• **Your child can sit still (on your lap or in a chair) for ten minutes.** You need to get them engaged long enough to experience different aspects of a program. What good is a great computer program if your child can't enjoy it?

M A R K :

Shortly after my daughter Nicole's second birthday, we bought a computer and she was banging on the keyboard in no time. We'd hit a key and something would fly out of a barn or a pig would squeal. She'd laugh—and keep banging. I was amazed at how easily she adapted to the machine. No one told her she was too young to learn or that girls weren't supposed to be good at computing. She just did her thing, learning as she went along. Today, at the ripe old age of four, she's pretty proficient at the computer and telling *me* what to do. So much for innocence and helplessness.

• **You have time to spend together with your child.** Avoid the temptation to use the computer as an electronic babysitter. Instead, make it a partnership affair, something you both share and enjoy. We call this shoulder-to-shoulder learning.

Getting Off to the Right Start (No Matter What Age)

Don't worry for a minute that your kid won't be interested in the computer. The bright colors and lights naturally draw in kids. The animated cartoon characters, sound effects and music of today's kid software programs also lure them. Your job is simply to help get your half-pint started—then hold on and keep up. We know many kids at all different ages who are cruising around the computer playing and learning all kinds of cool stuff:

- In Vallejo, California, six-year-old Mandy uses the word processor to spell words and the names of family members and friends. She loves to change the size and color of the fonts. She's becoming quite a speller while having a great time.
- The music and graphics of *Reader Rabbit* mesmerize Zach, a four-year-old boy in Colorado. He doesn't even notice that he's learning pre-reading skills; he just laughs at the rabbit's antics.
- In Atlanta, the six-year-old son of a TV correspondent is fascinated with the *Crayola* art program and will spend up to an hour flexing his creative muscles.

Once you've decided it's time for your kids to get computer smart, there are a few things you can do to give them a good start. First up: protecting your investment.

Kid-Proofing Your PC

You've spent good money on your PC, so the last thing you want is a kid spilling milk or dropping pizza on it. You also don't want to be so paranoid that your kids are afraid to go anywhere near the thing. The idea is to balance accessibility with respect for the hardware—not an easy deal with young-uns. Here are some tips to keep you from pulling your hair out:

• **Placement:** We always advise parents to get the computer away from the craziness of the kitchen and den so you can enjoy quality time with your kid. But you don't want it so secluded that you can't keep an eye on it; in other words, don't put it in their room. You want to be able to monitor activity easily. A good compromise is placing the computer in a study that's near a main traffic area, allowing you to pop in and check up on the kid. This makes it easier to keep an eye on your child *and* the computer while demonstrating the PC's importance.

• **Order:** Even if you're a slob, try to clean up your act near the computer. Pick up the coffee cups, business cards, pens and other junk. Put the CDs back in their jewel cases or, better yet, in CD booklets that hold up to twenty disks. Discipline yourself to provide a good example so your children learn to take care of their stuff. Also enforce a cleanup rule. Everyone must clean up after themselves; break the rule and you lose computer privileges for a while.

• **Cords:** Don't allow dangling cords around the computer. All those tangled wires sticking out are a safety hazard for everyone, but especially for small kids who can pull on the cords and send something crashing down on themselves. Make sure to tape the wires together and put them out of reach.

• **Backups:** Keyboards are cheap and replaceable, so even if your daughter spills juice all over it, it's not the end of the world. But critical files, like financial or family files, are a different story. Be sure to back them up regularly on a tape or other backup device. Our favorite backup device today is the Iomega Zip drive, a gadget that you can pick up at almost any computer store.

Keep in mind your child's age and interests as you fire up the computer. Technology is going to be a way of life for your kids. The best thing you can do for them is to get them comfortable, excited and interested in the computer *without* overwhelming them. Every child is different; using a computer is a little like walking and talking. Each kid does it in her own time with her own unique style. Getting your child computing has at least as much to do with using good parenting skills as it does with technological competence.

Toddlers and preschoolers have short attention spans and limited eye/hand coordination so keep it short and easy. Seven- and 8-year-olds typically regard the computer as a toy and see being on a computer as play. Capitalize on this now and your child will reap the benefits for years. The 9- and 10-year-old crowd gets a lot of gratification from being good at what they do and having control over something. These kids generally want to master *something* and feel a sense of competence and achievement. It's like they've discovered that practice makes perfect, so it's a great time for them to learn to touch type and expand their computer skills. At this age, they want to be recognized as something more than a little kid or so-and-so's big brother or sister, so don't forget the positive reinforcement.

Five Ways to Make a PC Kid-Friendly

1. Give it a "kid look." First impressions count, and children should feel good about the computer. Add-on programs like Microsoft's *Plus! For Kids* for Windows 95 and Edmark's *Kid Desk* Family Edition present children with colorful customized opening screens, friendly animated guides and simple start-up buttons. In other words, they get to create the look and feel of the computer, tailoring it to their tastes. These programs also make it a snap for young kids so they don't have to ask Mom or Dad every time they want to play a program.

2. Tack on kid-size controls. Brightly colored keyboards featuring extra-large keys are now readily available for about $60. Microsoft has a huge track ball device called Easy Ball aimed at 2- to 6-year-olds, and you can find large digital drawing tablets for about $100 that allow kids to use a pointing device to draw pictures or operate programs. All these make it easier for little fingers to manage the PC.

3. Splash on some color and fun. Consider colorful screen savers: the crazier the better (for us and the kids). Another cool tip: buy comical screen saver programs or "picture frames" that attach around your monitor featuring cartoon characters, animals or super heroes. You might even want to buy a piece of white poster board and let your children create their own decorative screen frame. To keep things lively, rotate screen savers and frames every week.

4. Upgrade to better sound. High-quality sound is just as important as flashy graphics to the little folks. Make sure your computer has a good set of stereophonic speakers, available for about $100.

5. Get an adjustable seat. For about $50 you can go to the office supply store and buy an adjustable desk chair (with rollers). Raising the seat and being able to move it close to the keyboard is heaven for tiny kiddies.

Toddler Tips

It's tough being a toddler. Just about everything, including the family dog, towers over them. They're Lilliputians in a world of Gullivers. Despite their knee-high view of the world, toddlers just plunge on ahead into every potential disaster they can find. You can minimize the computer calamities in your house and enhance their experience by using these tips:

• Start with them in your lap, and continue making it a lap experience as long as needed, with you directing their early moves.

• When your toddler graduates from your lap, set up a special chair for her and encourage good posture. The child should sit sixteen to twenty inches from the screen.

• Keep the volume at a level that's comfortable for both of you. (Tip: Learn how to set the master volume for your speakers. On a PC, you can set volume via the Windows operating system, using your manual for guidance.)

• Give your child a container for CDs. That way you can control access while giving the child a chance to find the one he or she wants to use. It also teaches the importance of order and taking care of things.

• Read to your toddler. Reading stories made for the computer is a great way to help introduce your child to words and language. But think about how you're using these stories and the computer to enhance language or pre-language skills. Computing can give kids many opportunities to hear and use language. Vary your tone and inflection. Pronounce the words clearly and use different sentence structures. Nursery rhyme programs are a great way to start for really little ones, as it allows them to begin discriminating between words and exploring the connections between words in a playful way.

• Repeat: repeat, over and over and over. Repetition is an important part of your child's intellectual development. Your computer never gets tired of reading *The Little Engine That Could* day after day. That's good, because we do.

• Seek balance and set time limits. Some kids will have had enough after ten or twenty minutes, while others stay glued to the computer if given the chance. Toddlers, in particular, need to explore their great big world. Their play is their work—it's how they learn. Make sure they have plenty of time to go outside, bang on the pots and pans and interact with other kids.

• Set a specific time for the toddler to use the computer. Toddlers have a hard time throwing their weight around. If there are bigger kids in the house, it's easy for the younger kids to get lower priority. Let it be known in the family that a certain half hour belongs to the smallest member of the house.

Let Them Explore

What's the coolest thing about a present to a child? The box. That's because before it's opened, the present—the box—could be anything. A toy submarine. A doll. A robot. Kids love to imagine, and if there's one environment where you can turn them loose, let them open everything, explore everywhere and not worry that they'll get lost, hurt or make a mess, it's a computer with a good software program. Let them explore.

 MARK:

I love turning Nicole loose on the computer. At first she was choosing the characters and objects she wanted to click on, and later the programs she wanted to play. By the time she was four she was confident enough to call most of the shots. She was really seeking freedom, and the computer seemed like a better bet than letting her run wild in her brother's room. She explored in a safe environment, and there were no serious consequences (except when her mom yelled at me because Nicole didn't want to come eat dinner). Giving kids the latitude to explore on their own is the first step in using the computer to develop independence and solid decision-making skills.

Using the PC to Foster Independence

From the "terrible two's" all the way to twenty-something, kids are working on gaining independence, differentiating and distancing themselves from their parents. You can use the PC to help with this very major task by fostering independence. Here's how:

- **Give them space to concentrate.** Kids are highly distractible, but if you help control the noise, they can focus. Try creating a quiet environment, free of noise and the hustle and bustle of the family room. Provide guidance when needed, but also step back at times and let them work the program. Let them have their space.

- **Give them the right tools.** Opt for age-appropriate accessories and programs so they can do more with less help. A software program like

Kid Desk that allows them to start up their programs easily means they can get in and out of the programs on their own. Children can design their own background environment, complete with cool pictures and sounds.

• **Designate storage space that's just for them.** Get a bin, a rolling cart, a cubbyhole, or a shelf that is theirs alone. This will allow them to organize their things and eliminate excuses for leaving the computer area a mess.

• **Give them incentives.** To keep fueling the independence drive at every age, provide new reasons to stretch and grow. For instance, reward them with tokens (which can be cashed in for programs or accessories later) if they work alone, quietly, for thirty minutes or so. Get creative. What would pique their interest? What about your old computer? If you just upgraded or are looking for an excuse to get rid of the old PC, why not put it in Junior's room and let him put a couple of programs on it? He'll feel a little ownership and it beats using it for a boat anchor.

THE ART OF THE DEAL

 MARK:

Much of parenting involves negotiating with your kids. There's a real knack to this. When you're about to try to force your will on them, try instead to compromise. You can do this with the computer and software. Left alone, my sons would play games until the cows came home or a buddy showed up. This is the equivalent of eating fast food all day; they needed veggies. For months I tried to cajole and pressure them into playing educational programs—no luck. Then I came up with a new system where I reward them with "credits" (we use poker chips) for every thirty minutes they spend on an edutainment program, which they can use to buy time playing their favorite games. So if they spend thirty minutes on a program like the *Encarta* encyclopedia, they get thirty minutes on *POD,* a high-tech racing game, or another favorite.

There's a kicker to it: if they save up enough chips, they can use them to buy a game. About twenty hours on edutainment programs earns them the chance to pick a nonviolent, low-priced ($30) program. This is a bonus.

We also keep a chart on the back of the door to the computer room where the kids log their time on the edutainment programs. This helps us all keep track, minimizes arguments—and mitigates reliance on my feeble memory. It also teaches them a little bit about project management.

 RALPH:

My 10-year-old son would stay glued to the PC if we didn't step in and manage the exposure. After much trial and error we hit on one idea that seems to work for both of our kids. From Monday through Friday he has a one-hour "electronics" daily budget. He can watch TV, play his Nintendo game, listen to the radio or use the PC—it's his choice. However, the combination of any of the above can't exceed one hour a day. This takes the emotion out of the issue, and it's a simple time-management system that everyone in the family understands, including Dad.

Learning How to Make Decisions

Good judgment comes from experience, and experience comes from bad judgment.
—Anonymous

One of the most important skills children need to learn is how to make decisions. This is actually the culmination of some pretty serious brain development. These skills go hand in hand with fostering independence in kids. Younger kids think in concrete terms; they can only deal with the here and now. The future is too abstract, and they can't understand long-term consequences yet. We know a few adults like this, but for the most part, the mental skills develop over time and with practice. As kids get a little older, they can begin to think in more complex terms. This may start around age four, but really kicks in at age five or six. ("You mean I can't choose a video if I hit my little sister?") That's when you begin to see some pretty interesting mental fireworks.

As children develop intellectually they begin to carry on some complex mental exercises. They can categorize concepts, for instance, drawing neat little mental boxes around different ideas. They can also follow an idea through and logically link it to other ideas. Parents can help facilitate the overall process of mental development, and the result is a child who can make a decision. It is one of the skills that will determine their destiny.

Here's how you can help using your PC:

• **Read to them.** It's no coincidence that many kids who grow up reading a lot tend to be better decision makers. Early on there's something about reading interesting stories to children of all ages that causes their little brains to click into action. Good stories have plots, action, characters—and consequences. Computer-based stories are the same way, with multimedia characters thrown in for added fun. Clearly, reading off a computer screen is a different activity than reading a real hardback book, but it's easy to do. Just make sure your child is comfortable facing the computer (or firmly in your lap if he's a toddler), and start up a program like one of *Living Books* series books (like *Just Mom and Me*) from Broderbund. You can sit back and let the book read to your child, page by page, as it highlights the text on the page; often animated characters move around. Your child can also stop the action and play around on the page by clicking on different objects; every object on the page does something. Click on a sea animal and it jumps up and plays a musical instrument; it's reading mixed with fun stuff, and it'll keep kids entertained for months. (Mark's daughter, Nicole, a four-year-old, still loves these programs.)

• **Let them make choices.** Do you want grits or fried chicken? Would you rather feed the chickens, feed the dog or set the table? The computer gives kids lots of choices to make: Do you want to choose the letter A or the letter T? Do you want to see what the pig does or hear what the farmer says? In virtually every situation there's a way to give a kid some choices. And kids need to practice making decisions in order to understand the consequences associated with particular choices. Understanding the relationship between cause and effect (choice and outcome) is a prerequisite to making good decisions (see Chapter 9 on Critical Thinking).

• **Encourage experimentation.** Children need to try things out and see what happens; they need to experiment. The computer gives children the chance to turn over options in their minds—to try one thing, see if it works and then try something else—at their own speed. Art programs like *Kid Pix* are wonderful for allowing kids to flex their creative muscles risk free.

• **Avoid the visual stew.** Making good decisions requires clear-headed thinking and the ability to link ideas and information together. Kids must be allowed to create their own mental pictures and wrestle mentally with complex concepts and ideas. This doesn't happen when they're watching TV sitcoms. Television gives it all to them in pretty, no-brainer visuals, robbing them of this opportunity, but computers can be almost as bad if they're not managed. Some of the new 3D games, for instance, can be overwhelming after a while. Keep it simple, limit time on programs and set a clear agenda so the kid's not glued to the screen (a friend calls kids who stay in front of a video screen constantly "screen faces").

• **Let them learn consequences.** The computer is a benign place to learn about consequences. When you screw up, it doesn't yell at you; get it right and you often get a reward. There's no scolding or humiliation. A wrong answer isn't a cause for shame. It's simply an opportunity to learn how to get to the right answer. The parent's off the hook too; there's no mess to clean up, nothing to have fixed, re-painted or incinerated. Your only job is to help the child understand the process and stay with it.

Homework and Home Schooling Help

For grade school kids, homework and school-related projects are often their introduction to the computer. Lining up educational resources at home to bolster school-work used to be a hassle, but CD-ROM encyclopedias and the Internet have changed all that. (See "Buying Software" and "Driver's Ed on the Internet, Parts I and II" for more information on these topics, respectively.) Whether your child is a super achiever or a perpetual struggler in need of a boost, they can

A Sampling of Educational Websites

FOR HOMEWORK HELP:

The Research Paper:
www.researchpaper.com

Study Web: www.studyweb.com

B.J. Pinchbeck's Homework Helper:
tristate.pgh.net/~pinch13

Homework Helpers:
w3.trib.com/%7Edont/hwhelp.html

Kids' Web:
www.npac.syr.edu/textbook/kidsweb

Yahooligan's School Bell:
www.yahooligans.com/School_Bell/
Homework_Answers

FOR HOME SCHOOLING HELP:

Train-up-a-child:
www.techplus.com/ncm/TUAC.html

MultiMag Homeschool Magazines on the WWW: multimag.com/home

National Homeschool Association:
www.n-h-a.org

The Homeschool Zone:
www.caro.net/~joespa

Homeschoolers' Curriculum Swap:
theswap.com

Knowledge Adventure:
www.knowledgeadventure.com/home

find helpful sites that can help them with homework and maybe pique their interests. In addition, if you're home schooling your child, you'll find a bunch of online resources for both parents and kids. These sites are full of educational

MARK'S HIGH-TECH HOME SCHOOL

Not long ago, the mention of home schooling drew suspicious stares. It's still off the beaten path, but it's getting more common in some states, including Oregon. My wife began home schooling our kids three years ago, when Matthew was in fourth grade and Michael was going into second. We were concerned about their progress in school. It just seemed to us that they were falling behind, getting lost in the crowd. We wanted to stabilize them and get them back on track before it was too late.

My wife teaches and has a strict curriculum like a regular school, with one twist: she has flexibility. If the kid isn't getting the math, she doesn't have to stick to a schedule. The boys don't waste a lot of time at recess and by 2:00 P.M., they're done.

We go to great lengths to tie learning to real life. Example: we spent a Sunday visiting the USS *Missouri*, the famous warship that was docked in Astoria, Oregon, for a week in late May. It was a three-hour wait in a cold Pacific wind, but it was worth it. All three kids got to tour the ship where the Japanese officially surrendered in WWII, giving them a rich history lesson. When we got home that night we fired up *Encarta 98* on the computer to do some more research. The articles featured realistic 3D views of the entire ship, including inside the ship's quarters and the gun rooms. You could move around within the ship and get a real feel for what it was like aboard. Extensive articles told about the rich history of "Big Mo," which endured three wars. Then we listened to a short audio clip of General MacArthur, grainy sounding but somehow chilling. The combined approach—a real-life tour and the multimedia lesson on the PC—did the job. The kids were fascinated with the ship, and still occasionally talk about it.

Computers make the job easier, but my wife isn't a computer nut. She only uses the PC to supplement the course. She also corresponds with others via e-mail when needed. To her, the computer is a tool, not an end in itself. She gets together frequently with other home schoolers to trade notes and, often, the kids will present reports and get human feedback. Being around other people is important.

Home schooling isn't for everyone. Kids do get more individual time and attention. But parents have to stay on top of it and—face it—not everyone's cut out (or has the time) to be a teacher. But for those who choose the home-school route, there's no better time for it thanks to the computer and the Internet.

---

material, bulletin boards for comments, curriculum swapping, and the ability to correspond via e-mail with other parents.

Keep It FUN

The most important thing parents can do for their children is to keep them motivated, and that means keeping it fun. Don't be overbearing, and do be flexible—some days the kid may not be inclined to compute. Let it go. And when you're playing the programs, keep it light. There'll be plenty of time for more serious matters later.

Give yourself a break too and check out some of the Web sites that offer parental support such as ParentSoup.com and its parent, iVillage.com. You'll get some helpful tips and maybe make a few new friends in the same boat.

FOCUSED QUESTIONS

- How ready are you to help your family become computer-smart? If there's anything holding you back, what steps can you take to gain the confidence to move ahead?

- How computer ready are your kids? Are they raw beginners or experts already?

- Is your family PC in an optimal location? Is the environment safe? (If you don't have a computer yet, where will you set up your PC?)

- What rules has your family established for the care and feeding of your computer? (If you don't have a computer yet, what rules will you need to set?)

- Knowing your kids' ages, how might the computer help them explore and experiment, or foster independence and decision-making skills?

8.

See Spot Run (and Surf)

COMPUTERS, READING AND WRITING

Reading and understanding language is still the key to knowledge.
—*The PC Dads*

Imagine not being able to read. How would you follow street signs? How would you buy a car, or find a job if you couldn't read want ads? For that matter, how would you read this book? More important, how would you think complex thoughts if you never learned by reading?

Not many years ago you could get some kind of job without knowing how to read. The jobs may have been in a factory in one of the manufacturing industries like automobiles or steel. There used to be thousands of low-level service jobs that required a minimum level of literacy. But those jobs are gone or fading fast. Today most jobs require reading skills and not just minimal skills. You not only need to read text, you have to be able to put it in context and make sense of it—that's what "literacy" is all about. It's not just being able to read a street sign or job application; it's a way of thinking. Companies are looking for people who can think. Period. Good readers tend to be able to "connect the dots," to think critically and make better decisions. That goes a long way in life.

If you think of your children learning to read as a battle, the personal computer is an effective weapon. It's a tool that can help you teach your kid to read, supplementing regular old-fashioned reading. While it's not a panacea, it *is* a valuable tool in helping your kids get ahead of the learning curve.

In short, reading helps develop:

- Mental organization
- Sustained effort
- Verbal logic
- Seeing/appreciating an unfamiliar point of view
- Making new connections (connecting the dots)

This chapter will touch on those issues and help you learn how to use computers to supplement your school's efforts to teach your kids to:

- Read better
- Write better
- Think better

Getting Started

Learning to read doesn't just happen; it's a complex mental process that takes years to develop. People have been talking to each other (or themselves) seemingly forever. But reading and writing are relatively modern skills that use more sophisticated brain processes.

Good parents know that learning to read starts well before kids hit first grade. In fact, it's almost never too early to start developing reading skills. A baby or toddler can listen with delight as you recite nursery rhymes, or sit on your lap while you turn the pages of a book or click through a book on the computer screen. They're honing their "pre-reading skills," and preparing to appreciate language and reading. Studies show that kids that obtain early pre-reading skills—even if the parent reads to them only fifteen to thirty minutes a day—do better in school.

Nursery rhymes are great for teaching a kid to appreciate language and learn the relationships of words—their meaning, how they work together and

so on. "The rhythm of language is one of the greatest helps to extending understanding, and the sounds of language are intimately bound up with meaning," says Margaret Meek, author of *Learning to Read*.

Computers can't replace having a parent read to you, but it's a pretty good
pinch hitter. Start off with interactive reading programs like Broderbund's *Living Books* series (example: *Just Grandma and Me*). These are neat books with
charming characters like Little Critter. Click on the screen and watch the story
as it comes to life; everything does something—mailboxes jump, crabs dance,
flowers sing and so on. Other reading programs we like include the *Arthur*
books (*Arthur's Teacher Trouble*) and the *Dr. Seuss* books (*ABC* and *Green Eggs
and Ham*).

Our kids love having the computer read to them. They can see the words
highlighted on the screen and go back and click on them and hear them again
. . . and again . . . and again. Click on the words and let your kids get familiar
with their sounds. Turn off your speakers, click on the words and have your
child sound them out. Later on, kids can have the computer read back sentences they write.

The PC is perfectly suited to help stimulate reading if it's used right. That
means exploiting the multimedia capabilities of the PC to play to the kid's passion. We don't just get information from words on paper; we use all our senses,
and the more senses involved, the more likely we are to remember something.
That's why the computer is such a great way to learn, since it can combine text,
graphics, sound, movement—a multi-sensory presentation of information. It
reinforces the information through many paths. On the other hand, be sensitive to your children and don't overwhelm them with cool graphics and multimedia. Balance the graphics and color with straight textbooks on the
computer—and with good old-fashioned book reading. Some kids actually prefer *not* dealing with the graphics when they're reading; to them, they're a dis-
traction. You'll have to make that call after working with your budding reader.

As kids get a little older, let them take the lead. They can point to words or
fill in the blanks after you read a few sentences. Try to be patient if they don't
want to read or fail to recognize words—that will come in time. Instead, en-

MARK GETS A BREAK:

Every kid is unique. My daughter loves the *Dr. Seuss* books and can listen to my reading them until my voice wears out. I always point to words as I read them, and she generally follows. By the time she was three, she was predicting the word before I said it. More recently she's wanted control over the story. She wants to read it herself—even though she knows she's not really reading. "I want to read that page," she'll say, then add: "I'm going to make it up, OK?" Of course it's OK. I get to watch her spin a tale and I get a brief break.

When we started playing the *Dr. Seuss* books on the computer, it added another twist: funny sounds, animated characters, and it even read the book to her. She'd click on a word, and a voice from the PC would sound it out. Wow! Now she tells me which stories she wants to read on the computer. If her mom or I can't be with her, she'll sit down and go through the tale alone. It's funny watching her talk to the characters and try to "read" the story. Experts would call this "building pre-reading skills"; we just call it fun.

---

courage them to talk about what they're seeing and what they think of the story. Get those little minds cranking.

The goal is to stimulate your kid's interest in reading, so use reading software to broaden your kid's interest in books. Find programs that are based on storybooks; then, after you play the computer game with your kid, head down to the library and check out the books by the same author. For example, remember Curious George, the goofy little monkey who was always getting into trouble? Now he's gone digital, with a program that teaches kids letters with their sounds and how to sound out words through phonics as it plays circus games. If your kids are old enough, ask them about similarities and differences between the book and computer versions—kids are experts at spotting differences and discrepancies. Ask what they liked or disliked about the two. Some computer reading programs even include little comic books or coloring books that can be used to further reinforce reading skills.

Growing the Independent Reader: Five and Beyond

By this age kids are starting to recognize words and, somewhere around first grade or so, are actually reading. This is where literacy starts to kick in. Most of us think of literacy as being able to recognize words and rattle off sentences. But experts say that literacy is actually understanding the context and the meaning of words. What good is it if a kid reads a whole book and doesn't understand what happened?

So at this point, parents have two goals: reading comprehension and motivating the child to *want* to read; in other words, developing an "independent reader."

This isn't easy. Children today are already bombarded with so much information in the form of dazzling videos and graphics—just turn on a kid's TV show—they can barely think straight. Reading, by comparison, seems boring, and to many of them the PC is just another entertainment channel.

To cut through the noise and get your kid reading, prepare to do some work. Here are some tips to help you get started:

- **Make reading fun.** Choose programs that are fun and educational, and make it a playful experience. A good program is *Let's Go Read* by Edmark. Kids put on a microphone and speak the words they see on the screen. The microphone picks up their speech, and an IBM-developed voice recognition system, tailored to children's voices, lets the kids command the computer, records the words and plays them back so they can hear themselves read. This system combines the best of whole language and phonics methods.

- **Use the Web to feed your child's passion.** Whether your future Einstein is into soccer or snakes, dolls or dinosaurs, you're bound to find Web sites that interest them. Kids can read information off the screen or print it out, and you'll find them poring over every detail. But remember, the goal with younger children is to stimulate them to read, not to drill down and force them to learn.

• **Ask questions.** Let your children explain what they've just learned. You don't have to grill them—it can be friendly and informal. Let them be the expert. You're just trying to find out how much they're comprehending. Don't stop every few sentences and try to get them to identify a word, though; this takes the fun out of the experience.

• **Make it relevant.** Encourage activities that require reading—exploring the Internet (using search engines), installing new software (following instructions), cooking (following a recipe) or bird watching (using references). Show your child how to use books, newspapers, magazines, and Web sites to check the weather, local news, local movies—or where the fish are biting. Make reading relevant to their lives.

• **Buy good software.** It isn't enough just to teach a child to recognize words; they need to understand what they're reading. Look for software that combines systematic phonetics instruction with an emphasis on the meaning of words—programs that combine the best of both approaches. The stress should be on meaning and reading comprehension. Children should work with large chunks of related text instead of bits and pieces of unrelated words. When the programs feature the study of words and phrases, these should be presented in the context of a story or some other framework that makes sense to the kids.

There are plenty of reader programs for 5- to 8-year-olds. The most famous is the *Reader Rabbit* series, which cover all the basics. The *Reader Rabbit 1* and *2* programs help kids practice phonics through a variety of exercises and games. Learned skills include recognizing letters, short and long vowels and rhymes. Other titles to explore: *Ready to Read with Pooh, Sesame Street Elmo's Preschool, Interactive Reading Journey 2, Reading Blaster 2000, The Great Reading Adventure,* and *Richard Scarry's Best Reading Program Ever.*

GROWING A READER

You're an avid reader, but your kid won't read anything but *Jurassic Park* or *Mad* magazine? We relate.

MARK:

Michael, 9, has always been a pretty good reader and reads well beyond his grade level. No problem there. But Matthew, 13, was another story. Getting him to read was like pulling teeth. On the other hand, he comprehended what he did read pretty well. He just didn't have a passion for reading. Then he became interested in cars—actually fanatical about them. Suddenly he was on the Internet every night looking for info about the latest hotrod. He had to read to feed his craving for information about cars. It primed the pump. While he still doesn't read as much as I'd like, and most of his reading is for his home-school lessons, he's doing better and will occasionally pick up a book or magazine and read it just for fun. That's what I want. He's learning to read for the sake of learning rather than learning for grades or praise. Nothing wrong with that.

RALPH:

I found I could use Jeff's fixation on video games to get him to read. First of all, just being into games as much as Jeff has forced him into reading. He had to read instructions with enough comprehension to get the games to work. Then he wanted to get the "Cheat Codes," and those are available mostly online. He had to be able to read enough to work his way through search engines and find what he wanted.

To get him started reading, I bought him subscriptions to gaming magazines. He reads them thoroughly and talks constantly about what he's reading. It's not Shakespeare, but at least he's reading with understanding, has learned to follow instructions and retains what he has read. When he's not reading manuals or magazines, he's surfing the Net and reading.

My daughter is interested in horses, so we bought her subscriptions to horse magazines. It's important to teach kids to read for pleasure and information rather than to overemphasize the learning to read process. Now she's dabbling on the Internet, searching for horse sites and reading whatever she comes across.

Role Modeling: Practice What You Preach

If you're reading this book, chances are good that you're a serious reader. But what are you doing to make sure your kids know you're serious about reading? It pays to be a positive role model, something kids need desperately today. If you start reading books, magazines or articles on the Web it shows you take reading and literacy seriously. You want the message to be clear: Reading is important, and it's part of your daily life.

Other role modeling tips:

- **Make sure both Mom and Dad support reading and using the PC as a tool to help kids learn to read.**

- **Make reading easy.** Turn off the TV and get rid of other distractions. Have quiet "reading hours" several times a week. Leave reading software, magazines and books where they're easy to get to. Make sure the child has a reading light by the bed. Provide a quiet space to read on or off of the computer, free of craziness and noise. Kids need to be able to concentrate, and that's hard to do when the TV's blaring or friends are calling.

- **Be flexible.** Sometimes that means backing off and letting your kids follow their passions. So what if they're studying horses or computer game tricks instead of reading classical literature? At least it's a start.

- **Show enthusiasm!** Change your voice when you read to fit different characters and feelings. Ham it up—act happy, grumpy or thoughtful. Bring reading to life. (Bonus for you: This is a safe way for you to hone your own public speaking skills without having the neighbors think you're crazy.)

Above all, make sure the material your kids are learning is at their level. If they're only ready for basic reading books, you're wasting your time trying to get them to read Shakespeare. The work should be challenging but not frustrating.

MARK AND RALPH:

We were on a plane recently beside a mother and daughter, who was about seven or so. The girl was reading a paperback book with a lot of interest; occasionally she turned to her mom to check a word, but for the most part, she was reading on her own. Her mother told me she personally had not been a reader growing up. She only read when required. Reading seemed like work for her. But that changed a few years ago, just in time for her to help guide her daughter. As we watched her work with her daughter, we could tell they had a good solid relationship. Reading was helping strengthen the bond. That's the magic of reading.

Typing Mania

We admit it. We're typing nuts. Maybe it was all those bone-grinding punch-and-drill typing courses we took in high school that pounded it into our brains, but we're adamant: Knowing how to type is critical. Sure, voice-driven computers are coming one day, but right now you need to know how to type to make the computer work for you.

This isn't always easy, since kids resist anything that requires a lot of repetition. But it can be done. *JumpStart Typing* and *Mario Teaches Typing* are good to get kids started and prime the pump. But we really like the latest versions of *Mavis Beacon*, the market leader. Mark gives his kids credits (poker chips) for spending an hour or so every other day on a typing program and extra credits as they improve their typing speed. They can use these credits to play other, more fun games.

The key is setting up a system and sticking with it. Maybe the child works on typing three times a week, for thirty minutes to an hour. Times will vary depending on the age and inclination of your child. The key with typing, like everything else, is to make it fun or something approaching fun. Children's typing programs include games and exercises that reduce the monotony, making kids more open to learning—they'll also stick with it longer. Try out two or three programs and see which ones work for your kid. Putting a little time in and learning how to type now will pay off down the road.

Writing

Remember the old manual typewriter? Make a mistake and—oops!—you had a mess to deal with, correction fluid and all that fun. Talk about labor and drudgery. Somehow many of us learned to type and compose essays on these contraptions and lived to tell about it. But our kids don't have to suffer; they have word processors.

Word processors are cool. You screwed up? No problem. Back up and delete. You can move whole paragraphs—and thoughts—around. You can highlight, boldface, add color, even add sounds and pictures. Put kids on a word processor and they're more likely to take to it, just because you've reduced the labor. Newer versions even highlight errors so the kid can quickly fix them, rather than repeating the errors over and over.

This is just one example of how the PC can automate tasks and make it easier to help kids learn to write. But like reading, writing isn't easy.

You need to develop a clear system, with a heavy emphasis on structure and organization. Think back to your school essays (if you can) and how you developed them. Every writing project goes through the same basic steps, whether it's a high school essay or a *Business Week* exposé. So if you want to help your kids develop their writing prowess, think of those basic stages and of how you (and the computer) can help.

1. Brainstorming

Let's say Junior has a topic—spotted owls (big issue in the Northwest, by the way). Why are spotted owls becoming extinct? What are the two sides of the argument? Talk through it with your kid. What do you like about owls, what do you or others want to know? What are some "issues" that people might be interested in? Once the ideas are flowing, have your child list every word and concept that comes to mind: birds, night animals, trees, logging, the Northwest and so on. Don't have them try to write anything yet—just churn out ideas.

Nothing is wrong at this point. You want a free flow of ideas, so encourage anything they come out with.

They can also draw pictures or do mind maps, where you have pictures connected to pictures. The idea here is that the brain thinks in visuals and constructs various kinds of connections on several levels, not just in linear (outline) form. A great software program for this is *Inspiration*, which automates the mind maps. The child comes up with an idea, then picks from dozens of different pictures to illustrate it, like trees, stars and letters. The program provides instant clip art and different templates that help you to connect the illustrations and ideas. Imagine a picture of a spotted owl in the center of a page, with connections to trees, food sources, lumberjacks and lumber companies and other issues you want to write about. Images like these help to spark creative imagination.

2. Organization

Now it's time to roll up their sleeves and begin organizing the clusters. The traditional way is some kind of outline. Microsoft *Word* is useful here—children can use its "outline view" to create an outline. Or you can stick with a child-oriented program like *Creative Writing Center* and *Creative Writer*, from Microsoft. One idea, used in speeches too, is to develop a point of view on a subject, then boil it down to three to five subtopics, each supporting your point. This eventually becomes the body of the paper. Another approach is to put your separate ideas and themes on index cards along with the subtopics. These can be easily sorted and organized.

3. Research

With the Internet at your fingertips, you no longer have an excuse *not* to dig up vast amounts of information on a given subject. You might look up "owls," for example, via a search engine like AltaVista or Yahoo. Be sure to use the "advanced" features of these engines that allow you to refine your search. (For instance, just doing a search on "spotted owls" netted 180,000 Web-page citations. But changing it to "spotted owls and Oregon" narrowed it down to 730 citations; adding "and clear cutting" to the two key words narrowed it down to 68 citations.)

You should also be able to find plenty of articles and documents on the Web, and be sure to explore bulletin boards. While BBSs are all over the map, in terms of topics and discussions, you might luck out and find someone who knows about your subject, and begin an online conversation with them. We knew a father in Kansas City who went online with his elementary-age daughter to find out information about ghost towns. He managed to hook up with several folks across the country who led him to ghost towns in their area and even an expert on ghost towns.

Last, be sure to check out CD-ROM encyclopedias like Microsoft's *Encarta*. These programs are packed with information, along with sounds, pictures and video footage that bring the subject to life. If you need fresher information, you can often click on a button and go to their Web page for additional material.

4. First Draft

Before you begin writing, make sure your child is comfortable with the word processor. Show them how to change fonts, delete text, cut and paste and so on. Then get the key three to five topic sentences down and start putting those thoughts on paper. Make sure the topic sentences are strong, but don't worry if the writing isn't perfect at this point; just encourage them to think and write.

With kids under twelve try *The Amazing Writing Machine*, from Broderbund, which helps kids organize their thoughts and create ideas. This program offers writing tools like preformatted pages for writing essays, letters, stories and poems, a password-protected journal, an address book, "Fun Facts" and more. It even helps reinforce correct grammar and sentence structure. (And it has 2,000-plus clip-art images.)

Emphasize to children that what they write ought to be valuable to someone else, so they need to keep the reader in mind. Quit thinking about your own perception for a moment, and think about how other people would feel about the subject. What would interest people about spotted owls? What are the hot topics or angles? Be there to answer questions, bounce ideas around, help direct where the story's going—but don't overdo it. It's the kid's project, win, lose or draw.

5. Editing

This is where the bulk of writing happens. Have your child take their first draft and rip it apart—not literally, but figuratively. What can they change, improve or completely overhaul to make the report flow, read better and communicate the intended message? A super editor, even an 11-year-old, can transform a mediocre piece of writing into a masterpiece. By the time you get to this stage, the kid may be getting tired, so take a break if needed and do whatever you can to encourage them. They're almost home.

6. Proofreading

Here's where the child goes through with a fine-tooth comb, hunts down errors and sharpens up lazy sentences. Be sure to introduce them to our good friend, Mr. Spell Checker. Be aware that the spell checker generally doesn't catch usage errors. For instance, if you use "your" instead of "you're" the spelling is correct, so the spell checker will miss it. Ditto with grammar checkers. They catch some of the blatant errors, but the best defense is always an eagle-eyed editor.

7. Publishing

Kids love to see the results of their work so print it out on an ink-jet or laser printer. If they've thrown in a color graphic or two they can print it on a color printer (if it's an ink-jet printer). They can also create a Web page based on the subject: "Kyle's Spotted Owl Home Page" (more on that later). Make it a big deal, show it off.

M A R K :

Michael likes the *Ultimate Writing & Creativity Center* from The Learning Compa
partly because it's easy to use. He starts on a kid's word processor with a bla
page. After he writes his story or his letter to Grandma, he goes into the art se
tion and adds a background—a moonscape, a beach or something else tha
dress up his copy. Then he'll add a little cartoon animation to bring it to life—s
a spider playing a piano tune. Editing is easy, since the program comes with a sp
checker, dictionary and thesaurus. When it highlights a misspelled word, it giv
him the choice of looking it up on a list of similarly spelled words. The program v
even read the text back to him. He gets a kick out of hearing a female "robot" re
his material, particularly with his misspelled words. Rather than agonizing ov
misspellings, he laughs about it and fixes them. Last he adds a few color
touches—a border, another graphic—and prints it out.

Here are some other ways the computer can improve your child's writing,
with your help:

- **Think about your child's personality**. With some kids, you must
  have a clear purpose for writing anything and it must be relevant to their
  world before they're interested. In these cases, encourage them to write
  a plan for a family vacation, an article for the local neighborhood
  newsletter, song lyrics, poems—something they're passionate about.

Other kids like to just write for the sake of writing. Great; encourage them
to keep a daily journal. What happened to you today? Expand it to cover other
activities—what did you do on your vacation? Make greeting cards for friends,
creating verse and adding clip art. Create a family history by interviewing

Grandma and Uncle Wilbur, importing files of old-time photos. Use programs like *Creative Writer* to add goofy art, funny sounds and colorful, stretchable fonts. This program includes a Web page maker, thirty-five music selections, 2,000 clip-art choices and an address book.

- **Expand beyond writing programs.** Get your kid writing on the Internet or chat rooms, in e-mails and so on. Find other programs that require them to keep notes or write.

- **Increase motivation**. Make it worth their while to write. Publish their story in a local newsletter or on the Web. A teacher in Vermont gets kids jazzed up to do their best by publishing what they produce on the school's Web page. The "extra incentive" of seeing it published on the Web keeps them going, he says.

SAMPLE SOFTWARE PROGRAMS

- *The American Girls Premier* from the *American Girls* collection of books. Girls can create their own plays, complete with dialog, action and props.

- *Logic Quest*. Thinking is closely related to writing. This software package builds thinking and creative skills in a 3D medieval adventure. Children develop key thinking skills including logic, problem solving, strategy, planning, mapping, patterning, spatial awareness and creativity. (See Chapter 9 on Critical Thinking for more suggestions.)

- *Student Writing and Research Center* from The Learning Company. Once your kids have to do papers for school, they need a good word processing program, and this one is tailored to their needs. They can wrap text around graphics and use templates to write reports, newsletters, journals, letters, bibliographies and title pages.

- *ClarisWorks 5.0* is great for middle and high school age kids. *ClarisWorks* even has a slide-show function that can turn a classroom presentation into a multimedia event. Its outline feature can help kids organize ideas before turning them into a complex report.

Don't feel you need to buy all of these programs; just look for the ones that work for you and your family. Reading and writing are hard work, and you can use all the help you can get. But the rewards are enormous. When children learn to read and write, they open a window to a new world of intellectual development. They train their minds to use language in a way that allows them to reflect, analyze and solve problems. They begin to get a better understanding of the world, to synthesize information, "connect the dots" and make sense of this crazy world. In other words, they're starting to think independently.

One Final Tip

It's easy to get sucked into thinking the computer can do it all, and use it like an electronic babysitter. That's a mistake. Parents need to make reading a shoulder-to-shoulder experience. The computer isn't a substitute for good hand-holding and direction when it comes to learning to read. In fact, it should be just one part of your child's overall reading program. Integrate the computer with books, magazines, newspapers and other learning materials. According to ERIC (the Educational Resources Information Center, www.aspensys.-com/eric), a clearinghouse of educational material, "Students need to think of the computer as one additional means of sharing and retrieving information and practicing skills in interesting and meaningful ways."

FOCUSED QUESTIONS

- What are you doing to get your child started reading, to build "pre-reading" skills?
- If your child is a little older, how would you rate them on a scale of 1 to 10 as a reading enthusiast (10 being a passionate reader)?

- With that in mind, what sort of programs are you using to build the reading skills? Which ones work for your kid? Which ones don't work? Why?

- Do you have a system set up to read thirty minutes to an hour a day? What programs are you using to supplement your reading program?

- What are you doing to make reading and writing more relevant, more fun for your kid? Do you have a clear system set up so your child knows the correct steps for writing a paper?

- What kind of model are you when it comes to reading and writing?

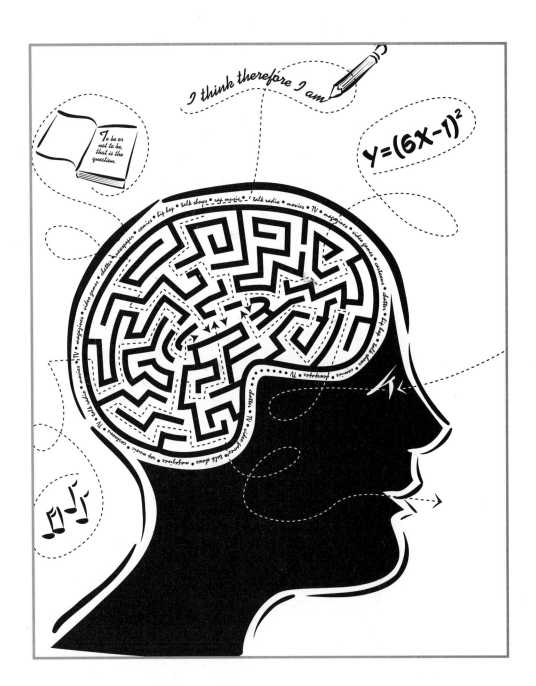

9.

Beyond MTV and Video Games: Thinking Straight

HOW THE PC CAN HELP DEVELOP CRITICAL THINKING

Most people spend more time trying to go around
a problem than trying to solve it.
—Henry Ford

Try this out on your kid. "A truck leaves New York City at 8 A.M. to head for San Francisco. It averages 65 mph for the next twelve hours. Another truck leaves San Francisco four hours later and averages 70 mph for the next sixteen hours. When they meet at a truck stop outside Chicago, which one is closer to New York?"

The answer, of course, is: neither. They're both in Chicago. But many young children would struggle with the question, trying to figure out some kind of magic formula that would give them the answer. They'd be tricked by all the extraneous information given. The clutter makes it hard to sort out which facts are essential to answering the question.

Here's another one. "If the length and the width of a room are both 12 feet, how much will it cost to lay new carpet in the room if the padding, plus carpet, cost $8.75 a square yard?" The answer is $140 (16 sq. yards @ $8.75 each). (*Encouraging Potential in Young Children*).

While these may sound like simple exercises to an adult, both questions require some relatively sophisticated thinking, the result of years of brain development. Unfortunately many kids would miss both questions because they are not thinking clearly. They may be able to reel off the names of popular musicians or find a Web site in Paris or Tokyo. But what good is all this fancy world knowledge if they can't apply it?

Jane Healy, author of *Endangered Minds*, argues that children do not think as critically as they did a generation ago. She points to mounting evidence to support this idea, including declining test scores in schools, poor reading skills, the way our "instant society" tends to erode attention spans and a slew of other issues. Heavy stuff, but we think she's on to something.

Computer-smart parents know critical thinking is like a map or compass. With good thinking skills, kids can cut through the fog and the mountains of information to find answers and make sound, logical decisions. Over time the ability to put problems under an analytical microscope and make good decisions can mean the difference between children who have control over their lives and children who are lost, reacting to the whims of the moment.

Helping your child develop critical thinking skills and stay on track intellectually is one of the most important things you can do as a parent. These skills include:

- Conducting logical analysis
- Wading through hype to find truth
- Listening with a critical ear
- Reading with comprehension
- Speaking with precision

The idea that kids need to improve their thinking skills is not new. Experts have been squawking about the subject for years. What *is* new is the rising tidal wave of information bombarding our children—TV, video, books, magazines and other publications. Young folks today are drowning in information and choices. We've gone from a culture of information scarcity to one of an information glut, and many children that we see aren't handling it that well. They struggle to put information into context, develop a clear perspective and ultimately to transform it into something they can use—real knowledge.

Today's lifestyles don't help much either. There was a time that kids learned trades and work habits as apprentices from their parents or other close relatives or friends; working through and solving problems was part of daily life. Much of that broke down with the advent of the Industrial Revolution and Dad went off to work outside the home, later followed by Mom. It wasn't just the absence of the parent, but the *type* of occupation—remote and detached from anything that affected people on a daily basis—that made it tougher for parents to teach their kids critical thinking.

There are exceptions, of course. Mark remembers his father, a part-time carpenter in the early '60s, showing him how houses were constructed, using plans and blueprints. Everything had a reason and an *order;* miss a step and you've got a real problem. But most of what kids deal with today are abstractions—visuals reflecting real-life issues and problems for instance.

Enter the personal computer, which by its nature *is* a logical machine. It doesn't care what kind of mood you're in or what your opinion is; it provides logical answers based on whatever you plug into it. With the parents' direction, it can help kids cut through this morass, sort it out and make decisions—in other words, think critically. Without a clear plan and system, it might simply add to the mess with more unguided information. So while the computer isn't a magic bullet in this area, it can go a long way toward boosting a child's critical thinking if used appropriately.

In this chapter we'll explore:

- Critical thinking and its importance
- The computer as a tool to enhance thinking skills
- Software to sharpen thinking
- The ultimate benefits of using the computer to develop thinking skills

Socrates, MTV and the Digital Generation . . .

To get a grip on critical thinking, you have to go back to Socrates. This guy had it figured out. First, he debunked the notion that the big shots—people in authority—have all the right answers. He established the importance of confronting and critiquing common assumptions, seeking evidence and analyzing thought for logical content. His method of questioning, known fondly as "the Socratic method," emphasized tough systematic questioning to ferret out the truth logically. He was the original Perry Mason. That was over 2,000 years ago (yes, people were thinking about thinking back then). Eventually Plato, Aristotle and other big-name thinkers like Thomas Aquinas (Middle Ages) and Descartes (seventeenth century) followed suit with supporting theories. Appearances, they said, could be deceiving. The best bet for coming to the truth is a well-trained, clear-thinking logical mind. These scholars' critical thinking paved the way for the emergence of science and even the concepts of freedom of thought and democracy.

Zoom ahead to the late 1700s and the Revolutionary War, and eventually the creation of the U.S. Constitution. It's been said that the U.S. was the first country *argued* into existence. Thomas Jefferson, Ben Franklin and the other original founders of the U.S. used reason and logic to argue for breaking away from Great Britain and, eventually, define the U.S. Constitution and laws that still govern this country. The separation of governmental powers and the rights of individuals, just to name two examples, were all determined through lengthy papers and debates and arguments based on some serious critical thinking.

Of course Socrates and Jefferson didn't have to deal with MTV, Madonna and Bart Simpson, not to mention shoot-em-up video games. You can't go anywhere today without being bombarded by media images. From tabloid journals and infomercials to news magazine TV shows and high-cost, high-tech, high-glitz advertising, an ocean of information is flooding us. It's easy to get swept up by the pretty images and compelling hype. That's where critical thinking comes in.

Young Kids: Nutrients for the Brain

As parents, we need to begin teaching thinking skills early on. Kids don't suddenly wake up when they're seventeen and start thinking critically; it's a process that gets under way very early in life and is heavily affected by their upbringing and surroundings. While genetics certainly play a big role, the brain is also very responsive to the outside world. It grows and develops areas for language, math, art, eye-hand coordination and just about everything else as it is stimulated and prodded. If areas of the brain aren't stimulated with experiences, they don't develop. We know a woman who always wanted to take piano as a kid but never had the chance. She started taking lessons when she enrolled her daughter. Guess who picked it up the quickest? It's much tougher to train an older brain than a younger one.

According to the authors of *Encouraging Potential in Young Children*, "Kids start in early stages with curiosity and the desire to experience, experiment, and understand." They move on to awareness and understanding of other concepts, including "the same, bigger and smaller; alike and different; first, second and third, more or less, before and after," and so on. Meanwhile kids are beginning to learn that numbers represent something—like "how many"—and that actions have results (plant a seed and it grows, make your baby sister cry and you get to spend time in your room). All these experiences are laying the foundation for critical thinking.

Think of these learning experiences as nutrients for the brain: a well-nourished brain develops better than one that's starved for knowledge and attention. Even if your child has reached the ripe old age of four or five, you can use the computer to stimulate his or her mind, fuel a sense of wonder and ignite a quest for adventure and knowledge. Over time this can be cultivated into inquiry, reflection, and analytical thought.

There are many ways you can use the computer to strengthen your young explorer's analytical abilities without buying a library of software. The tricks:

What does it mean to think critically?

Critical thinking means being flexible and disciplined in your thinking, being able to organize information, conduct sound analysis and then employ logic to solve problems and make decisions. That can take several forms in the real world. Examples of thinking critically:

- Proving the Earth is round when everyone says it's flat.
- Saying no to drugs despite relentless pressure from peers.
- Writing a document declaring liberty for your nation that affirms life, liberty and the pursuit of happiness for all.
- Calling 911 at age five when your mom just collapsed.
- Identifying a weakness in the opposing football team and scoring as a result.

• Emphasize thinking, not just remembering a bunch of facts. And emphasize the importance of critical thinking. The battle over the founding of this country and development of our Constitution is a good example. What were these men *thinking*, and how did critical thinking play a role in the formation of the Constitution, the Bill of Rights, other laws that govern the U.S.?

• Ask provocative questions related to your child's interests and schoolwork.

• Make exploration of the unknown a family pastime.

• Encourage questions and thoughtful consideration of answers.

• Use the computer as a resource to assist in obtaining, classifying and analyzing information.

Older Kids: Virtual Forest Trips and Financial Discipline

You probably can't drop everything and take your children to the rain forest to learn more about that biosystem. But you can support their efforts (and their teacher's) by doing some exploring on the computer. The next best thing to a trek to the tropics is a virtual trip that brings the rain forest to you—minus the rain. (Oregon readers take note.)

Try this. Create a Rain Forest Scavenger Hunt in which you send your little researcher on a computer safari. All you need is a CD-ROM encyclopedia, on-line reference materials and Web sites to gather information. Get them to dig up material on various plants and animals that live in the rain forest, the locations of some of the world's rain forests and the importance of that ecosystem.

The problem with many lessons is that kids can't relate them to real life. Ask your son or daughter to come up with five products used in everyday life that are derived from the rain forest. Next, head to the grocery store and buy the ingredients for a tasting party of rain forest foods. By then they should be relating the lesson to their own lives. (Don't forget the Ben & Jerry's Rain Forest Crunch!)

Here's another exercise, one that might actually imbue some financial discipline in your little gold-digger. Use a spreadsheet program such as *Lotus* or *Excel* to create a budget, then have your kids manage their money (allowance or money earned from doing odd jobs) for a few weeks. Spreadsheets demand rigor in thinking and precision in constructing formulas. If kids get sloppy, they'll get an error message. Garbage in, garbage out.

These programs can also do forecasting and projections that will help reinforce seemingly foreign concepts. Say your daughter needs to save a certain amount of money for a class trip at the end of the year. She can calculate how much she can earn under various scenarios and determine the most efficient means to reach her goal. She can create charts and graphs to mark her progress.

These kinds of exercises enhance reasoning and analytical abilities—and, just maybe, show kids that money doesn't grow on trees.

Using Software to Support Creative Problem Solving

Children today seem to have short attention spans, which can undermine critical thinking. Solving problems requires the ability to stay with the issue and work it from different angles, using creative thinking and approaches. But that doesn't mean they can't focus for long periods of time if they're motivated. Watch a 10-year-old boy play a video game, and you'll see him glued to the set for an hour or more, oblivious to the outside world. The trick is to channel that energy and focus into activities that will actually support creative problem solving. There are a variety of software programs designed to work those mental muscles, and some of them are so much fun your kids won't even know they're building thinking skills.

One of our favorites is Edmark's *Thinkin' Things* series of games and exercises for kids ages 3 to 13. Featuring enchanting little creatures called Fripples, the activities allow kids to work on spatial relationships, memory, musical skills, creativity, auditory skills and much more. In one game, customers order Fripples with specific characteristics: "One Fripple with polka dots, straight hair and a hat, to go please." Kids then examine a dozen adorable Fripples to find the match, and drag it to the correct place in the Fripple shop. This helps kids become adept at visual discrimination and detail orientation.

Another *Thinkin' Things* game blends music, art, science and play, allowing kids (and their dads) to create unique multimedia visual effects. This lets the kids experiment with motion and the illusion of depth. Our kids like this game because they can go wild with various creations that appear to dance around to the music. They also like another game, which demonstrates how gravity works by allowing users to increase or decrease gravitational pull by altering a course—say, creating a hill structure—and effecting the behavior of a metal ball bearing. The kids have to concentrate on the task at hand, think through various steps and anticipate consequences. Sometimes we have to kick them off this one so we can get our turn. Very cool.

Scholastic's *I Spy* is another engaging program. It's designed for kids ages 5 to 9, and it works on logic, visual discrimination, classifying and sorting, associative thinking, strategic thinking and problem solving. *I Spy* is similar to the game that we played as kids. You remember—one of your buddies or siblings calls out clues ("I spy something gold") and you hunt for it. In the software version, children solve riddles by searching for objects, unraveling secret codes, analyzing relationships and making their own games. There are eight different games within the program and most have different levels and options, so there's lots of variety. Children use reading and listening skills as they work through oral and screen clues, while the sound effects and animation keep it entertaining. Don't expect a lot of fancy fireworks or special effects; these are clever games with more subtle and frequent rewards.

Don't forget chess, an older classic. Chess helps children sharpen their strategic thinking skills and anticipate consequences, among other things. As the game evolves, they must refine their tactics, evaluating multiple scenarios and weighing alternatives. They must also practice restraint—that's a tough

MARK: CHESS AND INCREDIBLE MACHINES

I've struggled to get Matthew, 13, to play programs that require more than fifteen or thirty minutes to master; if it takes more time, and a lot of thought, he begins looking for the exit. I've had good luck with games like *Thinkin' Things* and, even better, one called *The Incredible Machine*, which allows him to create wacky puzzles out of thirty or forty gizmos, gadgets and contraptions. By stringing these together in certain ways he can create his own little interactive exercises, say, sending a ball through pipes, whirling blades and bouncing it off various kinds of walls and barriers, until he finally blows it up. It looks silly, but to make these work he has to calculate distances, angles and even density and weight of certain items. He loves it.

But my favorite game with him is chess. It's about the only game where he'll sit and play for a solid ninety minutes or more, glued to the screen as he tries to outwit me with a clever move—hoping to catch me offguard. It's still hard to get him away from his friends long enough to play, except at night, so I use every opportunity. Whenever we travel together, I make sure a chess game is loaded on the PC and I carve out time to play. When I took him with me to Philadelphia to the National Speakers' Association convention in July 1998, we played for almost two hours—nothing else to do, so why not? The quiet moments are rare, so plan ahead and take advantage of them.

one. There are chess software packages for every level, and some provide easy, step-by-step tutorials. Most packages let kids play against the computer, which is nice because the PC never loses patience or stomps away angrily, and the newest versions like *Chessmaster 5500* feature nifty graphics and a wide range of boards, views and chess pieces to choose from.

Simulation Games: Teaching Children to Think Ahead and Anticipate Consequences

One long-running complaint about public education is that much of what's taught doesn't strike the child as relevant. Remember how hard it was to learn Shakespeare?

Software is no different. The more realistically a program mimics real-life situations, the better. The new crop of simulation software programs do this by placing kids in real-life situations with the authority to make decisions that impact entire cities, parks, financial markets and ecosystems. These games also hold kids accountable for their choices. Raise taxes too high and people leave. Pollute the environment and they march on your city. Most of these programs are designed for kids ages eight and older.

Simulation games also take pretending and role playing to a new level. We've watched our kids play *SimCity 2000* for hours. They love being able to build bigger and bigger cities. They're always looking for new ways to bring in new "Sims" (people) by cutting taxes, offering new city services, and so forth. *SimCity* is chock full of graphs, maps and charts to help. They've gone broke before, and gotten battered by hurricanes and other natural disasters, but it never seems to faze them. That's the beauty of a game like this. Unlike real life, you can just start over.

Recently our sons picked up a new program called *The Streets of SimCity*, made by Maxis, maker of the *Sim* series. The game lets them build hot rods and race them down the streets of one of fifty pre-built Sim Cities—or they can import their own city. We felt a little let down seeing one of our favorite classics, *SimCity*, being transformed into yet another high-action, super-charged action game. But our sons are car nuts so they felt like they'd discovered the best of both worlds. They're in, well, *Sim* Heaven.

SIMULATION:
THE ART OF IMITATING LIFE

Check out these cool programs, but evaluate your child's needs before you go into the store. What aspect(s) of critical thinking are you trying to improve? What are their strengths, weaknesses? Also, keep in mind your child's age, computer skills and game interests as you wade through all the titles. Some children enjoy going to elaborate lengths to build cities or ecosystems, just to name two; some like other games. Find out before you buy the program.

- *SIMPARK* (MAXIS, AGES EIGHT TO TWELVE)

Children become rangers responsible for building and managing a park in any of nine North American climate zones. They can use more than 100 different animal and plant species to create any kind of park imaginable. The animals come to life and move, stalking each other amidst the natural sounds of the environment. The field guide that's included is full of helpful information. The ranger or park manager even receives e-mail from patrons or their boss if they do a good job—or screw up.

- *SIMTOWN* (MAXIS, AGES EIGHT TO TWELVE)

This is a very user-friendly simulation game for the preteen set. Junior planners must develop a community from the ground up or use a Starter Town or Fixer-Upper Town to get going. The idea is to balance the town's people, natural resources, and buildings. The visual appeal of the things they can put in their towns is high: pizza parlors, haunted houses, kids on wheels and all kinds of other interesting choices.

- *SIMISLE* (MAXIS, AGE TWELVE AND OLDER)

Kids rule the world, or at least this Southeast Asian island. They balance tourism, a fragile environment, wildlife, rare animal species and economic growth on the island. They have the help of twenty-four agents, each with a unique talent. This gives children the aid of informed advisers who can help them forge successful strategies if the young ruler is open to counsel.

- *OREGON TRAIL III, AMAZON TRAIL II, MAYAQUEST* (THE LEARNING COMPANY, AGES TEN TO SIXTEEN)

Children test their mettle as they try to survive treacherous journeys. The adventure is uncertain and survival is always on the line as weather conditions, supplies, pioneering skills and health all influence success. Children must use their wits, historical information that's provided and all the creative and critical thinking skills they can muster. The graphics and animation make you believe your wagon is crossing a river, your bike is careening down a hill, or your canoe is shooting the rapids.

A Call for Clear Thinking

A lot of kids struggle with math, and especially with word problems. You remember the kind: Sam's mom sends him to the post office. She asks him to get four 20-cent stamps and the rest 32-cent stamps. She gives him $3.00 and says that there's enough money there to buy him a candy bar at the convenience store. The candy bar costs 60 cents. How many 32-cent stamps can he buy? (Answer: 5)

Why do word problems make children sweat? Part of the problem is that many kids have a hard time sorting out the relevant facts, organizing them and solving the problem. They tend to want to plug numbers into a formula mindlessly just to get to an answer. And even if they remember the formula and get the right answer, they may not be developing the thinking skills they will need for tackling more complex problems in the future.

Listen to your children and how they speak. The careless way many children speak and listen reflects fuzziness in their thinking. It's like . . . well, you know what we mean . . . sorta . . . don't you? How many times have you heard that? The way children speak—the words they use, the way they string them together to communicate complex thoughts—affects the way they think and vice versa. In other words, if you can't talk and think clearly, you're going to struggle with these types of word problems and problem solving in general.

In some ways, modern technology encourages sloppy thinking. It's easy to slap together an e-mail message, with little regard for punctuation or grammar. Spell checkers make it easy to gloss over errors in hopes you can catch them later. While others have celebrated the new "Net generation," and how easily they communicate with peers across the globe, we've been disturbed by more fundamental trends. Just to take one, the discipline of carefully choosing words, putting together a series of thoughts in a logical fashion, and arguing a point is lost on many kids. It's like, well, uh, you know. . . .

You can help by demanding clearer thinking at every level. When you hear your child use vague words in a report, e-mail message or conversation, make them aware of it—and discuss ways they can sharpen their message. It's really not ok to just string together words haphazardly and hope the other side "gets it."

You can also help the cause by emphasizing math and science as part of your child's daily life. These subjects demand precise thinking. You can't solve an algebra problem if you don't understand the rules and know how to apply them. (Those are the rules that tell you to work inside parentheses first, raise powers, then multiply and divide, and finally, don't forget to add and subtract.) Likewise, how can you conduct a science experiment if you don't follow the scientific method?

New Ways to Teach Old Math Concepts

Many children would rather floss their teeth than work a math problem, so you're going to have to spend some time finding programs that fit your kid's learning style and appeals to them personally. This would have been a challenge a few years ago. The old math programs lacked much entertainment appeal and mostly focused on drills—basically electronic flash cards. But luckily, today's software tools are available that feature dynamic, fun exploits *and* teach math concepts using sound educational principles.

There are many advantages to using these programs to augment kids' math exposure:

- The technology encourages new approaches to math concepts that may just click with your kids where other methods fell short.
- There is less pressure, so kids feel freer to explore. Instead of freezing out of fear of getting the wrong answer, kids tend to experiment more. That means they'll practice more.
- The presentation of information is so engaging it often holds their attention longer.
- The variety of programs available means you can find ones that match your child's learning style. Choose puzzles, beat the clock, journey into other worlds, game shows, head-to-head contests, shopping and much more.

Our kids like *Math for the Real World* by Davidson and the Edmark *Mighty Math* series (*Number Heroes* and *Calculating Crew*). The *Real World* plot is geared to the preteen set. You're managing a rock and roll band and touring the country. Along the way to ten cities, kids have to stop and answer math problems. Solving the problem earns them bonus cash, which they can use to create their own music video. They also have to answer math questions to get food and gasoline. The goal is to create ten music videos and make it to the top of the music charts. "I think it's pretty cool for a math program," says Mark's son, Michael. "I like creating the videos."

Math Heroes are superheroes with names like Captain Nick Knack and GeoBot who teach math concepts (grades three to six) through various colorful games, quizzes, and challenges. In one game, for instance, children create their fireworks display by solving fraction problems (an example of the easy level asks you to "launch a fraction that's 7/12 yellow," with the aid of a visual pie chart; other more complex problems require you to add or subtract fractions). The result is a colorful fireworks display—in this case, featuring seven yellow parts and five other colors. Another one is set up like a virtual game show, where you play against an animated opponent. You get to choose from categories like "patterns" and "multiply." Miss the problem and the opponent gets a shot at it. Our children find these exercises challenging and entertaining—and you can bump up skill levels as they master the problems.

One more program worth considering is *Math Heads*, which appeals to children ages ages 9 to 13. This one capitalizes on kids' infatuation with television by presenting the program as an outrageous game show where the kids become contestants with their own faces made up on screen. Users solve word problems, do estimation, spend their prize money and receive tips on how to solve problems, all while enjoying jokes and tricks and poking fun at convention. It's almost enough to make them forget they're learning math.

Wanted: More Critical Thinking

Imagine there was a marathon contest for brainwork and mental achievements. How would you prepare?

We don't expect athletes to go out and run a 10K (6.2 mile) race without training. The same is true of our brains. Just because we are born with a brain, doesn't mean it's charged up and ready for calculus, complex decision making, creating an artistic masterpiece or even deciding whether to watch a TV show or not! Our brains have to be warmed up; they need to stretch, grow and train. Think of the computer as a virtual training camp for your little all-star's brain. You are only limited by your imagination.

To recap, the computer can help develop critical thinking skills like:

- Planning ahead
- Finding alternative solutions
- Balancing choices
- Thinking with precision
- Enhancing visual spatial reasoning
- Understanding cause and effect
- Classifying and sorting information
- Increasing flexibility and strategic thinking

But it CAN'T:

- Think for your kids
- Do their homework for them
- Instill values
- Replace a caring parent or teacher
- Get them to eat their vegetables (sorry, you're on your own)

FOCUSED QUESTIONS

- On a scale of 1 to 10, how would you rate your child as a critical thinker (with 10 being a super problem solver who relishes math and science problems)?
- How would you rate their math skills and attitude toward math?

- How would you rate their curriculum at school and at home for encouraging critical thinking?

- What sorts of programs are you using at home to build math and science skills, while encouraging critical thinking?

- \What steps are you taking to encourage critical thinking in other areas, such as written communications?

- \What sort of role modeling are you doing to encourage clear thinking (and discourage fuzzy thinking)?

10.

Raising a Computer-Smart Daughter

GROWING COMPUTER SKILLS, GROWING SELF-ESTEEM

Who said girls can't use computers?
—Kristen Helmer, 14

Just on the surface, it appears that many girls are being left behind when it comes to computers. Parents and educators tell us the boys tend to dominate the computer in the classroom and at home, and there are still more male engineers (and presumably computer nuts) than females. If you doubt the fact that boys are taking over the PC, simply stop by a computer store and see who's playing the demo games.

But if you look a little closer you'll see that the situation is changing. There are an increasing number of girls who *are* getting into computing. The best evidence is online. More than 50 percent of the subscribers on America Online, for instance, are female. And while there are still more males than females on the Internet, the gap is narrowing. Many of these are younger girls, 10 to 18, and they can be as computer savvy as their male counterparts. While the picture is still mixed, it appears that many girls are catching on that computers can be a cool thing.

The reason for their interest is pretty simple: the computer is a great social and learning tool and may even help build self-esteem at a critical time. It's also a great equalizer: girls online are judged on their thoughts and ideas, rather than their personal appearances. This is pretty cool at a time when they're facing crushing social pressures.

We have deep personal interests in this issue (Ralph's daughter is 14, Mark's is 4). While they're years and worlds apart, we share a common concern:

neither one of us wants our daughters to be left behind as we move into the Digital Age. Both girls and boys will need technical knowledge to get almost *any* kind of decent job in a few years, and the choice jobs will require technical expertise and skills, "technology literacy" as the experts call it. To prepare for whatever new jobs emerge in the next ten to twenty years, girls will need to be versatile and techno-savvy. In other words, they'd better know their RAMs, ROMs and CPUs.

In this chapter we'll give you some tips to help get your daughter interested in the computer, including:

- A look at how girls and boys differ in their play and what it means for computing
- Software choices designed for girls
- Why the Web appeals to girls
- Organizations and activities to help girls become more technologically literate

Background

Young girls are generally just as interested in computers as boys are. Mark's daughter plays the same computer programs as any four-year-old boy. But when they get to be about 12 or so, something happens. Many girls abandon anything that smacks of being technical or scientific, including mathematics and science. Many begin to view computers as boys' toys.

You can see it at our PC Frontier shows. Observe two twelve-year-old kids, one boy and one girl, and you will see that the boy, typically, is all over the computer. About half the time, the girl will join in too. But many times, she'll stand back, passively watching or talking to a friend, observing as the others have fun.

There's probably a lot going on in that little girl's head, as girls are undergoing deep changes at this age. The teenage years seem to be a particularly difficult rite of passage for girls. In her landmark book, *Reviving Ophelia: Saving the Selves of Adolescent Girls,* Mary Pipher points out:

> *In early adolescence, studies show that girls' IQ scores drop and their math and science scores plummet. They lose their resiliency and optimism and become less curious and inclined to take risks. They lose their assertive, energetic and "tomboyish" personalities and become more deferential, self-critical and depressed. . . .*

The issues are complex. While twelve- to fifteen-year-old girls are undergoing major physiological changes and social pressure, they're also facing cultural biases that tend to discourage them from pursuing interests in science and technology. Studies by groups like the American Association of University Women and Center for Equity and Cultural Diversity indicate that girls and boys act differently in the classroom, and are treated differently. While boys tend to be more aggressive in asking questions, many girls hold back; girls also tend to get less verbal praise and feedback from teachers. Some studies show that teachers often give them fewer explanations about *how* to solve problems. When it comes to technology, math and science, girls aren't given the same level of detail that boys are about the logic behind the solutions.

The upshot is that many girls get the idea that they aren't as important as their male peers. They begin to feel that their contributions, insights and questions are not valued. This carries over into math, science and computer studies, with girls deciding that they're not as good in these areas. Self-confidence tumbles; they look for easier subjects to tackle. Soon they start doubting that they belong in these areas.

In the book *Does Jane Compute?* Roberta Furger tells of a research project that clearly illustrates this point. Researchers observed a class of twenty-nine seventh and eighth grade kids for the better part of a school year in Ontario, Canada. Their goal was to observe the different ways they used the computer, and how gender affected their habits and attitudes. After seven months they put the kids into seven classifications, from "hacker," defined as children who loved using computers, exploring new software, playing games and creating games and programs on their own, to "Luddites," students who basically hated computers. There were several boys who were labeled as hackers, the ones other students looked up to as experts.

Of the twelve girls in the class, three were categorized as "eager tool users"— students who were adept at using all the tools at their disposal. They knew their way around a computer and a wide range of programs, and they were confident in their computer abilities. But none of the girls were categorized as hackers.

One girl, in particular, was equally fanatical about the computer and was as competent as any of the boys, but she wasn't regarded in the same way. The hacker label had a "social aspect as well as a technical one." Hackers, under the researchers' definition, were the students that the others went to for help. Although the girl was adept at the computer, no one in the class, including the teacher, went to her for answers. Strange but true.

It doesn't have to be this way. We know lots of computer-smart parents who are successfully helping their daughters through these tough times. They're doing it by encouraging technological pursuits, working together on the computer and capitalizing on their daughter's interests to make computing relevant. Their daughters emerge from high school with newfound confidence, ready to tackle the world. Used appropriately, the computer can be a great antidote for some of the trials of female adolescence.

New Hope for Girls

Clearly things are getting better. Parents and educators are addressing the issues, and software companies are waking up and producing quality programs targeted at girls. There are new support programs like "girls only" computer clubs, camps and groups springing up across the country. These provide wonderful computer and technical opportunities for young women. It's also encouraging to know that no matter how old your daughter is, you can do something to enhance her technology literacy.

What we see when we take our show to schools is that girls get jazzed when we use the computer to do something fun and relevant to them. We show them a Web site where they can meet other girls, and they all want to jump online.

That one simple demonstration gives them a chance to learn a bunch of skills: getting online, finding a site, selecting activities, setting up a chat room, going off-line and knowing how to get back to the site next time.

Another point to remember is that most—and we emphasize *most*—girls have different tastes in computer software than the boys. Boys tend to favor action/adventure games that depict them vanquishing the enemy with force and physical domination. They relish destroying alien invaders, conquering other civilizations and outwitting opponents. They like the taste of battle.

Girls, by comparison, reject destruction for the sake of destruction. They tend to favor programs with more finesse, subtlety and complexity. In 1993 Interval Research Corporation undertook a massive study to find out why girls were being left out of the technology industry. They spent more than two years studying gender differences in play among 7- to 12-year-olds and examining girls' interest in (and use of) technology. Here's what they discovered:

- Girls didn't play computer games as much as boys because they found violence-centered games boring.
- Girls want to use the computer to do role-playing games, adventure games, drawing, creative writing, problem-solving and clue-based games.
- Girls like the social opportunities the computer can offer: e-mail, chat rooms and multi-player games.
- Girls and boys are equally competitive, but they compete in different ways; girls favor covert competition, establishing relationships and determining social status by associations and exclusions. Boys prefer overt competition, power and physical superiority and evaluating status by achievement and physical domination.

The best news can be found on the software shelves. Finally there's software that caters specifically to girls. This is a big deal. Since the first PC rolled out of the factory, most entertainment offerings for kids over the age of six have been tailored to boys. Now we're seeing new companies, like Purple Moon, whose mission is to create software for girls. Purple Moon was created by Interval Research Corporation to develop and lead the "adventures for girls" segment they identified through their research.

RALPH: RALPH'S DAUGHTER GETS BACK IN THE SADDLE

Not long ago my wife and I wondered if our daughter Christina would ever see the home PC as something more than a glorified typewriter for homework projects. She showed great promise in the beginning and then lost interest. At age three she loved puzzles and drawing colorful pictures with every pencil, crayon and marker she could lay her hands on. My wife and I wanted to introduce her to the PC so we started looking for computer programs and activities that would tap her interests. After a couple of trips to the local software store our home PC was loaded with computer puzzle games featuring everything from the popular Berenstain Bears characters to unicorns, farm animals and landscapes. And for artwork I showed her the ropes of the *Paintbrush* program that comes with the Microsoft Windows operating system and bought her titles such as *Kid Pix* and *Crayola Art Studio*. She was hooked.

As the next few years zoomed by we watched her rapidly graduate to more sophisticated educational programs and creativity software for making banners and greeting cards. Things were going great until she hit fourth grade, then the bomb hit. Brother Jeff, then age five, caught the action game bug and was spending way too much time on the Nintendo unit and our home PC playing the latest car race or flight simulation games I kept bringing home to satisfy my gaming-addiction habit. It was starting to get out of hand. As Christina recalls, the PC in her eyes had turned into a glorified Nintendo machine that left her cold. Gradually her time on the PC dwindled and before we knew it she only touched it to do word

processing for homework projects and research using one of our PC encyclopedia CD-ROMs.

That's when the alarm bells went off in my head. My wife and I wanted her to
keep her computing skills sharp. We knew it was important for her to continue exploring learning and entertainment software and to become familiar with navigating the Internet. The burning question became how to bring her back to the PC.

To turn things around, we thought about what worked in the beginning—tapping her personal interests. By age nine, when Christina began shying away from
the PC, she had become an avid horse lover after starting riding lessons when we
moved to Oregon. She read every book on horses she could find and talked all the
time about getting a horse. To bring her back to the PC I decided to see if Prodigy
(the online service we used at the time) had any special information sections for
horse nuts. One Saturday morning we sat side by side, fired up the PC, went online to Prodigy and began poking around. To her delight, we found a special bulletin board section covering every imaginable aspect of horses. She dove right in,
reading all the posted questions and answers and scoured the classified sections,
pretending she was in the market for the horse of her dreams.

Using horses to get her attention did the trick. From that point forward there
was no stopping her. She quickly moved from the horse bulletin boards on Prodigy
to surfing of the World Wide Web at large for horse Web sites. She learned how
to run a browser, how to keep a record of her favorite Web sites and all about information links. Most important of all, she began to fight brother Jeff for her fair
share of PC time.

By age 13 she had developed into a Web-surfing veteran. Suddenly she started
listening to rock music and buying CDs. She discovered that each rock group's CD
cover art included a Web site highlighting the group or artist. Her favorite Websites
list grew to include these addresses and she found out her best friends were creating lists too. Phone conversations about swapping favorite rock group Website
addresses with her buddies led to a big question in the summer of 1997—"Dad, do
I have an e-mail address? My friends want to send me messages and

pictures." After a few minutes of training she was e-mailing messages via America Online like a pro. A few days later I came home to find that she had taught herself how to set up a private chat room with her two best friends. She was now a total cyber kid running online private chats, downloading audio and video files, playing them back, and building quite an extensive library of digital pictures featuring her favorite rock stars. She was doing stuff I didn't know how to do!

The lesson was clear: For many girls the personal computer itself, and certainly most PC action games, just don't hold their interest. To get and keep my daughter excited about computing we had to tap *her* personal interests creatively.

Intriguing Software for Girls

The market for girls' adventure software is opening up and lots of companies are jumping on the bandwagon. Here are three examples:

• ***Rockett's New School***: Purple Moon created a series of friendship adventure games for girls ages eight through twelve. In *Rockett's New School*, the plot revolves around an eighth grade girl's first day at a new school. There's plenty of teenage angst, peer pressure and decisions to be made as Rockett navigates her way through her class schedule. The program has an eclectic bunch of characters, and the dialogue is right on the mark for the preteen set. The homeroom teacher is a little melodramatic but still effective. Girls control the story line as they select Rockett's responses to different scenarios. You get to peek in lockers, pass notes, and deal with annoying peers, cool friends and tough choices. Your daughter will appreciate the realism and the cast of characters. Behind the plot is a clear message: be yourself.

• **The American Girls Premier:** The Pleasant Company brought its successful series of dolls and books, *The American Girls Collection,* to the computer screen by partnering with The Learning Company. The program is called *The American Girls Premiere* and is targeted to girls 7 through 12. Girls create and direct plays by selecting one of five main characters, each representing a different historical era. The girls then populate the drama with a supporting cast, design a set using authentic props, add music, dialogue and sound effects. This program has plenty of depth, allowing girls to start as simply as they wish and advance to more complex performances as their skills improve. Although it's supposed to be for kids as young as seven, we found it too intricate for the younger kids. This program really capitalizes on girls' creative interests while allowing them to learn about American history from a female perspective and to explore the intricacies of making theatrical productions.

• **Pure Fun Programs—Cosmopolitan Virtual Makeover:** If you want to go for pure fun, check this one out. Once you get your mug shot on the computer,

Other Favorites with Girls

These programs may not be "pure girl" titles, but a lot of girls think these gender-neutral programs are pretty cool:

• **The Magic School Bus Series:** These games are packed with science, space and a great bunch of characters led by their indomitable teacher, Ms. Frizzle.

• **The Carmen Sandiego Series:** Kids test their detective skills solving mysteries and showing off their geography knowledge.

• **Myst:** For the 13 and over crowd, this ethereal adventure has a growing following of passionate "Myst-ics" who love this game.

• **Creative Writer 2:** Bursting with art, Web page design ideas and a bunch of publishing tools, this is a great program for girls who want to create newsletters, diaries and other cool stuff.

• **3D Movie Maker:** Kids try their hand at making animated movies and designing 3D special effects. They can create entire kid flicks working with others or solo.

• **American Greetings Creatacard Plus, Hallmark Connections Card Studio, and Greetings Workshop Deluxe:** Three feature-rich programs that make it easy to create greeting cards, invitations, posters, calendars, banners and stationery.

you have 150 different hairstyles to choose from, along with various other kinds of makeup (including hairstyles for guys). Also check out *Barbie Fashion Designer,* which lets girls design and create clothes and fashion accessories. While these might make a politically correct parent cringe, a lot of girls love them, and anything that piques their interest in computing can't be all bad. Plus, it beats hanging out at the mall or Dairy Queen, right?

Let Your Daughter Lead

Teenagers and two-year-olds have a lot in common. Adolescence is round two of your daughter's search to find the limits, push the boundaries, assert independence—and put space between her and you. The bottom line: Go with the flow. Don't try to shove technology down her throat. Find out what works for her. Remember that many girls see technology as a tool to accomplish something else. Capitalize on this by using the computer to further her interests, and don't forget that every girl is unique. Some will roll up their sleeves and jump in and develop an intense interest in computing; others will continue to hold back, viewing computers and technology suspiciously. Let them move at their own pace.

What does your daughter like? Leverage those interests and find ways the computer can enhance them. Rock music, Leonardo DiCaprio, saving whales, stargazing, Rollerblading—it doesn't matter. They all provide a springboard to catapult her into a higher level of skill that's essential to success. Spend some time perusing the software section of local retailers. There are programs for all kinds of hobbies and interests, with the list growing almost daily.

The Great Equalizer: The Web

There's no better place to pique your daughter's computing interest than on the Internet. The Web is particularly appealing to adolescent girls who are struggling to establish their identity. They get to explore a new world of information, while interacting with other girls with a wide range of interests and perspectives. We're referring mainly to chat rooms and bulletin boards, where girls meet and communicate. These forums are highly interactive; kids come and go, make connections, communicate about subjects close to their hearts, and move on. It's very fleeting but potentially rewarding. Compare the possibilities of discovery and interaction on the Web to TV, which spoonfeeds images and ideas to girls in a way that precludes any interaction—a passive medium. The bottom line is that the Web, with all its problems, offers a much better medium for girls to try out new ideas, discover new friends and define their identity than TV.

Not only does the Web provide plenty of opportunities for girls to get connected, it allows girls to express themselves in a safe haven. They don't have to worry about how they look online; people have to deal with them on an intellectual level. All those personal biases—appearance, clothes, race—vanish in cyberspace. You are what you say you are. That's why we call the Internet the great equalizer. According to Jupiter Communications, an estimated 5 million girls are already on the Web, and that number will increase to 15 million by the year 2002.

The feeling of being connected is particularly powerful for girls who feel isolated. Introverted kids who are struggling to find their place among their peers might feel more confident as they make friends online. Of course there are dangers online (more on that in Chapters 12 and 13), but if they're careful, girls can enjoy their time in cyberspace.

Monitored chat rooms and cyber pen pals are great starting points for girls. Take a look at some of the sites we've listed here. Practice so you can be a positive role model for your daughter. It's particularly important that girls see Mom using the computer with confidence; they need that model. Mom's lack of interest and competence in technical areas passes on negative messages to daughters. If a mother can't do it, actively seek a female mentor who can fill the gap. Here are a few other tips for having excellent online adventures:

- **Go exploring together.** Take a cruise down the information superhighway and let your daughter drive. Be inquisitive. Check out something you've never looked at before. Discover something new and talk about it. It'll kindle her curiosity and remind her that you're never too old to learn new tricks.

• **Get lost in space.** Wandering around the cyber-galaxy will boost her self-confidence and improve her skills. Pick out a few interesting topics and turn your cyber-journey into a treasure hunt.

• **Ask your daughter for help.** Teens always think they know more than their parents. This will give her a chance to be the heroine. Let her teach you a few tricks. You'll learn more, and she'll be able to exhibit her prowess at the computer.

• **Give her an e-mail address.** Setting up an e-mail account on America Online or another Internet service is easy. Let her have some cyber-independence. Give your daughter space and privacy. Let her write and talk to her friends for a specified amount of time without someone looking over her shoulder. The more she can connect with other girls, the more time she'll spend on the computer.

There are a slew of cool sites and resources on the information superhighway for you and your daughter. Following are sites that offer parenting guidance and information on teen issues, along with various resources to assist parents and links to other relevant spots. Girls will find sites filled with software titles, monitored chat rooms (where someone is monitoring activity and chats, assuring generally that discussions don't turn nasty), online magazines, games, activities, creative writing opportunities and more. Spend time surfing through the teen sites to become acquainted with them. It's a great way to keep your finger on the pulse of your daughter's world without being overly intrusive.

Here are some options for online adventures:

• **Women Online** (*www.women.com*). Sort of the ultimate girls' yellow pages, this is a directory listing hundreds of sites in a variety of categories that are of particular interest to girls and women.

• **Expect the Best from a Girl and That's What You'll Get** (*www.academic.org*). A great site for parents to get information and advice on how to support their daughters. There's a wealth of information and resources on lots of meaty topics.

• **Club Girl Tech** *(www.girltech.com)*. There's a section called Raising Healthy Daughters that's loaded with research, resources and ideas for parents and mentors. The Club Girl Tech site is a wonderfully supportive destination for girls. It actively attempts to enhance self-esteem and build a sense of community among girls. There are six areas for girls to explore plus links to other sites.

• **New Moon** *(www.newmoon.org)*. This is an online magazine written by and for girls. The online version is not as extensive as the print version that's available by subscription.

• **Purple Moon** *(www.purple-moon.com)*. A very interactive site allowing girls to join in adventures with characters from the Purple Moon stories, go on scavenger hunts, solve mysteries, contribute ideas to plots, create personal pages and find postcard pals. There is a "three strikes and you're out" policy on offensive language; if a user tries to use vulgar or profane language three times, they're kicked out.

PURPLE MOON: SHINING NEW LIGHT ON THE GIRLS' MARKET

Purple Moon, Mountain View, California, started from day one going against the grain. While many companies raced to churn out action-packed games, Purple Moon set out to provide quality and entertaining software programs for young girls. No blood and guts. No screaming and yelling. No brutal competition. Just plain fun and some social interaction and educational experiences along the way.

Girls don't want blood and gore, says Karen Gould, Purple Moon's Public Relations Manager. "They want experiences that are personally relevant to them with characters that they can imagine having a relationship with and through story lines and narratives that are relevant to their own life."

Purple Moon's answer: interactive multimedia programs that play to girls' interests, featuring personal stories and subplots, relationship issues and characters that mimic real life (check out their CD-ROMs or Web site (www.purple-moon.com). Girls get to live life vicariously through the stories and characters.

The company has done well too. Their *Rockett* series, centered around a friendly teenage girl experiencing life, has been a big hit with the third to sixth grade set. (Rockett receives more than 2,000 e-mail messages a week from her fans.) Meanwhile the Purple Moon Web site has 165,000 registered users who visit the site on average 1.5 times a day and spend thirty to forty minutes on the site. The girls can make friends with other girls who share similar interests and can exchange virtual postcards with them. Throughout the site girls can find and collect hidden treasures and exchange them with other girls. Girls can also create their own personal pages.

Not only has the site become its own girls' community, but it also teaches girls valuable computer skills they'll need for the future. There's definitely something here. Even Mark's four-year-old daughter fell in love with Rockett, and now she's kind of a hero for her.

Purple Moon's current CD-ROMs include: *Rockett's New School, Rockett's Tricky Decision, Rockett's Secret Invitation, Rockett's Adventure Maker, Rockett's Starfire Soccer Challenge, Secret Paths in the Forest* and *Secret Paths to the Sea.*

• **Parent Soup** (*www.ParentSoup.com*) Good overall site for parents to get tips on a wide range of parenting issues, including raising a daughter. Lots of community activity.

Growing a Digital Daughter

Whether your daughter is 5 or 15, your job as a computer-smart parent is to understand the issues facing her and help her confront them head-on. You've got to pay attention, engage her in technology, support her, be involved, nurture—and nurture some more. Here are some small things you can do to make a big difference in your daughter's life:

• **Help her become technologically savvy.** Find ways to integrate the computer into her life as a matter of routine. Make sure you provide equal access to sons and daughters. Let your daughter buy software that interests her. (Put her in charge of some part of a project that involves using the computer, for example, designing the family's holiday card or party invitation, planning a vacation, searching for colleges, rotating screen savers that your kids design, creating a family Web page, sending fun e-mail to family members.) Have her take a computer-related course that interests her—possibly with a friend. Enlist her help in putting a family photo album on the computer. Let her update your look with a computer-generated makeover. You'll both get a kick out of it.

Camping—Without the Insects

Computer camps are similar to the summer camps parents have been sending their kids to for years, with one twist—the emphasis is on developing computer skills. Many computer camps for kids are offered by colleges and universities around the country, and they vary quite a bit. Some mix other outdoor activities generously—hiking, boating and so on—while others have more of a focus on computing-only activities. There are day and overnight camps that offer a wide variety of topics for novices, experts and everyone in between, and of course there are longer-stay camps. Most camps house kids in student dorm rooms on campus, giving kids a unique opportunity to experience some world-class college facilities. (Whether dorm food is any better than camp fare is a toss-up.) Check out these Web sites for more information:

• **American Computer Experience** (*www.computercamp.com*)

• **Kids 'n Computers** (*calgary.shaw.wave.ca/~knc*)

• **Kids' Camps** (*www.kidscamps.com*)

• **Praise curiosity and encourage exploration.** Ask questions, investigate and be a role model for life-long learning. Help your daughter explore the unknown. When she asks questions, help her figure out how and where to get the answers. Initiate new adventures to go on together. Take up a new hobby or let her see you digging deeper into one of your own passions. Enroll in a class or seminar and talk about what you learned. Let her see you puzzling over something. Show her that gaining knowledge and expertise takes time and practice. Do something for the very first time while your daughter is watching.

• **Send her to camp.** And while we appreciate the great outdoors, we mean computer camp. They even have real beds there.

 ## MARK: NEVER TOO YOUNG

Here's a bonus tip: start young and early. My wife and I have been working with our daughter Nicole, now four, since she was a tiny baby. We read to her, played games, puzzles, anything to stimulate her mind. Then when she got old enough to sit in my lap and play on the computer, I made special time for her. I made her brothers step back so she could have her time on the computer and begin to learn about technology as they did. Of all the programs in the house, at least 35 percent are her programs—and they get a lot of use. I let her pick her favorites, but I also slip in the ones I think will help her advance. There's a lot of hands-on support, but other times she just wants to play alone. (*Putt-Putt* is a good example— "I can do it," she'll tell me, and she does.)

I've already noticed how she loves to explore these programs. For instance she'll spend an hour or so on *Kid Pix*, creating her own little paintings, adding goofy bell and whistle sounds and mixing everything up with the "crazy mixer." Then she'll sit back and laugh. This is my goal: to help stimulate her interest so she sees the computer as a tool for fun and learning. While it's still early in the game, so far she's right on track.

• **Get down and dirty.** Get her involved in organized sports programs. It's great for the body and the self-esteem, and she may make some new friends. Roll up your sleeves and practice with her.

• **Join a girls-only organization or activity.** This will give her an opportunity to see how girls and women solve all kinds of problems and provide an unparalleled opportunity to develop leadership skills. See if your town has a girls-only computer club. If not, consider starting one.

• **Encourage mechanical and technical interests.** Oftentimes girls won't take the lead but would relish the chance to have a chemistry set, learn how to use a set of socket wrenches or help paint the house. Jump in and teach her. Surprise her with her own tools for her bike or a subscription to a sporting or technical magazine.

DEAR SOFTWARE INDUSTRY . . . GIRLS SPEAK OUT!

Software makers, watch out! Teen girls are on the warpath, and they're armed with loads of ideas. We found this out first-hand when we asked preteen and teenage girls on America Online to send us ideas in early 1997. The message came through clearly: Girls are tired of the usual fare of blood and guts games on one end of the spectrum and Barbie games on the other. They want more variety, and programs that are relevant to their own personal worlds.

Kristen Helmer, 14, of Saginaw, Michigan was typical:

Being interested in computers is being interested basically in words. It helps to have a big vocabulary right off the bat. Stop at the bookstore on your way home from work, find a large colorful book, and make a gift of it. I cannot stress how important that is in everything we do today.

If I could create the perfect program it would be colorful. Kids would first be able to step-by-step put together their own characters. Face, eyes, weight, ears, design their own clothing, giving them thousands of choices. The game would include interactive racing, word games, role playing for specific age areas, and levels, moving them up from barely literate to expert. It would include ages 6 to 17, and immediately boot anyone that utters a dirty word before it hits the screen.

Before you decide to get your children involved, you have to ask yourself, "Do I want my daughter's face glued to the screen twelve hours a day?" Try limiting their time on the Internet, encouraging them to realize how valuable it is.

Girls at a young age often have trouble expressing themselves. Bottling up can have bad effects. Give them their own folder. Show them how to create their own diary by putting their own password on a word processor. Give them their own space, don't rearrange the order they put things in. If they make mistakes, correct them, but also leave them to fix some things on their own. They learn to experiment that way.

If they have their own Internet service, set their home page at their level and interests. For teenage girls, do some research and find a Web page with a lot of information, suitable for their age.

I've won typing contests, along with several awards for my home pages and for my stories.

Who said girls can't use computers?

• **Be a role model.** Walk the talk. Lead by example. Your words and actions are powerful influences on your daughter. As a computer-smart parent you can give your daughter skills and tools to expand her career options and be a leader in the techno-revolution.

FOCUSED QUESTIONS

• What is your daughter's level of computer interest on a scale of 1 to 10. Is she confident of herself on the computer and proud of her skills?

• If she's less than enthusiastic and competent, what's holding her back? How can you, as a computer-smart parent, help her move ahead?

• If she *is* enthusiastic and competent, how can you help her stay challenged on the computer?

• What are her interests and how can she use the computer to go further with them? Who can she exchange e-mail with? (Get Grandma online, and those post-birthday thank-you notes get lots easier to write!)

• How are you as a computing role model? If you're not comfortable with the beast, what steps can you take to become more confident? Who else can you enlist to act as a role model or to share their computer enthusiasm?

11.

Boys, Game Addiction and Violent Software

RAISING A GOOD SON IN THE AGE OF ENTERTAINMENT

My son is driving me nuts. I bought a PC for the kids to do homework, but all he wants
to do is play games. Every day after school he runs to the PC and plays these battle
games. When he cranks up the speakers, our den sounds like an arcade.
—Parent attending a PC Dads workshop
at the Rice Elementary School, Houston, Texas

It's a classic dilemma. You buy a computer intending to use it for finances, educational programs, word processing and a few other select programs. But within hours of getting it home, Junior has taken over and turned it into a game machine, playing around the clock. Many of the games have a violent tone, with explosions and bodies flying around. He loves the games and is glued to the PC several hours a day, but you wonder if it's gone too far. This isn't what you had in mind.

Computer-game addiction is one of those nagging problems that drive parents crazy. It usually afflicts boys between 8 and 14. While there are a few girl game addicts, we've found that the boys are usually the biggest culprits. Game addicts want to play all the time, and they can never get enough action. Throw in a thirst for violence on the screen and you have the makings of an unhealthy situation—again, not exactly what you intended when you lugged that new computer home.

Luckily computer-smart parents can take steps to regain control of games. In this chapter we'll discuss how to get a grip on the situation: how to control games in your home, how to judge a game in terms of violence, how to work out a peaceful compromise with your kid—and how to keep your sanity along the way. We'll also show you how to choose "high-action, low-violence" alternatives to the usual blood and gore programs. When you're finished reading the chapter, you'll also know how to be a smart games buyer.

Breaking the Game Addiction

Computer games, like TV, are ok up to a point. It's when they become an overriding obsession that they become a problem (as if parents need more of these, right?). You can see it coming. The kid's glued to the PC. He skips dinner so he can play. He's back on it at night, missing his favorite TV show. He talks about it constantly. He can't break away or play other programs because he's so caught up in the latest game.

Some experts worry that this is an extension of an already negative trend in society, where TV and other modern electronic mediums replace the child's natural need to think, explore—and imagine. This worries us. Boys should be allowed to use their imaginations to create a world in which they can grow and feel comfortable. In their book, *Raising a Son,* authors Don and Jeanne Elium state that "A boy creates a world where he is in charge; his own powerful acts affect people and events . . . which enables him to accept his place in the everyday world. Thus, imagination helps a young boy learn how to relate to the people with whom he comes in contact." In other words, imagination helps kids cope in an otherwise tough world. According to Waldorf educator Margaret Meyerkort, it even helps provide the foundation "for the vision to love."

We had plenty to imagine when we were kids—there wasn't a lot else to do in many cases. Times were simpler. We'd have sword fights with sticks or drag out the toy soldiers, build imaginary forts and stage mock battles. John Wayne was a big deal back then. A trip to the beach or countryside was a new adventure, a chance to explore and let our imaginations run wild. One of our favorite games as kids was playing around in the backyards and acting out "What if" games. "What if we could go to another planet? "What if we could be whoever we wanted to be?"

You'll still hear some of this if you hang around kids long enough, but imaginative play is being overshadowed by new electronic tools—arcade video games and computer programs with 3D graphics, fast-action shoot-em-up cop shows and movies and so on. Many of the new games allow kids to blast their way through buildings and bodies with ease or blow up a city with a single click of the mouse. How can a quiet night under the trees and stars compare with bodies and car parts exploding into pieces on the screen?

The result, we fear, is that the new mediums—TV, video games, fast-action TV shows—are crowding out our child's imaginative abilities. "The characters he sees on TV then become the playactors in his dramas, rather than the soulful images and emotions that are alive within himself," note the authors of *Raising a Son*. "The result is that he begins to rely on what is outside of himself for sources of creativity, ideas, entertainment and enjoyment."

The most disturbing part of this is the ever-increasing violence children are bombarded with today. Some experts believe that kids today, particularly boys, have been desensitized by the overload of violent images and information being thrown at them, particularly by TV. They come to see violence as a part of life, and a basis for entertainment. You can see examples in even the most harmless situations.

One example: We were demonstrating the *Adventures with Barbie Ocean Discovery* game at a technology showcase in Scottsdale, Arizona, when a 10-year-old boy came up and started playing. The game, of course, is mostly played underwater, where Barbie hunts for special treasures. It's all clean and safe, with no violence. But the boy soon got bored with swimming around. He was about to leave when an idea hit him: "Can we get a shark in there and chase Barbie?" he asked. It's not enough to swim around and find treasures; he had to have Barbie facing a life or death confrontation. "It'll give her something to do," he added, grinning.

We don't mean to overplay this issue, and we're the last to argue for any kind of ban on exciting games for children, for there are better ways to deal with this issue. The key is to realize that what kids really want isn't violence as much as it is empowerment—a sense that they're in control. A study by an In-tel research group of twenty-eight families in the Portland area, with thirty-six children, found that kids simply like being in control of something. The typical 8- to 14-year-old boy is desperately seeking a way to have more control over his life. He's not old enough to drive, date or do many "adult" things, so he looks for alternatives. Along comes a program that allows him to control a character with some power, and he's hooked. *He* gets to decide what the character's go-ing to do, who he's going to annihilate, where he's going to go, which weapons he's going to use and so on.

The key, then, is to find programs and other activities (including noncom-puter activities) that help the boy meet his needs for action, and to feel "in con-trol," while putting reasonable limits on games.

How can you help your son find healthier ways to feel in control? Here are a few tips we can pass along based on our own experiences and ideas we've picked up from parents all over North America. (This can also apply to the ded-icated game machines like Sega Genesis, Nintendo and Sony PlayStation too.)

• **Find a substitute.** Don't try to ignore the kid's desire for action and drama; just find acceptable substitutes. Racing games and flight simulator programs are just two examples of programs that offer action without the violence. Our sons love games like *Need for Speed, VR Sports Powerboat Racing* and *Motocross Madness*. They enjoy configuring the performance of "muscle" cars with engines, wheels, and other special gears much like they do if they were choosing weapons in one of the shoot-'em-up games. Play the program with your kids; they'll get a kick out of beating you!

• **Set up a family agreement.** Call the family together and agree on some ground rules. What's acceptable in terms of violent content? How much time should each kid be able to spend playing games? It's going to vary by age and family, depending on your values and priorities.

• **Set up a time-management system or budget.** Ralph's son has a one-hour-a-day electronic entertainment "budget." He can watch TV, play his Nintendo N64 game unit or play games on the PC; it's his decision. But he has a maximum of one hour per day (you may want to go with ninety minutes, but less is better).

• **Make kids earn game time.** Consider making your kids earn their game time. Mark admits that his sons play more games than he prefers. To manage this, he substitutes "high-action, low-violence" games (more on that later) and makes them earn game time. They get credit for playing educational software programs, which they can use toward playing PC games—one hour of *Encarta* or *Reading Blaster* earns them one hour of games. Rack up enough educational program hours and they can even buy another game—on his dime.

• **Turn the darn PC off!** Tell 'em to go outside. Get some fresh air. Throw a baseball. Mow the lawn.

Special PC Dads Tip: Look for Educational Value

Believe it or not, there are action-packed games that have some educational value. With *Flight Simulator 98* from Microsoft, for instance, you can learn quite a bit about flying a plane. Another Microsoft game, *Age of Empires*, lets you learn about different ancient cultures. It's one of our favorites. With this one, you pick your culture (Babylonians, Persians, etc.) and learn a little about the way the people lived back then. The idea is to build a civilization, using the tools and resources of the day. Of course, much of the action centers around beating back the enemy. Like the popular game *Command & Conquer*, there's mild violence (bodies falling down, some groans) as you fight it out, but parents can use the game to teach their kids about ancient cultures.

Players start by choosing an ancient culture. You get to pick from the Egyptians (5000 to 30 B.C.), the Hittites (2000 to 1200 B.C.) and the Persians (700 to 332 B.C.), among others. Then you start building your civilization—gathering resources like gold and stone, creating villages, developing a military, trading with other civilizations. You can win the game through several means: conquering the enemy militarily; gaining and maintaining control over all the ancient structures like Stonehenge built by "lost cultures"; or controlling a

"Wonder" for 2,000 years (a Wonder is a crowning achievement of a culture, like the Great Wall of China or Egyptian Pyramids). And while 2,000 years may sound like a long time, it zips by on the computer.

Each culture has unique economic systems, geographic challenges, religions and government structures. There's always a "rise and fall." The Persians, for instance, started out strong around 700 B.C., expanding their empire from modern Iran across the Near East to the eastern Mediterranean coast, south into Egypt along the Nile to Sudan and beyond. It peaked around 500 B.C. The poor Persians suffered with weak kings later on, wasteful government spending and frequent battles with the Greeks. Our knowledge of the Persians, and many of these cultures, is really limited, but the game does a pretty good job pulling it together.

Age of Empires is a great example of the potential of games. With adult supervision and some direction, children can learn about ancient civilizations, something you won't see on TV, unless you're lucky enough to catch a good documentary. You may even tie it into other studies or activities. Have your child look up more information in your CD encyclopedia or create a trivia game based on what they learn in the game. Without parental involvement, many kids will revert to just trying to blow up the enemy or blast their way through the enemy lines. See the pattern here?

 RALPH: RALPH MEETS DOOM

When my son was 6, the era of ultra-violent PC games was just getting off the ground. One Saturday we went to the local computer superstore to pick up some supplies. Off in the corner was a PC running a demonstration of a new high-action game called *Doom,* a violent game that involves blasting creatures and enemy characters, almost randomly it seems at times. You actually feel like you're inside the character blasting your way through strange, cavernous rooms. In less than a second my son had the joystick—a curved sticklike device that connects to a port in back of the computer and acts as the central controller—in his hand and was blasting everything that moved. He was hooked, and so was I. It was my first encounter with what would become the hottest segment of the PC game market—ultra-violent shoot-'em-up games.

We picked up the trial copy of *Doom,* went home, installed it, and that's when the bomb hit. When my wife saw all the mayhem flashing on the screen, she pulled me aside for an immediate parent conference. I didn't see any problem—it was pure fantasy (of course, I'm a guy). I figured my son could tell the difference between fantasy killing and mayhem and the real thing. After all, I grew up watching *The Three Stooges,* with Moe banging Larry constantly, and didn't turn into a maniac.

My wife, however, made the point that for a child, the issue is glorifying violence or associating violence with fun or excitement. Her comments stopped me dead in my tracks. It was clear we needed a family policy to deal with this sensitive issue.

After a lot of discussion we came up with a three-part compromise that's worked well for us:

1. Graphic violence involving close-up views of bodily harm (blood, guts and dismemberment) is out. My trial copy of *Doom* is now in my PC software history archives, safely tucked away from my son.

2. A game may contain elements of violence, but not if it's too graphic (close-ups, detailed). Our answer and compromise: the *Command & Conquer* genre of games from Westwood Studios. This is one of the biggest game title hits of all time. In the game you maneuver a host of tiny soldiers, tanks, ships and planes over a vast landscape viewed from high above. There is violence (you shoot tiny soldiers and blow buildings up), but it's tame compared to the real violent programs.

3. The game has to offer more than just violence. With *Command & Conquer,* you manage budgets and resources and think out a strategy for your army and air force.

So we reached a compromise. My wife wasn't crazy about it, but felt it was acceptable. My son loves it and his friends think it's cool, so we haven't damaged his social standing. My daughter couldn't care less, so there's peace on the homefront—for today. Now if I could just get him off the computer so I could play! (Be sure to do your homework before you get the program home. For more tips on checking out game software, keep reading.)

Set Up a "Visitation" Agreement

An in-home family agreement won't do you much good if your kid roams over to a friend's house and plays ultra-violent games. Both our sons were working this angle, playing *Doom* and *Duke Nukem* on their buddies' machines until we got wise. You know the argument: "Hey, Jimmy gets to play *Duke Nukem*, why can't I? His parents don't have a problem with it. I'm the *only* guy who isn't allowed to play these games!"

The answer was simple: a visitation agreement, similar to our family policy for movies. We don't allow our kids to rent R-rated movies or view ultra-violent or adult content at home or at their friends' homes, and we just carried it over to computer games (see the games rating sidebar, page 201). The rule applies everywhere they go. We recommend that you consider establishing consequences too, just as you do at home. If you find out they've been playing forbidden games, consider taking away access to the computer for a specified time—a week to ten days is a good start. They begin to get the message.

Also consider talking to the parents of your son's buddy. They may not realize that a certain game is violent. If they do realize it's violent, and allow their son to play it anyhow, it should serve as a clear warning to you. Do you really want your son hanging around someone who spends hours blowing bodies apart or running over pedestrians in fast cars (the object of one game)?

So far you've learned how to break PC game addiction and set up some family rules regarding violent content. Computer-smart parents are hip to all of this and more. They've also learned how to research, analyze and test drive the games their kids want to buy. Most important of all, they've learned all about the rating systems the software industry uses to warn parents about the content of the games. Now it's time for you to learn the ropes and become a smart PC games buyer.

How to Be a Smart PC Games Buyer

Computer-smart parents know they've got to spend a little time learning the lay of the land if they're going to be smart PC game buyers. Rule No. 1: Test drive before you buy. Find a neighbor or friend who has the program. Check out the demos at your local computer store. Spend some time playing the games at stores like CompUSA or check them out at the local video store—many offer good selections. Also check out the gamer magazines, which often include "free" CD-ROMs with a dozen or more game demos.

It's not always feasible to test drive programs in the real world. The computer store may not be featuring a demo of the program you're interested in or the lines may be too long and of course there's always one or two kids hogging the programs. Eventually you'll be able to request a program and try it out—just like you can with a CD in many music stores. But right now that's rare, so you may have to find other ways to explore the programs.

If you're online you can download copies of some games so you can try them out. Downloading a game is not much more difficult than recording off of a video cassette recorder. Once you're online, using a service like AOL, you simply go to one of the hundreds of game Web sites and look for the software section. The site will probably walk you through each step until you get to the part where it allows you to download or transmit the game to your computer. The transmission can take up to several hours on a slow modem, and even an hour or more on a speedy modem, depending on the size of the game.

That's one option. Another is to just talk to friends and get their opinions and read the game reviews in the computer magazines. The game reviews in PC games magazines like *Computer Gaming World* and *PC Gamer* show the level of mayhem in the newly released games. (Parents' bonus: watch your kid's jaw drop open when you start rattling off the names of the latest action-game hits.) Get online and get advice on good games from online services like America Online. Ask fellow parents and software salespeople for advice. Do your homework.

One final tip: Get hip to the ESRB rating system. Most PC game makers

Warning: Horsepower Needed

Games often need a lot of horsepower—processor power, that is, plus a bunch of memory and hard disk storage space. Before you hop over to the computer store and shell out $40 or $50 for a game, make sure you've got enough horsepower to do it justice. Go back to the software chapter and review the audit charts. Read the recommended system requirements on the side of the game boxes, which will tell you how much memory and hard disk storage space and what kind of microprocessor you need. You'll be able to see if your computer has the "right stuff" to drive today's games. If not, you could wind up with jerky video and slow response times—and a frustrated kid.

Besides processor power, memory and storage, check out your graphics add-on card, which is inside the PC and is responsible for putting images on your screen (see Chapter 2 on Buying a PC for a review of the key components of a PC). As of this writing the two most popular ways to get 3D thrills are by using either a 3DFX technology-based graphics card, or an AGP (Accelerated Graphics Port) card (see Glossary). Just be aware that if you want the games to look as good at home as the pictures on the boxes, you may need to beef up your graphics hardware. It may set you back $200 or so, but you would have spent it on something else anyhow. Why not enjoy it?

have voluntarily adopted the Entertainment Software Rating Board (ESRB) ratings system. The ESRB system rates games by age group—Early Childhood, Kids to Adults, Everyone, Teen, Mature and Adults Only.

Following these smart buyer tips will help you win the ultra-violent games battle with your kids. Understanding the ratings system and test driving software puts you back in control.

Bonus tip: Sit down and play the games with your kids. On a couple occasions we've discovered offensive elements of games that we missed during a test drive. But we've also been pleasantly surprised by other programs, which contain hidden nuggets of educational information (example: *Age of Empires,* mentioned earlier). You've got to look for it though. No kid's going to come screaming into the den or study saying they discovered a new enlightening fact in their new game. Not going to happen.

An Alternative: High-Action, Low-Violence Games

As we mentioned already, we've found that our boys and their friends gravitate toward programs that provide empowerment and action. The good news is plenty of games provide super action that's low- or nonviolent. Car racing, flying or sports simulation games are wonderful alternatives. Here's our Top 10 list of great high-action, low- or no-violence games that the whole family will enjoy:

1. *Redline Racer* (UbiSoft) A dazzling motorcycle race game with beautiful landscapes. You actually *feel* like you're flying through the air when the motorcycle soars off of a hill or jump.

2. *Pod* (UbiSoft). A sci-fi futuristic car race where the object is to win a spot on the last space shuttle leaving a doomed planet.

3. *Monster Truck Madness II* (Microsoft). Pure heaven for racing nuts. Kids zip through mud, rivers and over rough terrain as they drive one of those trucks with the insanely huge tires. Incredible graphics.

4. *Need for Speed* (Electronic Arts). Kids try their hand at driving the world's coolest high-performance sports cars. Learn the cheat codes and they can drive a school bus or even an old VW Bug.

5. *Test Drive Off-Road* (Accolade). A straightforward race simulation game easy enough for the younger crowd (5 and up) to operate.

6. *Jet Fighter II* (Interplay Productions). Most jet fighter simulation games for the PC are just too complicated for kids who want to get to the thrill of flying quickly without having to memorize a bunch of complicated steps. *Jet Fighter II* lets kids set the level of difficulty and zooms them into heart-pounding action over a wide selection of real-world terrain.

Learn the ESRB Ratings Stickers

The most popular rating system with game and educational software makers these days is the ESRB (Entertainment Software Rating Board) system. Below is a roundup of their rating system labels with a brief explanation (at the time of this writing). Study these symbols before you go shopping, and be sure to check out the ESRB Web site (www.esrb.org) for updated ratings symbols.

 Early Childhood (EC)—Content that's okay for kids 3 and older. Clean as a whistle. We call it Disney clean.

 Everyone (E)—Content suitable for kids 6 and older. Low violence and slapstick comedy.

 Teen (T)—Okay for 13 and older. Warning: may contain violent content and mild or strong language or sexually suggestive themes.

 Mature (M)—For ages 17 and up. Crank up all the violence and sex themes in the T category. May also include hate messages. Most stores will not sell these titles to kids without proper ID or an accompanying adult. Ask your store about their policy.

 Adults Only(AO)—Graphic depictions of sex and/or violence. You get the picture.

7. *SWIV* (Interplay Productions). A remarkable helicopter simulation game in which youngsters pilot their way around dramatic landscapes as they blast opponents from the sky and land and pick up supplies to stay alive.

8. *Flight Simulator 98* (Microsoft). Realistic flight simulator that requires players to learn how to handle everything from a one-engine prop plane to a jumbo jet.

9. *NHL Powerplay 98* (Virgin Interactive). Nonstop NHL action captured in an on-the-fly 3D environment.

10. *VR Soccer* (Interplay Productions). A real-time 360° 3D virtual soccer field with players a kid can control from any perspective. Another cool sports game along this line is the *Hardball* series.

MARK'S FAVORITE: BEYOND RACETRACKS AND SPORTS CARS

My favorite game, hands-down, is Microsoft's *Monster Truck Madness.* The game is a wild free-for-all romp in which you take the controls of a wacky monster truck with the giant tires and grinding engines. There's no blood or guts, just a good old-fashioned romp in the dirt. The controls are clean and easy to understand and navigate and the graphics are stunning—you really feel like you're racing across mountains and dangerous terrain. The controls are neat. You can control the type of vehicle you're racing, whether you want traction or speed and the type of tires you want. What else could a Monster Truck nut want?

The latest (*Monster Truck Madness II*) version threw in nine new trucks and crushable car bodies, eleven new tracks and even better graphics that take advantage of advanced faster processors and other new hardware that makes your games play better. The game will even allow you to hook up special joysticks and wheels that give you the real feel of the car—when it rolls over, your joystick shakes.

I was never a great racer with the traditional games, but now I have new options. If I can't beat 'em, I'll run over 'em.

While titles will come and go, the key is to look for games with high-paced action, a KA (Kids to Adults) or E (Everyone) ESRB rating and room to grow in terms of lots of levels to keep kids engaged.

RALPH'S FAVORITE:
A FROG WITH AN ATTITUDE

Back in the early 1980s the video game craze was just getting off the ground. My wife-to-be, Carolyn, and I were single, childless and hopelessly hooked to wacky games like *Pac-Man, Centipede, LadyBug*, and *Frogger*. We spent hours dropping quarters in the video-arcade machines, just like Vegas gambling addicts. Finally we bit the bullet and coughed up a whopping $400 to buy our first "home computer," an Atari Model 400, to play all our favorites from the comfort of our respective living rooms. We bought *Frogger*—and our lives changed forever.

The original *Frogger* used flat solid-color graphics that would make my kids laugh today. The sound track was an infectious ditty of digitized notes, and the object was simple but devilishly challenging. Using a joystick you had to help your frog hop around all kinds of zany obstacles, from floating logs to cars and trucks racing across a multi-lane freeway. It was a pure sugar-high blast.

A few years ago I stumbled across the old Atari 400 and fired up some of the games to show my kids some of the artifacts from the infancy of the computer gaming world. They toyed with it off and on, but always came back to the powerful PC with its flashy 3D graphics and stereo sound tracks. I figured *Frogger* and all of its kin were buried forever in the past. Think again.

Thanks to Hasbro Interactive, my beloved *Frogger* is back, and this time it's packed with the latest 3D graphics and sound. This title remains true to the original simple premise—hop well or get squashed or zapped (isn't that like real life?). But that's where the similarity ends. This baby is loaded with features we could not have imagined nearly twenty years ago. You can have up to four simultaneous players right at your PC or connected via the Internet and explore dozens of brand-new wild environments and advisories. You can't beat *Frogger* with a stick.

GAMES 2001: A GLIMPSE
OF THE FUTURE IN GAMES

If you want a glimpse of the future, check out the annual E3 convention, a showcase of the latest gaming technology. We attended the show in spring 1998, in Atlanta and were amazed at how the gaming technology had progressed. Dazzling 3D graphics, super animation and mind-altering sounds and visuals—it was all there. The show even had its own superstar, Lara Croft, the star of the ever-popular *Tomb Raider* series. Never mind that Lara is an animated character; game nuts worship her anyhow. We're talking about a different crowd here.

The new realism is a double-edged sword. The more realistic the characters and action, the easier it is to suck young children into the game. When Lara gets nailed by a goon or a wild beast, she doesn't just vanish—she flails and flops down on the ground. At times it looks like she's actually out of breath, huffing to catch her breath. And when she shimmies across a wall, her hips actually . . . well you get the idea. The realism impresses even hardcore gamers, who can't get enough.

The good news is that some of the graphics and animation once found in only hard-core violent games are finding their way into high-action, low-violence games. The graphics in programs like *Monster Truck Madness, Rayman* and *Redline Racer* (UbiSoft), are staggering. Expect to see a whole new crop of these programs over the next year or so, including new versions of stellar war programs, like the *Star Wars* series. Sure, there are guns ablazing and bombs flying, but the action stops far short of the blood and guts found in the *Doom*-type programs.

The other cool trend we saw at E3 (along with more realism)

was the revival of old arcade and board games in new super 3D action-packed games. Hasbro, for instance, is releasing *Life* on CD joining *(Monopoly* and *Sorry)*, and it's full of fun animation and funny twists. *Frogger* and *Centipede* are two arcade games that have been brought back to life.

FOCUSED QUESTIONS

- How many hours a day does your son play games? Does he pass up other opportunities (or meals) to be able to play? Does he like to play alone? How does this compare with other kids his age and/or your expectations?

- How much do you know about his games? How much violence is involved?

- Are you up to speed on the ESRB ratings system?

- If he's playing games too much, what are you doing to cut back (example: limit hours per day, set up a "credit" and earnings system?). What are you doing as a role model?

- What are you doing to become a smart software buyer (reading reviews, test driving programs, etc.)?

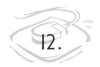

12.

Making Cyberspace Safe, Part I

PROTECTING KIDS ONLINE

We really monitor our daughter's use of the Internet, but she says her friends' parents
aren't as vigilant and they can surf the Web at will. I'm not sure what to do.
—Mother calling into our weekly "Downhome Computing
with the PC Dads" show, Portland, Oregon

Many parents are up in arms about what's going on on the Internet, and no wonder. When we were kids, parents would go ballistic if they found *Playboy* under a boy's bed. Now, kids can bring XXX-rated content right into the living room via the Internet with the click of a few buttons. They can also interact with people they'd never come into contact with otherwise—bigots, political extremists, even pornographers and child molesters.

A few highly publicized cases have fueled the flames of concern. Reports that another teenager has been attacked by someone they "met" on the Internet makes even computer-savvy parents cringe. How do you control something you don't understand, that's based on a technology that never stands still, and is used by people you never see?

It'd be nice if there were a simple, straightforward solution. Unplug the computer. Ban the Internet from the home. Slap a techno-monitor on the machine that buzzes every time your kid even thinks about going in the wrong area.

Sorry. At least for now, there are no easy answers or silver bullets. Even if you ban your kids from using the Internet at home, chances are they can go down the street to a friend's house and go online. Still, there's plenty you can do to improve your kids' chances of having a safe cyber experience at home, with friends and even at school. It requires a certain amount of trust between you and your kids, some thoughtful preparation, constant monitoring—and good ol' common sense. Sure, it's work, but the rewards are well worth it. There's too much good stuff on the Net to have a few losers with too much time on their hands scare you off.

In this chapter we'll walk you through a series of home-tested, common-sense steps you can take, then review some of the technology weapons at your disposal to help keep your kids from stumbling into the dark side of the Internet. For simplicity, we've divided the steps and tools into Good, Better and Best.

After completing this chapter you'll know how to:

- Set clear rules of cyberspace engagement, while teaching your kids how to protect themselves online.
- Monitor what's going on as your kid surfs the Net.
- Take advantage of cyber safety technologies, including "parental control" features offered by the major online service providers, special Internet search engine features and software that blocks adult content.
- Audit your kid's school cyber safety policies and talk to the parents of your child's friends about your family rules.

Before You Begin . . . Establishing the "Rules of the Road"

Children can be pretty gullible when it comes to online experiences, so you need to help them learn some healthy skepticism. As the famous *New Yorker* cartoon puts it, "On the Internet no one knows you're a dog." The online acquaintance who claims to be a fourteen-year-old cutie could just as easily be a 30-year-old creep. To keep kids safe, you also need to give them some clear rules. Remember the old rules of the road? Don't talk to strangers. Don't take food from a stranger. Don't believe a stranger who says Mom or Dad sent them to school to pick them up. Children have had these rules drilled into their brains since they could see straight, and for the most part, they work. As a computer-smart parent, you can approach the Internet in the same way.

Every computer-savvy family needs a Net version of the rules of the road. We've looked at a bunch of Internet behavior contracts, especially samples of agreements many schools use with students. As you craft your own verbal or written agreement, be sure to keep these three golden rules in mind:

• **Protect your identity.** If someone communicating with you on the Internet (via e-mail or in chat rooms) asks for your name, address or phone number don't respond. Watch out for other questions that might on the surface seem harmless, such as "What school do you go to?" or "What state or city do you live in?"

• **Watch out for messages from strangers.** Don't read text messages or open/view attached files (most commonly picture files) from strangers. If you don't recognize the e-mail address of the sender delete the message or show it first to Mom or Dad. By the same token, don't send a digital picture of yourself to a stranger.

• **Never agree to call or meet with a stranger.** If someone you meet in cyberspace suggests you call him/her, or that you should meet in person, immediately alert Mom or Dad.

For a ready-to-use agreement popular with many parents and schools check out the one created by Larry Magid for the National Center for Missing and Exploited Children Web site (www.missingkids.com). Printed copies of his rules are also are available by calling 1-800-843-5678.

RALPH'S HOUSE RULES:

When my kids started surfing the Net, I applied the concepts from the three golden rules just outlined. Since we subscribed to America Online, I used the parental controls (details to follow later in this chapter) to set up a "teenager" account for my daughter (age 14) and a "kid" account for my son (age 10). No problems with my daughter, but the highly restrictive Web site access limitations of the AOL "kid" account immediately frustrated my son. Jeff loves PC games. He and his friends wanted to hit the game manufacturer and magazine Web sites to learn about the latest games. The "kid" controls on AOL basically block access to all but a very limited set of preapproved, screened sites. The solution: I reset Jeff to a "teenage" account and drilled him again on the engagement ground rules. And, on top of that, whenever possible I'll sit by his side when he surfs the Net.

MARK'S HOUSE RULES:

I've tried to set up a partnership with Matthew, 13, rather than rely on technology controls (Michael, 9, is just getting interested in the Internet). Like everything else, he needs to feel like he has a vested interest in the deal to really buy into it. I do use America Online's parental controls and dabble with the browser controls at times. But for the most part I rely on the trust I've established with my son. I've bumped him up to teenage status and sometimes adult status on AOL at times so he can play some games and "chat" with his buddies online (more about chat rooms, e-mail, newsgroups, forums and bulletin boards in the next chapter). We have a working agreement: he doesn't do aimless surfing on the Net when I'm not around. He doesn't surf at his friends' houses either. In return he gets to play online games, check out kid sites on AOL and the Web and help me review cool software. He knows he has to hold up his end of the deal or he loses a lot of privileges.

The Good, Better and Best Ways to Protect Your Kids in Cyberspace

As promised, we're going to outline the steps and tools available to help control what comes into your home PC from the Internet. The wide range of options can be confusing so we've organized them (in terms of effectiveness) using the old Sears product catalog "Good," "Better" and "Best" approach.

None of the technologies or services cited in the following pages provide absolute cyber safety protection. If your child is computer hip, runs around with Internet-savvy kids, and is bound and determined to visit adult content and other objectionable material he/she *will* find a way. You can build a nearly airtight wall of protection around your home PC only to find out that your kid has been walking across the street to a friend's unguarded system. Bottom line: no technology Band-Aid approach can replace a strong bond and relationship with your child.

With that "truth in lending" statement out of the way, let's walk through the three levels of protection available:

1. GOOD PROTECTION—ONLINE SERVICES' PARENTAL CONTROLS

The major online services have set up easy-to-use parental controls that can save you a lot of headaches. These services, such as America Online, Microsoft Network, Prodigy and CompuServe, offer controls you can set that determine the level of Internet and e-mail access your child will be allowed to experience. America Online, for example, has a comprehensive parental control center that allows Mom or Dad to manage entry to certain areas and features. You can go through a series of menus to customize chat, downloading, newsgroup, e-mail and general Web access for your child's account, or select adult content "block out" filters designed for kids under 12 and for teenagers. Cool, huh?

A CLOSER LOOK AT AOL'S PARENTAL CONTROL SYSTEM

America Online's parental control system has packages for kids 12 and under, young teens (ages 13 to 15), mature teens (ages 16 to 17), and 18 and older (an adult with no restrictions of any kind). The kids package restricts access to the features and Web sites found in the proprietary America Online "Kid Channel" (one of a host of special sections presented to subscribers from the opening screen menu). The child can't send or receive instant member-to-member screen messages, enter member-created chat rooms or use any paid service not covered by the base monthly subscription. E-mail is limited to text only (no pictures can be sent or received). A similar scheme applies to the young and mature teens packages but with greater freedom. They can access more chat rooms, but may only visit Web sites approved by America Online for these age categories. The 18 and older category, no surprise, allows unbridled access to all proprietary AOL services and general Web sites, newsgroups, you name it.

2. BETTER PROTECTION—CYBERSPACE MONITORING SOFTWARE AND WEB RATINGS

Monitoring Software

If you want more protection than the parental controls provide, consider installing a Web-filtering software package. You can set these programs up as on-line watchdogs that constantly monitor and block access to adult sites and other "hot spots" on the Internet. Most of these products also let you set up a custom vigil for specific words and topics. For instance, you might tell the software to block any sites with words describing human genitals; "erotic," or "sex."

Once you've assigned one of the age-level packages on AOL to each family member using your master account, you may use "Custom Controls" to fine tune access to chat rooms and newsgroups, determine what they may or may not download from the Internet, what e-mail they can receive and their level of access to the Web. Here's what the Custom Controls menu looks like:

Custom Controls

Custom Controls

- Chat
- Downloading
- Newsgroups
- Mail
- Web

Chat is an online live dialogue with other members of America Online. Parental Controls has four chat features you can choose to block— how many of these you select to block is up to you. Parents can block the following:

1) BLOCK INSTANT MESSAGES. Instant messages can be thought of as instant e-mails — two people can have a live conversation that can only be seen by the sender and receiver. BLOCK INSTANT MESSAGES turns the

Ask AOL   Chat Controls

AOL Custom Controls

There are drawbacks to these programs. You can't be a couch potato with these programs. You have to install the software and keep it updated, which means frequently downloading or buying new versions. Computer-hip teenagers may be able to find ways around the programs, so it's definitely not a silver bullet. Then there's the problem of filtering programs that work too well, blocking your child from legitimate sites (for example, the keyword "breasts" may block legitimate health-related or educational sites). Still if you do your homework, learn how to use the programs and manage them appropriately, they can be effective tools.

Leading cyber filtering programs for desktop computers include:

- *Cyber Patrol* from The Learning Company (www.cyberpatrol.com)
- *CYBERsitter* from Solid Oak Software (www.solidoak.com/cysitter.htm)
- *Net Nanny* from Net Nanny Software International, Inc. (www.netnanny.com)
- *SurfWatch* Software from SurfWatch Software (www.surfwatch.com/home)

Web Ratings—For Advanced Super-Hip Parents Only

To be completely candid, the system we'd all like to see does not exist: a universally applied, easy-to-understand ratings system, much like we have with movies, that would allow parents to carefully monitor and control content coming into their homes. When we rent movies for the kids, the first thing we check are the ratings—PG is ok; PG13, maybe; R and X are out. That makes it easy.

New ratings systems are starting to emerge for Web content, but sorry to say, they're not simple to grasp, and they're based on the Web site creator volunteering to be rated. In fact, the situation is a mess. But if you're serious about managing the Internet in your home, it's worth your time to bone up on this stuff. So keep reading.

Battle of the Web Ratings Bands . . . RSACi ,
SafeSurf and ESRBI—Rating the Ratings System

On the surface it looks simple enough: The RSACi (Recreational Software Advisory Council on the Internet), SafeSurf and ESRBI (Entertainment Software Rating Board Interactive) Web-site ratings systems essentially rate content on Web sites. Each has a different approach to doing its ratings and, worse, you have to "ask" your browser to use one or multiples of the ratings systems. It's as if there were several ratings systems for movies, and you had to ask your newspaper to send you the special edition that uses or displays the ratings.

Let's look at these ratings systems; then we'll talk about yet another technology (of course with its own acronym) that will help you set your browser to take advantage of them.

RSACi Descriptors and Levels

	Violence Rating Descriptor	Nudity Rating Descriptor	Sex Rating Descriptor	Language Rating Descriptor
LEVEL 4	Rape or wanton, gratuitous violence	Frontal nudity (qualifying as provocative display)	Explicit sexual acts or sex crimes	Crude, vulgar language or extreme hate speech
LEVEL 3	Aggressive violence or death to humans	Frontal nudity	Nonexplicit sexual acts	Strong language or hate speech
LEVEL 2	Destruction of realistic objects	Partial nudity	Clothed sexual touching	Moderate expletives or profanity
LEVEL 1	Injury to human beings	Revealing attire	Passionate kissing	Mild expletives
LEVEL 0	None of the above or sports related	None of the above	None of the above or innocent kissing; romance	None of the above

RSACi at a Glance

The RSACi ratings system uses categories to rate Web sites. Under the category of "violence," for instance, Level 1 means there will be some scenes of "injury to human beings" (rather mild) while Level 4 could include "rape or wanton gratuitous violence" (see chart). This gives you a pretty good idea what you're getting into. If you instruct your browser that you only want to see Level 0 Web sites, all others with a Level 1, 2, 3 or 4 rating will be blocked.

Here's the catch: the RSACi ratings are purely voluntary. The people who operate the Web site decide whether to employ the ratings or not. So, your browser *will* display unrated sites unless you tell it not to. As with so many of the tools for cyber safety, this solution is not bulletproof. You still need to be personally involved monitoring your child's wanderings in cyberspace.

SafeSurf at a Glance

The SafeSurf ratings system applies a complex and comprehensive series of numeric codes relative to these considerations:

- Age Range
- Profanity
- Heterosexual Themes
- Homosexual Themes
- Nudity
- Violence
- Sex, Violence and Profanity
- Intolerance—(Intolerance of another person's racial, religious or gender background)
- Glorifying Drug Use
- Other Adult Themes
- Gambling

For each of these areas the SafeSurf system provides a detailed breakout. For Violence, for example, the levels are:

1. Subtle Innuendo
2. Explicit Innuendo
3. Technical Reference
4. Nongraphic-Artistic
5. Graphic-Artistic
6. Graphic
7. Detailed Graphic
8. Inviting Participation in Graphic Interactive Format
9. Encouraging Personal Participation, Weapon Making

Once again, use of this ratings system is completely voluntary on the part of Web site designers. Also, use of the SafeSurf logo (one for "safe for all ages" and one for "adult") on the opening page of a Web site is optional.

ESRBI at a Glance

Like the RSACi system, the newer ESRBI Web-rating system uses content descriptors to evaluate Web sites. The ESRBI system differs, however, in that it provides a ratings symbol that is displayed on Web pages that elect to be reviewed by this organization. (These symbols are similar to the ESRB games ratings discussed in Chapter 11 on Boys and Games.) Once the ESRBI reviewers complete their review an ESRBI rating symbol is assigned to cover all or parts of a Web site such as chat rooms, e-mail and bulletin boards. When you call up a Web site rated by the ESRBI, you'll see one or more of the following symbols:

Websites/Webpages and online games rated "Early Childhood (ECI)" have content suitable for persons ages three and older.

Websites/Webpages and online games rated "Everyone (EI)" have content suitable for persons ages six and older. These sites will appeal to people of many ages and tastes. They may contain minimal violence, some comic mischief (for example, slapstick comedy) or some crude language.

Websites/Webpages and online games rated "Teen (TI)" have content suitable for persons ages 13 and older. Sites in this category may contain violent content, mild or strong language and/or suggestive themes.

Websites/Webpages and online games rated "Mature (MI)" have content suitable for persons ages 17 and older. In addition, these sites may include more intense violence and language and more mature sexual themes and strong hate speech than products in the teen category.

Websites/Webpages and online games rated "Adults Only (AOI)" have content suitable only for adults. These sites may include graphic depictions of sex and/or violence. Adults Only sites are not intended to be viewed by persons under the age of 18.

Warning: There are drawbacks to the RSACi, SafeSurf and the ESRBI systems. For one thing, they're competing standards, and Web site authors have to choose one or the other scheme to adopt. Not all Web sites have a rating. And, as we've said before, they're purely voluntary, unlike movie ratings, which are uniformly applied to movies produced in the U.S.

Still, they're better than nothing. You can teach your kids to be aware of the levels and, if they see a labeled Web site, to avoid those that are beyond the levels your family has established. Much better is to have your Web browser (e.g., Netscape or Internet Explorer) automatically detect and filter out Web sites based on one or more of the ratings systems it's been set up to use. To do this, you need to know a little about an arcane Internet technology called PICS (which stands for Platform for Internet Content Selection).

By now your eyes are probably starting to cross with all these acronyms (don't forget to check the Glossary), but bear with us: there's light at the end of the tunnel.

How to Activate a PICS-Based Ratings System in Your Browser

Here's the dream: one day there'll be one ratings system and a simple software program loaded on your PC that will watch out for your interests. You'll fill out a short form on screen, and your agent will link up with a smart browser and block all the bad content before it gets to your house, maybe even including seedy e-mail solicitations. But the reality is we have at least three Web rating systems and the PICS standard, which is backed by more than twenty companies. It's not bad, but it's got a long way to go before it's as easy to use as a toaster or microwave oven.

Anyway, for now, here's how to put the PICS technology to work in your browser so the ratings systems can do their thing.

Activating a PICS-compliant ratings system is really very easy if you're willing to follow some precise steps. You don't even need a degree in computer programming! To give you an idea of how it works (and to fill you with confidence that you can do it too), here's how to activate the RSACi ratings sytem in Microsoft's Internet Explorer 4.0 browser:

1. Turn on the PC.

2. Fire up the Internet Explorer browser by double clicking on the program icon (you don't need a live connection to the Internet to do this procedure).

3. From the top toolbar menu of Internet Explorer, select "View."

4. Then select "Internet Options" and click the "Content" tab. Look for the "Content Advisor" area on the Content tab menu and click the "Enable" button. This step will allow you to create a "Supervisor" password. (*You*, by the way, are the "Supervisor.")

5. After you set up a password the "Content Advisor" menu pops up with the "Ratings" tab displayed showing what Internet ratings system is currently active. If you're using Internet Explorer 4.0 or higher chances are good the RSACi ratings scheme is already active. If so, you can move on to adjust multiple "filters" to adjust the levels of language, nudity, sex and violence you deem suitable.

6. Clicking on the "Language" filter call-out makes a menu with a sliding bar from 0 to 4 appear on the screen. Using the mouse cursor, move it right and left across the slide bar and you see messages appear explaining each numeric level. For example:

- Level 0—Inoffensive Slang
- Level 1—Mild Expletives
- Level 2—Moderate Expletives
- Level 3—Obscene Gestures
- Level 4—Explicit or Crude Language

7. For totally clean language set the level for "Language" to all zeros (your tastes may differ, of course). Then follow a similar process to set the other filters.

8. The last step is to click on the "General" tab located to the right of the "Ratings" tab to let the browser know if you want your kids to be able to see sites that don't have an RSACi rating. If you check the box with the legend "Supervisor can type a password to allow users to view restricted content" every non-RSACi-rated Web site encountered that does not match your settings will cause a pop-up message to appear requiring you, the Supervisor, to override the system using your password. It's a great power trip, but there is a tradeoff. There are a ton of wonderful Web sites for kids to visit that don't use the voluntary RSACi or any rating system. Just because a site does not elect to use a rating does not by default mean it carries content you may find inappropriate. The bottom line: it's not a perfect system by a long shot.

Tip: for a step-by-step, illustrated tutorial for activating PICS with Microsoft's Internet Explorer browser, visit the RSACi Web site at www.rsac.org.

Another tip: Netscape and Microsoft's Internet Explorer can support multiple ratings systems at one time. Activate all the ratings systems offered by your browser. If you only find one, see if a newer version of your browser offers more, or go to the Web sites of the major ratings groups and see if you can download software you can install to add more ratings systems to your browser. Here's how to reach the three major Web-ratings players:

RSACi   www.rsac.org
SafeSurf   www.safesurf.com
ESRBI   www.esrb.org

3. BEST PROTECTION—CYBER-SAFE INTERNET ACCESS SERVICES, KID-SAFE SEARCH ENGINES AND WEB SITES LISTED IN DIRECTORIES FOR CHILDREN

Cyber-Safe Internet Service Providers

For once, taking the easy way out also turns out to be a very powerful solution. A new crop of so-called Internet Service Providers (ISPs) designed to appeal to subscribers willing to pay someone to provide cyber-safe surfing are popping up these days. With powerful Internet filtering software running on their computers, and teams of programmers constantly updating their defensive tools, they provide a potent twenty-four-hour, seven-day-a-week Web traffic cop.

Mainly these ISPs focus on serving families, schools, libraries and businesses that need "filtered" web access. Portland, Oregon, based Integrity Online is a star example (www.integrityonline.com). For a flat monthly fee (competitive with the big national services), its subscribers have access to the Web and full e-mail capabilities. Unlike the major national services and most small local access providers, Integrity Online's computers have powerful filter software designed to block Web sites and material their team of reviewers deem to be offensive. The ISP does the work of installing and constantly updating the filter databases that block adult, hate group and other content they believe would not be appropriate for public school, library and general home use.

These services aren't foolproof, but they do a darn good job and they're convenient. That's a nice feature for busy parents. At this point in time we believe services such as Integrity Online provide the best line of defense.

Kid-Safe Search Engines

One of the most popular "search engines" (special service Web sites that act like information operators for the Internet) is Yahoo! The creators of the famous

Search Engines for Kids

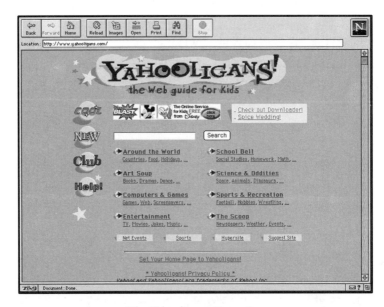

The Yahooligans Home Page

Super Snooper Home Page

Yahoo! search engine offer a kid-safe version called Yahooligans! (www.yahoo-ligans.com) that lets kids search the net using adult-content filters the Yahooligans! team maintains on their computers. Although other kid search engines are out there, such as Super Snooper (www.snooper.com), Yahooligans! is the best kid search engine we've found to date. Kids can do general searches or select from a number of information categories for links to safe learning and fun Web sites and resources.

Surf the Sites Found in Internet Directories for Kids

Another real safe bet is to surf Web sites published in Internet books for children. Here's a taste of what's available in most bookstores:

- *300 Incredible Things for Kids on the Internet,* by Ken Leebow (VIP)
- *Animal Lover's Guide to the Internet: More than 500 of the Most Educational, Fun Web Sites for Animal Lovers,* by Bonnie Marlewski-Probert (K&B Productions)
- *Cybersurfer: The Owl Internet Guide for Kids,* by Nyla Ahmad and Martha Newbigging (Owl Communications)
- *Internet Directory for Kids & Parents* (1st Ed), by Barbara Moran (IDG Books Worldwide)
- *Internet for Kids* (Teacher Created Materials)
- *Kids on the Internet: A Beginners Guide,* by Kim Mitchell (Instructional Fair)
- *Kids Rule the Net: The Only Guide to the Internet by Kids,* by Michael Wolff (Wolff New Media)
- *Online Kids: A Young Surfer's Guide to Cyberspace,* by Preston Gralla (John Wiley & Sons)
- *The Internet Kids & Family Yellow Pages* (2nd Ed), by Jean Armour Polly (Osborne McGraw-Hill)

FOCUSED QUESTIONS

- Have your kids gone online and visited Web sites yet? Have they encountered anything that's made them uncomfortable? Have you?

- Is your PC located where it's easy for you to keep an eye on what's happening?

- Have you created your own Online Safety Agreement, and have you reviewed it with your kids?

- What are you doing (software, etc.) to protect your kids online? What filtering services does your Internet Service Provider offer?

- Where, other than at home, are your children likely to go online? What steps can you take to ensure their cyber safety away from home?

13.

Making Cyberspace Safe, Part II

DARK ALLEYS AHEAD:
CHAT ROOMS, BULLETIN BOARDS
AND UNSOLICITED E-MAIL

For the past three weeks my fourteen-year-old and his friends have been coming over to
our house each day after school to go on the Internet. I thought it was great they
were learning so much about computers and the Internet thing. I had no idea how
easy it is for kids to be exposed to porn and other stuff. Now I'm wondering just
what they've been up to. I did wonder why they had the door closed all the time.
—Newly enlightened parent attending one of our
"Cyber Safari" shows, Providence, Rhode Island

Surfing the Web isn't the only place your child can get into trouble. It's hard to believe, but simply opening their e-mail mailbox can open a Pandora's box of unsolicited sexual come-ons and other weird messages.

Then there are all those chat rooms and bulletin boards (newsgroups are cousins to bulletin boards and very similar), places where you can communicate with other folks, mostly strangers. While bulletin boards and newsgroups allow you to post messages that are read over time—not when you're posting—chat rooms are live discussions. Chat rooms, bulletin boards, newsgroups and electronic mail are all different ways people communicate online, and they're powerful resources and tools. But they can also be cause for alarm if your child isn't aware of the issues and dangers. As we've said, it's like going out into the real world; street smarts are required to navigate safely.

Following are some tips to help enlighten you a little about these intriguing forums. The primary focus of this chapter will be on chat rooms, which are notorious for attracting weirdos. But we'll also discuss bulletin boards, newsgroups and unsolicited e-mail. You can go online and enter a chat room dealing with nearly any subject under the sun, from gardening and chemistry to rock and roll and, of course, pornography. Although the majority of chat rooms are legitimate and worthy forums for connecting people, they're also easy to slip in and out of anonymously, leaving little trail of the participants. They're a little like convenience stores along a busy freeway, tempting targets for folks with bad intentions.

The Lure of Chat Rooms

In a chat room, you can't see who is talking and can't tell anyone's age, sex or any other identifying aspect. In this strange room you start bumping into people and having random exchanges. You may read a dialogue going on between two or more occupants and enter into the conversation for a moment, then drift off and jump into another exchange. Everyone communicates via written text messages (although some now feature sound effects to allow users to express their emotions); it's all very fleeting, somewhat unsettling for a newcomer accustomed to face-to-face communications or being able to hear someone's voice over a telephone.

Welcome to the wonderful and weird world of chat rooms. Chat rooms are real-time (meaning *happening right now*) online conversations (via text you key in on your PC) between just a few or hundreds of people. At any moment of the day or night, thousands of chat rooms are buzzing with activity.

Finding chat rooms is easy. The major service providers like America Online, Microsoft Network and CompuServe host chat rooms, as do thousands of individual Web sites. On AOL, for example, you go to the "People" section or do a search using the keyword "chat" and up pops a long list of chat rooms. Select a room to join and in seconds your PC screen begins to fill with text exchanges that form a loosely organized conversation. If you want to jump in, all you have to do is type in a line or two of text and hit the enter key. In a flash your message mixes in the general soup of conversation. Other participants in the chat room may respond back to you directly or not.

On AOL, you can choose from discussion about a slew of hobbies, sports, finances and hundreds of rooms where people just hang out and talk. You can choose from chats in categories like "arts and entertainment," "friends," "town square," and "romance." Twenty or thirty cities (and several foreign countries) are listed under "places," so if, say, you want to talk to other folks about Houston, just click on Houston and you've joined a dozen or so chatters. But the most intense activity seems to be going on in what amounts to virtual singles bars, with names like "chance encounters," "tonightsthenight" and "romance connection." With as many as twenty people coming and going, and people constantly chattering, these forums pulse with energy and electricity.

To give you an idea of what a chat room looks like we created a mock chat room below. In this chat room, which is for kids who love animals, we find three players: Chatter1, Chatter2 and Chatter3 talking about rats.

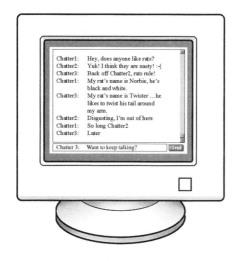

Chat Room

Once you're in a chat room you can type your message in a box (see the box above with the "Send" symbol to the right). Bang out a brief message and then click the "Send" button and your comments are presented on the ever-scrolling chat room page within a few seconds. People can respond to or ignore your entries.

We skip the romantic spots and venture into one of the "Seattle" chats, where there's a lively conversation under way about one of the male user's, uh, sexual habits. Services like AOL have rules on behavior and language to try to keep the discussions from deteriorating into raw gutter talk. Still we've seen some conversations that would make a sailor blush and, after all, AOL can't monitor all 13,000 chats a day. So, like it or not, some of these weirdos are going to slip through.

Many participants have clever ways to get around the rules, yet still make suggestive sexual remarks. This guy—let's call him DogBrain8 (everyone has a name, like TwoDads)—continually refers to the size of his "fonts." Others chime in what he can do with his fonts, and eventually he's shamed into shutting up. But the conversation rarely improves beyond basic grunts, howdys and "who's online?"

Although you can never tell, it always seems that there are more males than females online. Guessing ages is also tricky, but from the tone and content of the discussions, we'd guess the average age would be between 16 and 22 on late-night chats. But there are also plenty of younger teenagers online. Every few minutes another male will enter the room (his name pops up in a little box of attendees), bravely identify himself and ask if there are any females around. Example: "WidowMak19, male, 19, any pretty females want to talk. IM me."

(An IM is an instant personal, or private, message and chat session that the participants can create separately from the main group. "IM" stands for Instant Message. So if WidowMak19 starts a conversation this way, only he and his participant see it. Private chat rooms are similar, and both are basically methods for having a one-on-one online conversation. It's like going into a private room at a nightclub, away from the chatter and lights.)

Minus visual cues, users must express themselves in other ways. Their names provide one clue about their personalities. "Bbeetleleg" is likely a different personality than "HotCelt," although, as we said, you can never tell. No one is who he or she seems in the weird world of chats.

Many online chatters have personal "profiles," which tell about their personal interests, sometimes their age, computers they're using and even a favorite quote. Amazingly, even some teenage girls provide their full names and ages—making them ripe targets for predators. On AOL, users can do searches through personal profiles to locate people. This has some benefit, say, if you want to find a long-lost relative or someone with your same name, just for kicks. But predators can also use them to zero in on personal profiles that interest them. Type in "female and single and California and dancing," and you'll come up with a list of single girls who claim to be from California with an interest in dancing. The searcher can then do a search to find out if these people are online at that point, and even if they're in a chat room. If so, he or she can zero in on them and start up a conversation. It almost seems too easy—and it is.

Again, most chat rooms are relatively clean. You can meet people with like interests from all over the world, making it a powerful communications tool for everyone from the home-bound elderly to people who simply want to share their interests. The other cool feature is that people must deal with you on some intellectual level rather than based on how you look or come across physically. But we're focusing on late-night virtual singles bars—one subcategory of the chat world—because they're potentially the most dangerous places for children.

What strikes us the most about chat rooms is how easy it is to come in and out of conversations. You don't have the real-world barriers or issues to deal with, and there are no physical cues to interpret. Want to strike up a conversation with a stranger? Just post a message—or send them a personal IM. You would never approach strangers in person on the street and ask intimate questions. But it happens all the time in chat rooms.

While we were "lurking" (online term that means observing the chat rather than participating), we received an IM from a teenager in Washington—unsolicited (this is typical; you may get them every ten or fifteen minutes if you hang around). "I liked your profile," she said. "Where are you?"

Soon we'd started a conversation, as if we'd known each other for years—or at least minutes (time is measured differently online). She liked the Spice Girls (big surprise there), roller blading and rock music. When we asked her why she went online, she said, "mainly to meet other people. I actually met a thirteen-year-old who lived across town. . . . We later talked by phone." What did she hate most? "Cussin . . . and guys coming on to me." (That, of course, happens a lot.)

She gave her name, although never offered her address or other identifying information. We never asked. Still if we were clever and devious enough we felt that she may have offered the information. After all, for all she knew, we could have been a clean-cut, fifteen-year-old male with striking good looks. You are whoever you say you are on the Internet, and that's the rub.

Chat rooms can be wonderful places for kids. Being on an equal playing field where your voice is heard can be a positive, self-esteem-building experience for kids. You and your child can talk with people around the world who share a common interest, and even interact with celebrities and experts. The sad truth, however, is that many chat rooms are a playground for raw language, hateful messages and bad guys on the prowl for innocent victims. So take steps to manage your child's chat-room adventures.

Protecting your child from chat-room predators requires some real work on your part and a strong, trust-based agreement with your kids. Forget the magic solution—it doesn't exist. But we can offer some quick and easy steps for protecting your family from chat-room abuse:

- Check out any chat room your children are interested in *before* you let them visit. Find out who, or what organization or company, is behind the chat room.

- Seek chat rooms clearly designed for kids and those that are moderated by a "host" who manages the discussion and the behavior of the participants.

- Send e-mail to the chat manager(s) asking them to state their policy for removing participants who act/communicate in an inappropriate manner.

- Have your kid use a gender-neutral code name. Don't create a screen name or "handle" that indicates the child's sex or age. Don't allow your child to create a personal profile on your Internet Service Provider's member directory.

• Tell your kids not to accept an invitation to enter into a "private chat room" unless they know the person. (In some chat rooms you can invite a participant to break away from the main group and enter into a one-on-one chat.) Private chats can be harmless and fun ways to conduct a one-on-one conversation. They are, however, one of the means the bad guys use to start dialogue with unsuspecting kids.

• Teach your child to report any problems to the host of the chat room and to you.

• Train your children to apply all the rules for online safety when they visit a chat room.

Dealing with Bulletin Boards

Compared to chats, bulletin boards (and newsgroups) seem relatively harmless. These are services on the Internet that let you post messages, read responses to your message (or other messages) and send or receive files. The files you can send (or "post") or receive can be text, computer programs, pictures and so on. There are bulletin boards for everything from antique-car collectors to canary owners, and they're often great sources of information.

One feature that makes bulletin boards a little safer is the messages stay up there—you can find them days or maybe weeks later—and hundreds or more people will see them on a busy board. Predators don't like a big spotlight and lots of eyes peering at their messages, although they can change screen names and slip in and out of identities. In general, the messages on bulletin boards tend to be written on a higher level as opposed to the grunts and come-ons in many of the chats. That makes us a little more comfortable, but not complacent. You still need to be vigilant. Some bulletin boards (no surprise) focus on adult material, and bad guys can still use your postings to stalk you and try to strike up communications. Think of it like a classified ad in the paper where you happen to discuss some personal issues; anyone can see it.

To protect your kids from inappropriate bulletin boards, just apply the same basic steps as for chat rooms. Again, common sense should rule—don't post any personal information, such as your phone number, e-mail address, home address or mug shot. These can be used by the bad guys to track you down.

Shielding Your Children Against E-Mail Abuse

It's not enough that your mailbox at home overflows daily with junk mail. Now you have to deal with unsolicited online mail—or "spam" as the cyber junkies call it. These are basically e-mail come-ons. These often come in the form of seemingly friendly overtures—"Cool site" or "How about a friend" or "Hi-remember me?" are typical subject titles. Then when you open the e-mail, you find that it's an invitation to a seedy adult Web site. Yuck.

Rather than blow your top, consider some of the tips and steps below:

- Tell your children not to open e-mail from an address they don't recognize (note: return addresses shown on e-mail can be fake).

- Whenever possible, be at your children's side when they open e-mail.

- See if your online service provider has special e-mail control features that let you block e-mail from specific companies or individuals. These controls work by allowing you to add the e-mail address of the offending party to a custom personal "block out" list you create and maintain. Once your list is set up, incoming e-mail is examined, and messages from any sender found on your blocking list are automatically deleted and never seen by the intended target.

- Try out shareware programs that will help you block unsolicited e-mail. Shareware is Internet talk for free or trial versions of commercial programs you can download. You can download these from www.zd-net.com and other similar sites.

- Be discreet about the chat rooms and bulletin boards you visit. Junk mailers use this information—your "footprints" to zero in on your e-mail account. Good tip: Set up a separate screen name and e-mail address just for surfing the Web. Let all your junk mail go there. Give out your personal, main e-mail address to just your friends.

• See if your online service provider has a feature that sends you a copy of all e-mail sent to your child.

• If you or your children receive offensive e-mail, immediately report the address to your online service provider and ask them to investgate it.

CHILD SAFETY RESOURCES IN CYBERSPACE

Once you're online, there's a world of help and expert advice at your fingertips. Here are some of our favorite kid safety Web sites:

- www.missingkids.com (National Center for Missing and Exploited Children)
- www.uab.edu/pedinfo/Control.html (List of cyber safety software programs)
- www.safesurf.com (The "original Internet rating system")
- www.cyberangels.org (Internet safety organization)
- www.safekids.com (Child safety on the info highway)
- www.larrysworld.com/articles/parentright.htm (See article: "Rights of Parents in the Digital Age")
- www.zdnet.com/zdnn/content/zdnn/1201/249786.html (See article: "Few Parents Use Filtering Software")
- www.larrysworld.com/articles/kidspriv.htm (See article: "Marketers Are a Bigger Threat to Your Kids Than Porno")

- www.zdnet.com/zdnn/content/zdnn/1201/249834.html (See article: "*FamilyPC Details* Findings of 'Net Parent' Survey")

Warning: Web addresses and offerings frequently change. These addresses were active at the time this book was produced.

Keep an Eye on the Ranch

One of the keys to managing what does or does not come into your home from cyberspace is keeping an eye on the ranch. That is, make sure you're close at hand when your kids surf the Net. If you're really worried put the PC in an open area like the family room or den. As we've said before we like to have some privacy, meaning a study or computer room—but one that's right off the main hall or traffic area. Consider setting aside some "quality time" and surf the Web shoulder-to-shoulder with your child. The key is to *be there*, not because you don't trust your child, but to protect them from content they may innocently stumble upon. A December 1997 survey conducted by *FamilyPC* magazine found that of the 750 families they contacted, 73 percent monitor their children's PC activities. But we've found that even in the most vigilant homes, it's easy to slip for a few days or weeks. You have to stay on top of it.

Cyber Safety Tools at a Glance

Here's a quick snapshot of what we've covered in this and the previous chapter, organized so you can determine where you want to invest the bulk of your effort. This chart uses a scale of 1 to 5, with 5 being the highest rating.

TOOL	EASE OF USE	EFFECTIVENESS	COST
Behavior Contract	5	5—Depending on your relationship of trust with the child	$0
Parental Controls (on major services)	4	3.5—They work, but often severely limit Web access	Included with monthly subscription
Cyber Safety Software	2.5	3.5—You have to constantly update the database	$30 to $50
Browser Filters	4	2—Web designers must volunteer to identify the intended audience	$0 if you use browser provided by your service
Filtered Access Providers	5	4.75—Constantly updated	Average $20 per month
Yahooligans! Search Engine	5	5—Only downside is limitations of the search engine's database	$0
Internet Directories	4	5—Very safe, but only list sites available at time of printing	$20 to $30
Common Sense	5	5—Highly effective	$0

Audit Your Kid's School/Library Cyber Safety

Now that you're an expert in cyber safety and you've got the home-front Cyber Safety Tools squared away, you may want to see what's up at your child's school. Using the Cyber Safety Tools at-a-glance chart as a guide, contact your school's computer manager, librarian or principal and ask what cyber safety measures and tools they have in place. Many of our local schools, for instance, have students sign and take home an Internet behavior contract for Mom's and Dad's signatures. You follow the rules or you lose Web access. Also, in many cases, teachers are required to monitor all Web activity. Some schools have also installed and use cyber safety software and tools. This gives us a lot more confidence.

Form Parent-to-Parent Understandings

In Chapter 11 we suggested you strike an understanding with the parents of your child's friends as to what kinds of games you allow your child to play. Apply the same parent-to-parent agreement when it comes to surfing the Net. Some parents have found it helpful to work up a little letter for fellow parents, and even the child's teacher, outlining your family rules for game and Internet access. Remember, no matter how much work you put into making your home PC kid-safe, all bets are off the minute your kid walks out the door.

Mom and Dad, Cyber Gatekeepers

There is no silver bullet to protecting your kids online, but you can improve your chances of a pleasant experience if you're involved. Many older kids (12 and up) are going to rebel if you simply slap controls on and walk away. They may look at it as a sign of mistrust. You need to work closely with them and explain to them why you're getting involved. Spend time surfing with them, show them cool sites you've discovered, get their opinions about their online experiences. Make it a partnership in which you're working together to explore the online world. Set rules, but be flexible and make it a fun experience.

Knowledge and communication is the key. The more you and your kid know about how the Internet works, and the more you understand each other's side and interests, the better off you are. Sure, we know kids are going to be tempted by peers and you're not going to be there every minute. But a strong bond with your child is going to be pretty good insurance. When it comes to cyber safety, all the parental controls, cyber-filter software and ratings schemes in the world pale in comparison to a strong parent-child relationship.

FOCUSED QUESTIONS

- Have your kids gone into chat rooms? Have they encountered anything that's made them uncomfortable? Have you?

- What rules do you want to set for chat rooms and bulletin boards?

- Are you or your kids getting e-mail spam? What did you suggest they do? What steps are you taking to reduce it?

- Have you determined if your Internet Service Provider offers parental controls with the ability to filter or block e-mail coming to your kids?

- Have you talked to your kids about the risks involved with accepting an invitation to join a private chat session with a stranger?

- Have you checked to make sure your child's online service profile does not contain any personal information, such as the child's real name, address, sex or age?

14.

Street Smarts

USING THE PC TO TEACH LIFE SKILLS

The best school in the world can't teach a kid how to operate in the real world.
—The PC Dads

Every year or so we get a brainy idea. Such was the case in the spring of 1997, when we decided to bring our families—five kids total—to Disney World in Orlando. *FamilyPC* magazine had invited us to do a "PC Frontier" show at its Epcot exhibit, and we couldn't resist. Mickey and the crew, fun rides, dazzling light shows, day-long events and activities—this seemed like family heaven.

Then reality hit us. As we sorted through the piles of literature, we realized you don't just *show up* at Disney and start having fun. You have to plan it. Every detail of every day had to be planned—the theme parks, the eateries, special events, ticket packages. Yikes, this looked like work. So we came up with another idea. The kids were the ones who'd be rubbing shoulders with Goofy and whooping it up on the rides. Why not put them to work planning the vacation and mapping out the daily activities?

To keep it simple, we established a budget and some other basic parameters (such as the number of days). Then we turned the kids loose. They jumped right in, went online and began poring over the Disney Web site, getting ticket prices and comparing package deals. They reviewed hotels (complete with photos), debated about which ones had the best swimming pools and looked at special events and theme days that were being held during our stay. Mark's kids bought the Disney CD-ROM, which describes all the theme parks and rides, and began picking out their favorites and planning daily schedules. Even little

Nicole made a list (with her brothers' help) of her ten favorite rides, assuring she didn't get left out.

Christina (Ralph's daughter) went the extra mile. She put together a slide-show presentation (using Microsoft's *PowerPoint* software) with Dad's help, illustrating her ideas for the Disney vacation. In her presentation, she demonstrated special events at the parks she wanted to see and showed pictures of the hotel and rooms she'd downloaded from the Internet. As her family gathered around the home PC, she compared hotel room rates and made suggestions.

Without realizing it, Christina had:

- Conducted research.
- Distilled important information down into key bullets (like this).
- Learned how to package her information into a presentation.
- Made her points lucidly before a critical audience.
- Closed the sale.

Soon Ralph's wife was ready to hammer out the details with the travel agents, and both families had an itinerary.

None of this is rocket science. Any kid who can wield a joystick and read a game manual can help plan a vacation. But these activities go beyond just picking one hotel or restaurant over another. They involve skills in planning, group decision making and budget management, just to name a few. Essentially, they're about learning how to operate, navigate and survive in the real world.

Children don't generally pick these skills up in school. Sure, they may develop these abilities later by stumbling through—and costing you some bucks along the way. But now, with a home PC and some creativity, you can give them a head start and teach them real-life skills that'll last them a lifetime. We call these "street-smart" skills.

This chapter will show you how to use the computer to cultivate some of these skills in your kid, including:

- Planning and organizing (project management)
- Setting priorities
- Preparing and following a budget
- Presenting a proposal
- Negotiating and compromising

Home Economics (And We Don't Mean Sewing)

One day, on the way to a movie, Mark stopped by the ATM machine with his son, Matthew. "I'm not sure if I'm going to have enough money to get gas, eat and see a movie," Mark commented. "No problem," Matthew quipped, "just get *more* cash out."

Easy for him, Mark thought. Daddy Warbucks slides a card into the machine, pushes a few buttons and out pops the cash. Financial management, from a 13-year-old's viewpoint, is easy. You just need to know where to find the ATM machines and remember your password. Matt was already starting to talk about having his own personal cash card.

Mark's wife had already helped Matthew set up a savings account. But now, it was time to push it a little further. It was time for him to start learning about managing a checkbook, budgeting and cash flow.

Mark set up an imaginary checking account for him using *Money*, a financial management program by Microsoft, and printed out his checks for him (complete with his own little clip art on the check). He started with an imaginary deposit of $10 in his account, plus $20 he'd earned earlier, so his balance was $30. When he wants to buy something, Mark now pays for it, and Matthew writes a check to him for the amount of the purchase. When he does a job, Mark "pays" him by making a deposit to his checking account. His job is to keep the checkbook updated and balanced.

Matt's Check

Matt likes having control over an account he can quickly call up. (Before, he'd bug his parents for days if they didn't pay him for his babysitting or yard work; now it's instant gratification.) He's also beginning to understand that if there's no money in the account, he won't be able to purchase a video game at the store. When he begins begging or bargaining, Mark simply points him to the *Money* screen and the zeroes. He's always been pretty good about saving money and realizing he can't have everything he wants. The checkbook merely confirms this and encourages him to manage his money wisely.

Children want to do grown-up things, so why not give them more responsibility like this? For older kids, say 14 and over, you can set up real accounts instead of imaginary ones. They can deposit money earned from part-time jobs and track expenses to see how much they spend on entertainment, clothes, fast food and CDs, and what percentage they're saving.

Understanding a little about managing money lays the foundation later for more sophisticated financial planning, budgeting—and discipline. Children begin to spend more effort setting goals and planning how to achieve them. Much of this, of course, is just common sense. But the computer gives you one more tool to help hammer the lessons home. Our children, like many kids, like seeing the numbers on the screen. Why, we don't know. But we'll use anything with our children that can help make a point about financial management.

The goal of these activities is simple: to give your children solid financial management skills, so they can budget, save, plan for and invest in the future. You're not trying to raise little Donald Trumps, just help them understand the basics of money management. It's all about helping children learn how to manage their own cash flow and budget for the future. Sure the $60 running shoes *look* nice, but are they worth it if you have to mow seven or eight lawns to pay for them?

Looking further ahead, these activities give kids the skills to determine if they can afford a new car and the insurance that goes with it and to analyze the differences between fixed and variable-rate mortgages. This can pay off big-time if you play your cards right. Put another way, if you *don't* work on these skills, your children may be calling *you* later to bail them out on the car payment or the bad debts. Is that what you want?

Just how far should you go in teaching street smarts? It's up to you. One woman we heard about loaned money frequently to her older son. When he couldn't pay her back, she had his car repossessed. Now that's teaching financial management the old-fashioned way. You don't pay, you don't play.

MARK AND MATT'S ONLINE INVESTMENT ADVENTURE

MARK:

I had a great idea. Why not set up an online investment account for Matt and teach him a little about investing? America Online had a cool online stock portfolio feature I could set up as an imaginary account. Matt could invest in stocks and learn a little about investing and the market. Maybe he'd grow up to be another Warren Buffett, the legendary Omaha investor.

This worked, sort of. Matthew, true to form, rejected mutual funds and traditional blue-chip companies as too boring. Instead, he chased down a slew of fast-growing, fledgling unknowns, thinking he'd strike it rich. "Why should I wait all year for one of the $100 stocks to move up a few dollars when one of these little $5 or $10 guys can double overnight?" he asked, using typical teenager logic. Our compromise: I let him invest in some of the small fry firms and he agreed to invest in a few larger companies that he knew, like toy giant Mattel (maker of Barbie).

It was a good lesson. Matthew discovered that companies are funded by equity and investors. He also found new ways to research companies, such as visiting their Web sites. Pretty soon he was racing to get online to check his portfolio. I had done it. He was actually interested in the market. We played around like this for six weeks. Then it was time to tally the results. At the end of six weeks his speculative portfolio netted him an $80 loss!

This created a problem. I wanted to show him how the market worked and that it sometimes punishes investors, but I didn't want to discourage him. I finally decided to give him $10 for his efforts and a few words of wisdom about the dangers of investing in companies without positive track records.

Will this lesson sink in when he finally starts investing for real; will he avoid the riskier investments and play it safe? Probably not, knowing his personality. But at least he'll go into it with his eyes wide open and Dad's checkbook firmly closed.

Digital Dollars: It's Kid Stuff

When we were kids, just after the dinosaurs became extinct, it was tough for kids to earn a buck. If you needed money, you had to slave away mowing monster-size lawns, delivering newspapers, babysitting a passel of kids or shoveling snow. Good paying jobs still seem hard to come by, but computer-smart kids have a new weapon on their side. With a little creativity and some inexpensive software, your budding entrepreneur can earn some pocket money and maybe even learn about managing a small business venture. Here are a few ideas to help you get them going:

• *Desktop Publishing.* This is a great business that builds multiple skills, from creativity and design to typing and working under deadline pressure. There are a bunch of neat programs that make it a snap to produce professional-looking leaflets, business cards, handouts, newsletters, calendars and signs for small businesses, clubs and nonprofit organizations. Desktop publishing programs like Microsoft's *Publisher* provide everything you need to make cool-looking documents complete with eye-catching art and graphics. (A good starting program for the little kids is the *Ultimate Writing & Creativity Center* by The Learning Company.) Our neighborhood watch group hired a couple kids to do some fliers for their group, and another kid got a ton of business from local real-estate agents who wanted inexpensive fliers made.

• ***Greeting Cards and Invitations.*** Kids can design greeting card samples and then get quantity orders. They can also put together packages that contain cards for different occasions and sell them as a group, and they can customize individual cards. There are any number of greeting card software titles that provide similar features. *Greetings Workshop* by Microsoft is a great all-around package, along with *Print Artist* by Sierra and *Kid Cuts* by Broderbund (an add-on to *Kid Pix Studio*). One caution: you need to start planning well in advance if you want to capitalize on holiday card shopping.

• ***Custom T-shirts.*** Using an innovative software package called *T-shirt Maker & More* (by Hanes), children can create custom T-shirts with photos, artwork, cartoons, awards and slogans. The software makes it easy for them to put their own computer artwork or photos on a T-shirt. The design is printed on an iron-on transfer that's included with the kit. Kids can sell shirts to local teams in their neighborhood.

• ***Web Page Building and Consulting.*** Many teenagers have already created their own home pages, so the next logical step is to take their skills to the neighborhood marketplace. First make sure they have the software to build impressive Web pages. In addition to popular Web-

PC Dads' Web Site Pick

The Web is a great place to start practicing financial management skills. Many Web sites teach the fundamentals of money and investing through interactive activities. Check out *The Young Investor Web Site,* (*www.younginvestor.com*), developed by Liberty Financial Companies. The site includes an investment-related game room, two libraries (one for kids 12 and under and one for teenagers), and a place called "Kid2Kid" where junior investors can learn from their peers and win a prize for correctly answering a money question. It also has some good tips on how parents can promote financial awareness in their kids.

building programs like *Hot Dog* from Sausage and *Front Page 98* from Microsoft, there's *Web Workshop* by Vividus, a Web page design kit that's just for kids. It gives step-by-step instructions to guide first-timers through creating their inaugural Web pages. It also offers information on how children can hook up with other kids' Web sites. Also have your child check out the "Home Computing" section of the Intel Web site which offers some cool tips and tools for building your own Web site (go to www.intel.com, click on "Home Computing" and then click on "Do More with Your PC").

You might want to start by having your child work with a local nonprofit organization, such as a senior center or community group. These groups may not pay anything, but they'd probably appreciate having a Web page set up, and it would be good practice. (They'd also need to decide who would maintain the page after it was up.) After that, they might start trolling locally for some contract work. Have them start with small businesses or entrepreneurs. Maybe a local Realtor, dry cleaner or hobby shop would like to have a home page for its customers. Your son or daughter's job would be to design and perhaps maintain it. Rates for design generally run from $50 to $200 at the bottom level (much more, of course, for big high-profile jobs).

In addition to building Web pages, kids can pick up extra cash by becoming a neighborhood computer consultant. Depending on the range of expertise your whiz kids have, they can install software, troubleshoot problems, give guided tutorials on the components of the system, help set up a new computer and show veteran tricks to novices. All they need to get going is a little motivation and a bunch of business cards (which they can make on the computer). Rates are based on whatever people will pay: $10 to $20 an hour may be a good starting point.

Taking Care of Business on the PC

Not every kid wants to be a Web designer or computer expert, but they can all benefit by putting whatever business they're interested in on the computer. Start with your children's existing business interests. Show them ways they can use the computer to increase efficiencies, produce sales, and track revenues and expenses. For example, kids can create a database of customers and log revenue, or take a look at which jobs are the most profitable and seek more of those commitments. They can create fliers to advertise their services and generate additional cash.

You can also get your children an electronic organizer to encourage them to keep track of their appointments and commitments. You can buy these pretty cheap at most discount stores. They're another way to incorporate technology into everyday life and increase their comfort level with the digital age. They're also very cool.

Take the electronic organizer one step further. You can go crazy keeping track of the entire family's schedule—there's soccer practice, band, school committees, social engagements and on and on. Here's what you can do: make each child responsible for entering all their activities onto a computerized family calendar. You might also use an electronic notepad on your computer to handle telephone messages, as well as to jot down all those reminders to your kids to do their chores and finish their homework. Microsoft *Word* comes with *WordPad*; it's sort of like having a tablet on your computer. You can design a format for taking messages, type in the message and then hit the "date and time" button to stamp those on the message. No more sheepish looks from the kids with the refrain, "Mom, I forgot to tell you that your office called. . . ."

The ability to manage projects, set priorities, juggle multiple commitments, use budgets, apply entrepreneurial talents and be technologically literate: These are all skills your kids will need later in life as they join the workforce. They can't learn them too early.

Driver's Ed 101 . . .

Few things are more important to 14-year-olds than the day they'll actually drive a car—and nothing's more frightening for a parent. Visions of twisted metal and outrageous insurance bills come to mind.

Now there's help. Sierra's *Driver's Education* program lets kids get behind the wheel and take a spin—with some direction. *Driver's Education* isn't a racing game, though; it's a training program. Players have to take a written driving test (a different one for each state) before they get behind the wheel. Then they pick from a series of different driving tests that teach them about dealing with traffic lights, making turns, even parallel parking. If they screw up, a voice named "Driver Ed" corrects them—sometimes caustically. Our children love this program, particularly when they steer with the driving wheel (made by Thrustmaster)—and they howl with laughter when Ed gets upset. It's entertaining to them and they're even learning a few rules of the road.

Vacation Planning

Don't forget vacation planning. This is one of the best ways to get kids involved in planning and project management. Start off small by giving them a few destinations to investigate; then add a budget so they don't go overboard. Check out sites like Citysearch.com, Expedia.msn.com, City.net and MapQuest.com, which let them research area attractions, restaurant options, lodging, local weather and special events; they can even download maps and get directions. They'll find sites for every aspect of vacation planning: information on states, parks, resort destinations, package deals, condos, airline tickets, car rental—the works.

We were blown away by some of the online services. When Mark needed to book a flight to Houston to see his folks, he jumped on Expedia (Expedia.msn.com), which helped him find the lowest bargain fares ($250 round trip in this case). Its wizard walked him through the steps to find the cheapest fares and other options such as direct flights, flights with no change penalties and so on. He was able to pick out a seat (using a graphical picture of the plane) and booked the plane tickets online. He even set up the fare tracker to alert him to special airfare deals between Portland and Houston. He's now hooked on online travel services and convinced it's easy enough for his sons to use.

If you're driving, get the kids to use the new mapping software like AAA *Map 'n' Go* and *Trip Planner*. These programs allow you to map out exactly where you're going, choosing between maybe the most scenic or the quickest routes. You can set up exactly how many miles or hours a day you want to drive and see it graphically illustrated on the map. Some offer articles and photos of cool sites (there's even a *National Geographic* version, complete with stunning photos and a video of scenic sites). Getting the children to think in terms of time, distances and comfort issues is a good exercise on several fronts. They begin to understand that planning a vacation isn't simple, but it can be fun!

After they've collected the information, you can all talk about the pros and cons of each and make a choice. Your children will be more invested in the trip since they helped create it, and who knows, they might even thank you for tak-

PARADISE ISN'T LOST . . . IT'S JUST A COUPLE MOUSE CLICKS AWAY

America Online and the major search engines feature travel services and information. Here are some other resources to get your in-house travel agent started. Don't forget the sunscreen and the snacks.

- **Travel Industry Association of America** *(www.tia.org)* This site is loaded with information. The links to tourism offices in all fifty states give comprehensive details about what each state has to offer, including attractions, events, lodging, restaurants, historical landmarks and more.

- **Preview Travel** *(destinations.previewtravel.com)* Preview provides one-stop shopping for airline tickets, vacation packages, car rental and hotel accommodations. They specialize in leisure and small business travel.

- **The Mining Co.** *(travelwithkids.miningco.com)* This site is packed full of ideas on using the Web to plan and finance family vacations. There are strategies for coping with travel, kid cruises, reviews of destinations and other touring essentials. Also check out its cousin site (*camping.miningco.com*) if your family needs help planning an escape to the great outdoors. It gives advice on gear and supplies, lists RV resources, and provides a backpack full of info on camping destinations.

• **Microsoft Expedia** *(expedia.msn.com)* Microsoft has opened its own one-stop travel agency offering a full spread of travel deals, car rentals, vacation packages and more. Good all-around site.

• **Disney** *(www.disneyworld.com)* Everything you ever wanted to know about planning a trip to the Magic Kingdom is right here.

• **MapQuest** *(www.mapquest.com)* This site is a gold mine of information about particular cities—how to navigate them, what to do and see, where to stay, eat and play.

ing them on vacation (imagine that!). No matter where you end up going, the kids will learn skills that will serve them well their whole lives.

Easing the College Blues

You think you already have enough stress? Try sending your kids to college! Every new study shows that you'll need more and more money to send your child to college. ("My gosh, Johnny's already crawling and I've only got a few thousand dollars saved up. He'll probably have to work in the chicken plant and be lucky to get in the community college.") Then there's the mountains of applications and paperwork. Last, after shelling out all the money, you wonder if your kid will even *like* the college.

Thankfully, there's some new help available online. Kids can begin exploring colleges on the Web, locating schools that specialize in their area of interest.

They can learn about admission requirements, get financial aid information and calculate costs. They can find current tuition for many schools at *U.S. News & World Report*'s education site (www.usnews.com/usnews/edu/home.htm). They can project future costs by going to the Web site of the College Funding Company (www.collegefundingco.com) and using a program to calculate costs. (Don't panic when you get the results. You still have time to plan, and you may qualify for financial aid. Plus there are numerous Web sites where your kids can get the scoop on colleges and help to get there without breaking the bank.)

Our kids are a few years (or more) away from college, but we witness this issue through our hapless friends. The daughter of one of Ralph's friends was in turmoil about her major and where she wanted to go to college. It wasn't feasible for Claire to visit the five schools she was interested in, since they were scattered across the country. So she hopped online and explored her choices through the Internet and even ended up chatting with some students and alumni online. She also expedited her search by corresponding with the Admissions staff via e-mail. This process helped her narrow her choices to a couple of schools fairly close to each other, allowing her to make an efficient, one-day visit. She ended up choosing an Ivy League school.

Claire's Internet expertise paid off. She conducted her search at her own convenience and didn't have to rely completely on the limited hours of her high school's career placement office. She downloaded each of her choices into a "favorites" file for quick access. Her parents were also able to take a look at the options at their leisure. They never felt buried by a blizzard of paper or overwhelmed by forms. Usually there's a premium for convenience, but not in this case—they saved time and money while gaining expedience. How often does that happen?

Living With Technology

Kids are growing up faster today, trying to meet a rising tide of society's expectations and their own. To fully participate in the new millennium, kids need to be competent with a wide range of technology, including stuff that hasn't even

SHOW ME THE MONEY

We can't take you directly to the hidden treasure, but we can point you in the direction of some online resources to locate colleges, financial aid and scholarships for your superstar kid.

- **Colleges and Universities** (*dir.yahoo.com/Education/-Higher_Education/College_Entrance*) This leads to the Web pages of a couple hundred of the nation's best-known colleges and universities. The Web pages usually give information regarding admission requirements, history of the college, majors, student life, maps to get there, online admissions packets and more.

- **The Financial Aid Information Page** (*www.finaid.org*) This site, sponsored by the National Association of Student Administrators, helps you calculate how much aid your child might receive.

- **FastWEB** (*www.fastweb.com*) This is a database of more than 180,000 private-sector scholarships, fellowships, grants and loans from more than 3,000 sources.

- **SRN Express** (*www.rams.com/srn*) This site is the Scholarship Resource Network's database of private-sector aid not based on need.

- **ExPAN Scholarship Search** (*www.collegeboard.org/-fundfinder/bin/fundfind01.pl*) This is the College Board's database of scholarships, fellowships, loans, internships and aid programs from 3,300 national, state, public and private sources.

- **The National College Resource Association** (*www.collegere-source.com*) This association provides a broad spectrum of assistance with career searches, college planning, locating free monies and more.

been invented yet. In addition to being digitally smart, kids need to have the same kinds of life skills we all need in order to survive. They need to know how to manage their finances, organize and plan, evaluate alternatives, build a future, juggle multiple tasks and projects, and take responsibility for their choices.

It's a lot to learn. The great news is that the PC can help children garner these skills easier than ever before. Your job is to lead the way.

FOCUSED QUESTIONS

- How are your kids' money management skills? How can you use the computer to help them grasp the fact that money doesn't grow on trees and to develop/refine their ability to manage money effectively?

- When is your next family vacation? How can the kids help plan it and what skills would you like them to gain in the process?

- With everyone involved in different activities, family life can be as hectic to manage as any business. How can you use the PC to help simplify your family's bookkeeping, scheduling and so forth?

- Are your children old enough to use the PC as a money maker? What interests and skills do they have that they might want to use in a PC-based business venture?

- Where are you on the planning-for-college timeline? How can you take advantage of Internet resources to get the information you need?

15.

The Winding Road Ahead

MANAGING THE NEW CHALLENGES
OF THE DIGITAL AGE

Man is still the most extraordinary computer of all.
—John F. Kennedy

henever a new technology appears, it's human nature to ask questions. Why? What's it good for? Where is it going or, more specifically, where is it taking me? When the first practical telegraph emerged in the 1800s, Henry David Thoreau quipped, "We are in a great haste to construct a telegraph from Maine to Texas, but Maine and Texas, it may be, may have nothing important to communicate."

But it's now clear that it didn't matter what Thoreau or anyone else believed. The telegraph emerged as a powerful communications tool, and it was the precursor for new communication and mass mediums that would come later—radio, TV, and, yes, the Internet. Technology has a way of moving forward, pushing ahead deeply into our lives.

As the personal computer and Internet become more a part of our daily lives, it makes sense to stop and look at just where these technologies are taking us—and how we can prepare to manage the changes they will usher in. We are clearly reaching a crossroads with this technology. The computer is no longer confined to the world of scientists and geeks. It's already in more than 40 percent of the homes in the U.S., and use is growing rapidly worldwide.

Normally as a mass medium business like television reaches critical mass, interesting developments take place. The media latches on and begins developing "The Story." Big companies with fat advertising and marketing budgets

BRAIN-CHECK:
WHERE'S IT ALL GOING?

The advances in the personal computer from its beginnings in the early 1980s are truly staggering. Comparing today's personal computers to IBM's first PC (introduced in 1981) is like comparing a Ford Model T to a modern high-performance luxury sedan—rarely has technology advanced at such a dizzying rate. The fuel behind this rapid technology evolution is the microprocessor or computer "brain," which roughly doubles in performance every 18 months or so (Moore's Law, remember?).

For a taste of just how fast things have moved in less than 20 years, consider these facts: Intel's latest Pentium II processor (at the time of this writing) is more than 1,800 times faster than the Intel brain chip used in the original IBM PC in 1981. Another measure is transistors. Today's Pentium II processors have 7.5 million transistors vs. 3.1 million for the 1993 vintage Pentium and 29,000 for the Intel 8088 chip used in the first IBM PC.

One result of this technology ramp is that, for the same amount of money, you can buy many times more computer today than just a few years ago. Gordon Moore, one of Intel's founders, once described the pace of microprocessor advancement by comparing it to automobile technology. He said, "If the auto industry advanced as rapidly as the semiconductor industry, a Rolls Royce would get a half a million miles per gallon, and it would be cheaper to throw it away than to park it."

It's wonderful that brain chip power keeps going up as the cost keeps going down, but here's why you should care: As processor power increases it opens the door for new applications. Intel has already publicly demonstrated a microprocessor running almost twice as fast as today's latest Pentium II processor. These speed demons will boost multimedia and graphics capabilities on the PC dramatically and unleash a tidal wave of new applications. Expect to see full-screen, super-quality video, games with startling realistic 3D features and a wide array of business, personal and entertainment programs that you can fully control with your voice. In other words, the fun is just beginning.

jump in. More capital flows into the business. Entrepreneurs and others, smelling opportunity, leap into the fray. Everyone, it seems, wants a piece of the action. In the case of cable TV, to take one example, this began to take place after the industry reached about 60 percent of households in the U.S. by the 1980s. But it's already happening with the computer and Internet. Witness the explosive growth in Internet subscribers, to more than 20 million from a few thousand just a generation ago, and the thousands of businesses that have staked out a claim on the Internet, from small fries like Boothill Western Wear in our (Hillsboro, Oregon) backyard to media giants like Time Inc. and Disney. This stampede will change the Internet over time, creating new opportunities and challenges for computer-smart parents.

The good news is that the PC and Internet are still young enough to get our arms around and influence—if we take steps now. More than TV, the PC and the Internet are capable of being shaped and influenced by the participants— you, that is. This chapter will briefly examine some of the key challenges facing parents as we enter the next century and the Digital Age, while offering some tips and guidance to help navigate through these wacky times. We'll also take a glimpse of what's around the bend—the PC Dads crystal ball and wish list—and offer some ideas that could make the computing revolution a little easier on the nerves.

To put the computer in perspective, some people like to compare it to broadcast technology, which also exploded on the scene. Like the PC and Internet, the TV ignited people's imaginations when the first shows appeared in the late 1940s and early 1950s. We still remember watching the early TV shows like *I Love Lucy*, gathered with our parents around the glowing black-and-white TV set in awe. By the 1960s cable TV had emerged, and as operators rushed to sign up cities to establish franchises, new promises emerged. It was the promise of a Brave New World. There would be hundreds of alternative channels to choose from (versus the three channels of the day), educational stations, interactive services like shopping and banking and everyone would have access to a TV studio—the community-access channel concept.

It didn't quite happen that way. Most of what you see on cable TV—sitcoms, high-action thrillers, sports and entertainment news and so on—isn't much different than network TV. Community-access channels never really took off. Most suffered from poor funding, lack of production and overall expertise that TV requires. The significant services that did emerge—like banking—came via the Internet, not cable TV. The exception was the twenty-four-hour news concept, launched by Cable News Network, but even it seems destined to be subsumed by the Internet. TV, in general, didn't pan out as many of us had hoped.

Now, some critics believe the computer and Internet is being overhyped and could fail to meet expectations as well. The comparison is flawed, however. They are two different worlds, two different technologies. TV is passive—you see what a small group of producers want you to see. Computers require hands-on management and are interactive—you see and experience what you want to see and experience. TV plays on the emotions. Computers and the Internet can play on the emotions or intellect (think about people falling in love online versus the intellectual discourse that goes on in some bulletin boards). You operate a PC from about fifteen inches away; you operate about a TV from about fifteen feet away. You get the idea.

Neil Postman, author of *Amusing Ourselves to Death, Public Discourse in the Age of Show Business*, says it's a mistake to compare new technologies or mediums with old ones. The automobile was more than a fast horse. The electric light was more than a powerful candle. And the computer with its connection to the Internet is more than a TV with thousands of channels—much more.

Still, TV has one advantage for parents: it's simple and predictable. People understand it, and whether you like it or not, to some degree the content is controlled. We can refuse to let our kids rent R-rated movies or watch questionable shows, at least in our house. And it's unlikely that an X-rated movie will appear while we're watching *Barney*. The Internet is a different animal, and along with the computer, requires more hands-on management and awareness. What we're saying is simple: you can't treat the computer and Internet like the TV; the day of the couch potato is over. Parents will have to roll up their sleeves and get to work or face getting left behind by their kids.

It's going to be an interesting time for most of us as we enter the next century. Below are just three trends and challenges that we see looming as we move ahead:

- **Manage Information Overload:** Children are being overloaded with information, and it's getting worse. American children watch more than twenty-three hours of TV a week, and then there are the video games, radio and stereo—all devices that pump out some form of information. The main culprits are the visual stimuli they see everyday, the dazzling and often sensual imagery designed to titillate, to rock the senses, to create an emotional experience. This includes the stream of information and correspondence, from Web sites to chat rooms, that the computer and Internet have brought into the home. Children no longer have any downtime to think. They're too busy being in touch, being connected, being entertained.

As we've said, parents are the information gatekeepers of the home. Start by setting limits: the TV can only be on so many minutes a day, for example. The home should be a refuge from the onslaught of information, from TV images to the constant news bombardment. The PC can be the central control for a home information management system, and a model for the family. Some tips:

- Limit the types of programs your kids play. Try to keep a mix of at least 50 percent educational, 50 percent games—or whatever fits your own agenda and family plan. Don't let your children pile up programs by the computer, and jump from one to another, machine-gun style. Encourage them to play one program at a time, exploring it fully before moving to another one.

• Limit time on the Internet. A good rule of thumb is to limit Internet usage to one hour a day and encourage thoughtful research and exploration versus random surfing. Limit chats and e-mail correspondence as well. Children don't need to be wired every moment.

• Be a model. Actions do speak louder than words, and children will follow your lead.

• **Maintain Positive Values:** Postman calls this the Age of Show Business, where everything is entertainment—news, politics, religion, the list goes on and on. Everything is packaged as entertainment. It's a "peek-a-boo world," here today, gone tomorrow, very fleeting, very strange.

It's not easy competing with Madonna or Bart Simpson with a computer—but it's possible. It depends on how heavily the parent gets involved. Make it a fun experience, turn it into an adventure. Every mutual trip a parent takes with a child on the Internet should be an experience, something they'll remember, at least for a while. By taking a strong personal interest and emphasizing certain programs and activities on the PC, you're sending out a message: This is what I see as important. One-on-one, shoulder to shoulder in the quiet of the study, you have a fighting chance of helping shape your child's attitudes, values and their perspective on this crazy world. While you can't control how much a professional sports star earns, or what the media determines is the news of the day, you can control what happens on your PC (you paid for it, remember?).

• **Maintain Balance:** Children need balance in their lives. Too much of anything, including the computer, isn't healthy. The child shouldn't be in front of the TV or computer more than a couple of hours a day. They should go outside, play ball, volunteer for charities, get involved in organizations like the Boy Scouts of America and Girl Scouts of America. Children grow up too fast today. Let your kid be a kid.

The biggest challenge might be simply managing change as it happens. Technology is being introduced at a much faster pace than even twenty or thirty years ago, giving us less time to adapt. Parents today need to think like futurists, always looking ahead and anticipating key trends and events.

People have gone through these shifts before. Back before 1915 fewer than one in ten American homes owned a car; by the 1920s nearly one in two homes owned a car, and growth exploded over the next three decades, changing the way Americans travel and live. The trend was fueled by the development of a vast network of roads and highways across the country. People and old-line industries, like the railroad companies, that failed to keep up were left behind and often never recovered. People were freer to migrate across the country to seek fame, jobs or simply on a whim. Life would never be the same as it was at the turn of the century, when families were more rooted, less mobile.

Today it's the personal computer that's driving changes. Two decades after its introduction, the PC is emerging as a household educational and business tool and communications device; personal computers are now in well over 40 percent of U.S. homes, and may keep rising to 70 percent or more. Meanwhile we're moving into the next phase, which involves the development of the communications infrastructure that will allow computers to easily and rapidly communicate with each other, and move massive amounts of information around. The Internet, faster communications devices, and more useful software and easier-to-use computers are all part of this evolving picture. Much like the national highway system and thousands of new roads made it easier for the automobile to emerge fifty years ago, the new information highway will pave the way for the computer to transform our lives in new ways. When the dust settles, you'll be able to do things on computers that most of us could have only dreamed about a few years ago.

The good news is that it's still early in the game, with the PC and Internet, and by following ideas and steps in this book and getting involved, par-

Historical Tidbit

People think of the computer as launching the Information Age, but information technology dates back years. The telegraph in the 1800s had a powerful effect on the flow of information, which until then moved at only the speed of a train or horse. Suddenly, information could be transmitted instantaneously; space was no longer a barrier or constraint. It doesn't seem like a big deal today, but think about taking days, weeks or months to get the word that your sister had a baby or Uncle Fred died and left you a fortune. Today, of course, you can not only telephone, but send video e-mails or sound files, post photos on a family Web page—even do real-time video conferences.

ents can still get ahead of the curve and manage the change. That's the essence of a computer-smart parent.

The PC Dads Crystal Ball: Seven Wishes That Would Make Us Happy Campers

What is ahead? Everyone seems to have an opinion, but no one really knows. Rather than act like we can predict the future and tell you everything that's going to happen, we decided to develop a "wish list." Some of this stuff is already on the way; some of it is mere fantasies we'd like to see sometime in our lifetime. Anyhow, here are our top seven wishes. Think of this as an open letter from the PC Dads and moms and pops everywhere to the PC industry. We wish for a world where:

1. COMPUTERS CAN TALK AND LISTEN

There's nothing natural about typing or mouse-clicking or scrolling across a computer screen. Our fantasy is to replace mouse devices and keyboards with programs that let you run your computer via voice commands. We want the computer to understand *everything* we say—and carry out the orders without back talk. We'd like *something* that listens to us and consistently obeys (how's that for a concept?).

Think about the possibilities. Just sit back and dictate a letter, figure your income taxes or play a game, all using only your voice. You could even give a game a personality. Imagine playing chess with the computer, making a wrong move (via voice), and the computer laughs, cracks a joke and suggests what you could have done differently.

The real dream would be a voice-driven PC "traffic cop" that would manage information and steer messages from one family member to another. You could call your PC, have it read you your e-mail, faxes or whatever, and even assign it tasks. For example, if you're stuck in traffic, you could phone your computer (using voice commands so your hands are still on the wheel) and tell it to find your kids and ask them to get home. The computer would be smart enough to leave electronic messages on the children's home computers or their pagers. The kids might still ignore you, but at least you tried.

We may not be that far away from seeing full voice recognition systems emerge. Voice recognition programs by companies like Dragon Systems and IBM have made great strides. While they still tend to miss too many words, they've improved dramatically. We can't wait until they're ready for prime time.

2. COMPUTERS ARE FRIENDLY

Believe it or not, computers are drastically easier to deal with than a decade ago. You can do almost anything on the PC by simply pointing and clicking. Computer and software makers continue to come out with new ways to make life easier.

We're glad to see the crop of new, more stylish computers. Now we're getting spoiled. We want screens that fit neatly on the desktop or even hang on the wall, using flat panel displays. Imagine being able to walk into a room, touch a screen on the wall and have it come on immediately—no booting up, it just happens.

Friendly computers should be able to talk to other computers easily—to share files and printers and serve as communication devices between various computers. Right now you need to be a networking expert to make this happen. We want a smart computer you could plug into a wall socket of some kind, enabling it to hook up with all the other computers in your house. Or the computers should all be able to communicate using wireless radio signals or the telephone lines in our homes. It should all be a snap to operate and maintain.

3. COMPUTERS ARE EVERYWHERE

We'd like to expand beyond the single, central computer model. What about smaller "component" PCs spread around the house—one for each kid? They

"Wish I May, Wish I Might . . ."

When we ran a contest on America Online to gauge people's attitudes toward their computers, we received some interesting answers. The question was "If you had one wish, what would you change (or improve) about your computer?" The range of responses fell into three categories:

- **Serious:** Amazingly, people want computers that work right out of the box. This vocal segment says PCs should be easier to use and upgrade and should work flawlessly, without goofy errors, freezes or crashes. About half the answers had to do with making computers more user-friendly.

- **Humorous:** Many people wrote in with suggestions as to how their computers, with new improvements, could joke with them, spout funny quotes or even tame their kids (keep dreaming!).

- **Futuristic:** Many people want voice recognition and computers that surf the Internet for you or do other menial work. We heard it all. Why couldn't computers be more "human-like?"

One male user wished "that PCs had the ability to sense the user's emotional state, I dunno, maybe have a heat-sensing, photo electronic, video electric eye that could sense your emotion by registering the changes in your face by noticing the invisible heat caused by muscles in the human face. The advantage or use of this invention, would be that when a person is perplexed, the PC would automatically come up with a voice-activated help glossary. If a person is angry, it could sense it by the heat or change in facial muscular changes and work faster."

might be the size of today's laptop computers and linked to a bigger computer in a closet or basement that acts as a master information manager. They'd allow everyone to do their own thing—no more fighting over the computer. Mom or Dad could be in the kitchen checking out recipes on a flat "tablet" PC with a touch-screen display. Susie could be upstairs doing homework and connecting with experts online, Johnny could be checking car engine specs on CD-ROM videos on his garage computer and so on.

4. YOU CAN COMPUTE ON THE FLY

The new generation of mobile PCs is truly impressive—light, powerful, and nearly equaling what you find on a desktop computer. But sometimes we feel like we're fighting an uphill battle. What if hotels, airplanes, conference rooms, schools and coffee shops, among other places, set up computer hookups that let you plug in wherever you went? You'd just carry a book-size device containing your hard disk, a microprocessor and some electronics. The hotel would have the rest—the computer electronics, screen, keyboard, modem, online hookups and so forth. We'd really like to see computer setups on airplanes, and while we're at it, enough room to move our elbows. Then we could be wired and working all the time. Just plug, play—and pray (because of course there'll be glitches—nothing's perfect).

5. THE INTERNET GETS REAL

You can find almost anything on the Internet, but . . . there's so much more. Imagine being able to go on the Internet and find a babysitter, get quick legal help, buy a house, learn when your daughter has her next soccer practice or check on how your son is doing at school today. We're talking about a personalized Internet service.

Search engines and so-called "agents" (programs that find news and other stuff for you) need to be smarter to cut through all the clutter. We want to be able to send out an agent with a specific request and have it come back with a personalized list of five or ten solutions. Search engines and agents should cater to people's personal interests and whims, based on detailed personal profiles (I want a babysitter with two years' experience, at least two siblings, a B grade average or above, 16 or older, three solid references and who lives within a three-mile radius of my house). While we're at it, the agents could also weed out all those stupid unsolicited e-mails. You can even give your agents personalities.

Let's say we collect rare Beanie Babies, and a collector in Madison, Wisconsin, is selling these on the Net. The system should be smart enough to alert us and put us in contact with him. Agents might even go out and negotiate for us, arm-twisting other agents to get the best deal—yes, we know it's weird, but think of the time it would save.

And, speaking of the Internet, it needs to be faster—a lot faster. No one wants to spend two or three hours downloading a video. Luckily, help is on the way.

6. THE PC IS A KNOWLEDGE MACHINE

In many homes the computer is still just a fancy calculator and word processor and maybe a game machine. We want it to be a "knowledge machine," with the power of the computer used not to blow up evil aliens, but to teach kids how to think.

COOL NEW WAYS TO CONNECT
IN THE FUTURE

Most Internet surfers use a plain old telephone line to connect their modem and PC to the world. It's simple, already in place and relatively cheap. The downside is speed. It takes a long time to connect to multimedia content such as digital pictures and movies.

For the past few years a lot of research and development has gone into looking for and field testing faster alternatives. Talk to a techie about these emerging technologies and chances are good they will rattle off a bunch of acronyms and statistics, usually speed indicators expressed in megabits-per-second or kilo-bits-per-second. All this obsession with speed and racing faster and faster is meaningless unless you know how it can directly change and improve your experience surfing the Internet.

To put each of these technologies into perspective we'll use a typical real-world example to illustrate the benefits of speedier communications. Let's say you want to download a free trial copy of a cool new car-racing game. It's not uncommon for these files to be as big as 12 million bytes (12 megabytes). In the world of modem communications today, 12 million bytes, when you add some bits for quality control, comes to a total of 101,449,728 bits. As we highlight each alternative to the good old analog phone line modem we'll calculate how much thumb twiddling time you'd have to endure to receive that file.

The following list of technologies is not the final word on all alternatives to the plain old telephone line and traditional modems. Instead, these technologies were selected as they are the most likely candidates for home or small business use in the near future. Also, the amount of time estimates are just that, estimates. Your speed and mileage may vary due to phone line conditions and traffic on the Internet.

ISDN Modems. ISDN (Integrated Services Digital Network) modems are designed to use a special telephone line to connect to the world. With this technology it is possible to get speeds of 64,000 up to 128,000 bits-per-second, which would allow the 12 million byte file to reach your computer in about twenty-six and thirteen minutes respectively. Compare that to the latest 56,000 bits-per-second standard phone line modems (that actually, due to regulations, can only support a maximum speed of 53,000 bits-per-second) which would need about thirty-two minutes to deliver the file.

The downside of ISDN technology, especially for home users, is installation and cost. First, your local phone service company must offer ISDN service to your neighborhood. If you're lucky, your phone company can switch the existing telephone line to your house to support ISDN. Otherwise, get ready to pay hundreds of dollars for the phone company to "pull" a special ISDN line into your house. ISDN modems for your PC go for about $300, and monthly phone service fees are often several times more than your standard phone service.

Satellite Modems. Many technology companies are pushing the idea of sending Internet data via satellites. Hughes Network Services' DirecPC service, for example, supports speeds of up to 400,000 bits-per-second. You install a small satellite dish on your house, run a line from the dish to a special modem in your PC and you're ready to go. Here we could get our game file in a fraction more than four minutes. The equipment, using the DirectPC service as an example, will set you back about $300, with hourly access fees of up to $4.95 for the maximum 400,000 bits-per-second speed. Note: The high-speed benefit here is one-way. You still need a regular modem and phone line to send outgoing requests for Web access.

Microwave Modems. One of the most interesting new schemes involves the use of standard modems and phone lines to send information out combined with a high-speed microwave transmission back to you. In Portland, Oregon, where we live, there's a microwave Internet access service called WantWeb. Using a special modem designed to handle this hybrid combo of standard phone line and incoming microwave transmission, WantWeb can deliver anywhere from 750,000 to 1,500,000 bits-per-second of data into your PC from the Internet. Here the game file could reach you in about two and a quarter minutes or a little more than one minute respectively. Bringing this technology home involves a small wire antenna receiver on your rooftop and a coaxial cable (like the cable serving your TV) running from the antenna to the special modem. Costs run around $400 for installation with monthly fees of approximately $50. Warning: you can only use this technology if the location (i.e., position of the antenna) offers a clear "line of sight" with the microwave broadcasting tower.

Cable Modems. If you have cable TV, you're a potential candidate for what are called cable modems. Instead of plugging a modem into your standard phone outlet, you connect to the cable that's now feeding TV signals to your home. Commercially available cable modems, such as those offered by 3Com, support speeds from 1 to 2 million bits-per-second. Using this technology we could get the game file in about 51 seconds.

Before you get too excited, there are a couple of realities about cable modems we need to point out. First, the 2 million bits-per-second transmission rate is the speed that data can come to you, not the speed you can use to send data out from your PC. For a host of boring technical reasons, cable modems and cable service providers can't support two-way communications. To send information out you must use a standard modem and separate phone line.

There are other challenges facing their real-world deployment. To make it all work, your cable TV service provider has to support cable PC modems. The cable TV service also has to build in a new subscription business. On top of that, cable modems are much more expensive than standard models—up to $300 or more. Unfortunately, these obstacles continue to slow the progress of bringing this technology home. But, if speed is critical to you, it's worth asking your cable TV company if they offer this service. In communities where cable modem service is available, monthly fees for basic service go for about $40.00.

Asymmetric Digital Subscriber Line (ADSL). This is a technology developed by Bellcore in 1989 that can support two-way data communications using the plain old telephone line already installed in your home. Technically speaking, it promises to deliver up to 9 million bits-per-second of data "downstream" (that's from the computer with the Web page you want to your home PC) and up to 800,000 bits-per-second speeds for outgoing requests and messages. It'll take about eleven seconds for the game file to reach your PC using this technology. At the time of this writing ADSL was still being launched in a limited number of communities throughout the U.S. Contact your phone service company to see if they now offer, or plan to offer, ADSL and what monthly rates they plan to charge. Bell Atlantic's InfoSpeed ADSL service, for example, offers three monthly pricing schemes based on speed: $69.95 for up to 640,000 bits-per-second, $109.95 for 1,600,000 bits-per-second service, and $189.95 for 7,100,000 bits-per-second speed (note: the 7,100,000 bits-per-second is the top speed they support).

INSTANT RECAP

MODEM TECHNOLOGY	SPEED TO RECEIVE A FILE	THUMB TWIDDLING TIME TO RECEIVE THE 12 MEGABYTE FILE
Fast traditional modem	53,000 bits-per-second	32 minutes
ISDN	64,000 up to 128,000 bits-per-second	26 or 13 minutes
Satellite	400,000 bits-per-second	4 minutes
Microwave	750,000 or 1,500,000 bits-per-second	2.25 to approximately 1 minute 8 seconds
Cable	up to 2 million bits-per-second	51 seconds
ADSL	9 million bits-per-second	11 seconds

* All time estimates are based on ideal conditions. Your phone line quality and Internet traffic may cause the results to vary widely.

For that to happen, educational programs need to get even better—better graphics, better animation, better stories and plots (in other words, the same thing you see in games). Luckily we're already seeing this happen. Now we just need kids and parents to jump on the bandwagon. Imagine if your kids played a math game with the same intensity they play a car race game.

Schools also need to get computer hip, toss out the old computers and get top-of-the-line PCs with speedy Internet access. This could open up all kinds of opportunities. Kids in rural schools could take video-conferencing lessons from big-city experts, or communicate with other classes around the globe. Parents could connect with teachers in new ways. Imagine teachers posting assignments, schedules and personal updates on a Web page and communicating by e-mail to parents. Parents could check every night to see how their kid is doing relative to the rest of the class and maybe even how that class is progressing compared to other classes. Bulletin boards would allow parents to meet, trade notes and discuss issues. Sounds like a dream, but it's one that's already happening in a few schools today.

Ultimate PC Dads Fantasy
(Next to Getting Wealthy and Retiring to Montana)

7. ALL PARENTS ARE COMPUTER SMART

Our final fantasy is of a world of parents who know at least as much about computers and the Internet as their kids. Then the kids have to listen to them. Now that's a dream!

CONCLUSION

When I was a boy of fourteen, my father was so ignorant I could hardly stand to have the man around. But when I got be 21, I was astonished at how much he had learned in 7 years.—Mark Twain.

Some children grow up and reach their full potential on their own; we've all heard the stories of stars and celebrities who endured tortuous childhoods to emerge years later to be successful. But most children need a strong family and parents to help guide them, to help them learn what they're good at to discover who they really are. Children rely on the parents' wisdom and direction to avoid the biggest pitfalls and make the best use of their short time as kids. Lacking a parent's direction and vision, they may drift like ships lost at sea. But with the parent behind them, paving the way, they can dare to dream, to grow and be the best they can be in this crazy world.

The computer, if used correctly, can be a critical part of a healthy home environment. Not because it's a wonderful technology, but because it provides an ideal environment for the parent and child to bond, to learn, to grow together, to create a future. That's why we're here.

Good luck!

Mark and Ralph, the PC Dads

KIDS ON COMPUTERS

We also asked a group of elementary age kids, "What is one thing you wish the computer could do for you that it can't do for you now?" Here's what they said:

"Make me an artist."
—Suzy, age 10

"I wish it could talk to you."
—Jake, age 8

"Fly and take me to Africa so I could see what it's like there."
—Cassie, age 9

"Do my homework."
—Hector, age 9

"Drive me places."
—Jessica, age 9

"Take me to New Mexico."
—Fernando, age 9

"Walk to the store and buy me stuff."
—Araceli, age 9

"Jump to school so it can do my homework."
—Gustavo, age 9

"Speed up time to Halloween every year."
—Eric, age 11

"Speak to you and do your homework."
—Rafael, age 11

"Read your mind so then you don't have to type anything."
—Alex, age 10

FOCUSED QUESTIONS

- What do you like best about your computer?
- What do you wish the computer could do for you that it can't right now?
- What would your family's use of the computer change if the PC Dads wishes came true, for instance, if you could control your computer by talking rather than typing, and the Internet was safe, fast and practical?

- How would your spouse, kids or parents answer these questions?

- Are there other people in your world you'd like to help join the computer revolution? Your parents, maybe, or your retired neighbor or your friend who designs quilts? How might you share your computer enthusiasm with them?

- What do you want to be doing on the computer next year at this time? In two years? Five years? Ten years?

- Are you happy you bought this book?

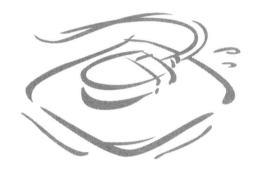

Glossary: The PC Dads Guide to ComputerSpeak

Get a few of these terms under your belt and you'll never fear computer sales literature again!

ADSL (Asymmetric Digital Subscriber Line) A technology that improves data communications over plain-old telephone lines. The "asymmetric" part is that ADSL divides up the phone line's bandwidth, using most of it for the Web-to-you communications (which usually involve a lot of data), and just a little for your commands to the Web (which are generally just a few bytes). The net effect is faster Web browsing and downloading. An ADSL connection to the Internet can support data traffic at up to 9 million bits-per-second.

Agent An automated program linked to the Internet that retrieves home pages of Web sites you designate and downloads the data to your hard drive so that you can read the pages offline. Sometimes called "smart agents" these little utility programs can also be used to scan information found in major online services. For example, America Online allows you to set up an agent program to search for news stories on a subject of interest to you. The information is gathered by the agent and delivered as messages to your electronic mailbox.

AGP (Accelerated Graphics Port) A newer type of PC graphics port that gives you better performance for games and other 3D graphics–intensive programs than older graphics cards that plugged into the standard PCI slots/connectors.

Analog Stuff that happens continuously rather than in discrete digits. Lots of the non-computer world is analog—for example, sounds, movies, photographs, ordinary phone lines—and has to be converted to digital codes or formats before it can be used by computers.

AOL (America Online) The largest online service; they provide you with a program that lets you connect (via a local telephone number) to their service, so you can send and receive e-mail, browse the Web and use other Internet services. In addition to Internet access AOL offers subscribers a slew of member services such as news, chat rooms and financial forums.

Application A set of instructions that tell the computer to do some useful work for you. Word processors, spreadsheets and databases are all examples of applications. Also called a program.

Back up To copy a file from one thing to another for the purpose of protecting your data should something bad happen to your hard disk. The simplest way to back up on a PC is to copy a file(s) from your hard disk to a floppy disk. Other ways include copying files from a hard disk to a tape drive or to one of many so-called "removable" storage products that can hold anywhere from 100 megabytes to multiple gigabytes of data. (Backing up important files is a good thing to do.)

Bandwidth The measure of how much data can move over various types of lines in a given amount of time. For example, ISDN lines, with the ability to handle up to 128,000 bits-per-second have much more bandwidth than ordinary phone lines using a standard 56,000 bits-per-second modem.

Baud An oldtimer's way of describing bits-per-second transmission rates when using modems. A rate of 300 baud is translated to 300 bits-per-second. Today the kilo-bits-per-second rating is king.

Bit The smallest unit of the digital code system computers use to represent text characters, numbers, pictures, sound or any other information. It's kind of like the genetic code for computers. 8 bits = 1 byte, and 1 byte can represent a letter or a number. You'll also see things like a 32-bit bus or a 64-bit sound card—those refer to how many bits of information the bus or sound card handles at a time. More is better.

Boot 1. To start up a computer with a software program (the operating system). 2. Part of the PC Dads western garb. Trivia: "Boot" comes from the word "bootstrap"—the handles on a boot. When you use a program to start up a computer it's "bootstrapping" itself—pulling on its own boots. Get it?

bps (bits-per-second) The basic unit of measure for the speed of data transmissions. Modems at your local computer store today range all the way up to 56,000 bits-per-second.

Browser The point-and-click software you use to navigate the World Wide Web. Netscape Communicator and Internet Explorer are the two big browsers.

Bulletin board system (BBS) A computer program that automatically answers other computers' modem phone calls and lets the calling computer upload and download files, post messages, and so forth.

Bundled The term used to refer to the practice of combining multiple products from several makers to create a package deal. The most common example is a PC system sold with a set of software programs "bundled" from different vendors.

Bus The "highway" that transports information electronically from one part of the computer to another (for example, from the memory chips, add-on cards, floppy to the CPU). A fast bus is good.

Byte A group of eight bits that represents a digit or character, and the basic unit for measuring the storage capacity of a disk, the amount of memory in your computer, or the size of a file. Your hard drive might have anywhere from a few hundred million bytes (megabytes or MB) to a few billion bytes (gigabytes or GB).

Cable modem A fast, new modem that connects your computer to the Internet by hooking up to the cable in your home that provides your TV signal.

Cache Special high-speed memory in your PC. Cache memory pops up in a couple of ways on a PC. A chunk of your PC's main memory (RAM) can be set up as speedy cache memory to hold instructions readily accessible that the brain chip will use over and over. A portion of your hard disk may also be set up as a virtual cache memory holder. Modern microprocessors, such as Intel's Pentium II processor, have their own close-to-the-heart cache memory. A system with lots of cache memory and a microprocessor with its own cache memory will run faster as the brain will spend much less time waiting for instructions to come from the hard disk to main memory.

CD-ROM (compact disk, read-only memory) A PC storage device that looks a lot like a CD player, except it runs PC software programs in addition to playing music CDs. Software manufacturers like CD-ROMs as they can hold up to 650 megabytes of data (equal to 700 floppy disks). CD-ROMs have basically replaced floppy disks for installing information on your PC; however, most can "read-only" and not record data. In other words you can't move information from your PC to most CDs, as you can with floppy disks. CD-ROM devices that can read and allow you to write one time to blank CD disks are now available for around $300.

Chat rooms These are like online coffee shops, except you can't see who you're talking to. You can find them hosted by major online services such as America Online, CompuServe or MSN or via Web sites on the Internet. Chat rooms are usually focused on one subject, like horses or marital issues. You communicate by typing messages in your computer and responding to other people's messages, all of which flash across the computer screen.

Client A computer that's receiving services from another computer. When you're on the Internet, your computer is the *client*, and the computer you're connected to is the server.

Clip art A collection of ready-made artwork, symbols and digital photos you can add to documents or your desktop publishing work. Many word processors, desktop publishing and graphics packages come with clip art; you can also buy separate packages full of clip art. Most clip art software packages contain royalty-free artwork.

COM port Short for communications port. A receptacle (usually on the back of your computer) where you can plug in devices like modems and printers. If your computer has more than one COM port, they're labeled COM1, COM2, and so on.

Command An order or direction you give the computer, or an instruction to the brain chip coming from a program. Command-driven programs wait for you to type in an instruction, while menu-driven programs let you pick a command or function from a menu displayed on the screen. Some new programs let you command the computer by speaking to it.

CPU (central processing unit) Essentially, the brains of the computer; the chip, or set of chips that receives and responds to your commands, the programs you run, and the automatic internal processes of the computer. Intel Pentium or Pentium II processors are the most popular CPUs for desktop PCs, with the PowerPC chips running Apple's Macintosh computers. Also called the microprocessor.

Crash The failure of a system, program or piece of equipment such as a hard disk.

Cyberspace Fancy term for the Internet, World Wide Web and the online world in general.

Data Information a computer can do something with (coded in the form of bits and bytes). Data is stored on the hard disk of your computer, comes in via the Internet through your phone line and modem, or is entered by you (using a keyboard). Once inside your PC, data can be stored or processed for you. The e-mail message to your cousin in San Diego, the photo you scan in for your family newsletter, the budget details in your spreadsheet—those are all considered data.

Database manager A computer program that stores, organizes and retrieves information. Popular database manager programs include Microsoft's *Access* and Borland International's *Paradox*.

Defragmentation program A utility program that gathers related data fragments from the hard disk and then lays them back down in a contiguous segment. Doing this regularly can speed up your computing tasks by making it faster for the computer to get information off the hard disk. Windows 95 and 98 include a disk defragmentation utility.

Desktop What your computer screen shows you when you first turn it on, e.g., the screen you see first when you start the Windows operating system is called your desktop. The desktop, in turn, displays the icons (symbols) for the programs you can run.

Desktop publishing (DTP) Programs that make it a snap to produce professional-looking leaflets, business cards, handouts, newsletters, calendars and signs for families, small businesses, clubs and nonprofit organizations.

Dialogue box The box that pops up on your screen and lets you enter commands or give information to your computer about your preferences. Sometimes called menu boxes.

Digital The opposite of analog. The digital world measures things by discrete units rather than smoothly continuous values. A watch that says you ran a mile in 8.23.57 seconds is digital; the face of a grandfather clock is analog. Computers are digital, and deep down, they record everything as a bunch of 1s and 0s.

Digital camera A camera that doesn't use film but stores pictures digitally in the camera's memory. You then download your pictures from the camera's memory directly to your PC. Once on your hard disk you can view, edit, print or attach your images to an e-mail message.

Directory A group of related files stored in a virtual "file folder" on your hard disk, floppy disk, or other storage device. A typical hard disk contains lots of directories, some created and named by the end user along with others automatically created by the operating system or programs loaded on the system.

Download To bring information or pictures into your computer from another computer or peripheral device to which you're connected (via a modem, cable, etc.).

DVD (Digital Versatile Disk or Digital Video Disk) A new generation of data storage device sometimes offered in addition to (or in place of) a CD-ROM drive. DVD disks (which look the same as an audio or PC program CD-ROM disk) can store a minimum of 4.7 billion bytes of data, as compared to a maximum of 650 million bytes of storage supported by traditional CD-ROMs. These babies can run DVD full-length digital movies, play all your existing CD-ROM PC software and even play your music CDs.

E-mail (electronic mail) Just like old-fashioned letters, except you compose them on your PC and mail them over the Internet. Transmission time is minutes instead of days.

Emoticons A combination of punctuation symbols and other characters that express emotion in documents, on e-mail, in chat rooms, e.g., **:-)** means happy,

:-(means sad or disappointed (look at them sideways if you don't see the connection at first).

ESRB (Entertainment Software Rating Board) An organization that rates PC software.

ESRBI (Entertainment Software Rating Board Interactive) A Web site ratings system that rates content on Web sites by using content descriptors. See also *RSACi* and *SafeSurf*.

File An accumulation of information stored as a single unit on a hard or floppy disk or CD-ROM.

Fixed disk drive A disk drive with nonremovable disks (as opposed to a floppy disk drive where you can insert and remove disks). The so-called hard disk inside your PC is a fixed disk drive. You can't remove the platters inside it.

Floppy disk A small, portable disk used to store documents and files that you want to save or transfer from one computer to another. (The floppy part is a holdover from the original floppy disks, which were flexible and larger than the ones we use today.)

Folder A directory on the hard disk or CD that stores a bunch of related files.

Font A set of characters of the same type size or style (typeface).

Forum An Internet discussion group.

Freeware Games and programs that you can download for free from the Internet. Most freeware software carries messages from the authors asking you to buy the program if you like it. Often, freeware software has a time limit. For example, you can download the program and use it for thirty days only.

Gigabyte (GB) A billion bytes. See also *byte, megabyte*.

Going online Accessing the Internet or the World Wide Web or a commercial online service from your computer.

Gopher An older search program that lets you find documents on the Internet by using menus to "go for" whatever item you request. Gopher was invented at the University of Minnesota and named after the school's mascot, the Golden Gophers.

Graphics adapter The hardware inside a PC that helps display pictures and video. Also called a graphics display card.

GUI (Graphical User Interface) A program with graphical features like windows and menus that allow for easy navigation on the PC, e.g., Microsoft Windows.

Hard disk A computer's permanent data file cabinet, the place where information is stored for later use. Also called a hard drive.

Hardware The parts of a computer you can touch and see, like the CPU and the memory chips. Often contrasted to *software*.

Home page The front door or starting point to a Web site on the Internet.

HTML (Hyper Text Markup Language) The code used for creating documents on the World Wide Web. These codes tell your Web browser how to display the text and how to connect a document to related information on the Web.

Hyperlink A "clickable" link (a graphical button or underlined words or phrases) on a Web site that lets you zoom from one Web page or document to another.

Icon A cute little picture on your computer screen that represents a document, a program, a file or other object. Clicking on the icon using your mouse opens the file or program.

Information ("Info") Highway City slicker word for the Internet.

Initialize To reset a program or computer to particular starting values. Some techies call formatting a floppy "initializing" it.

Ink-jetprinters The most popular type of printer for home and small business use. Ink-jet printers squirt teeny tiny droplets of ink on the paper.

Internet (the "Net") A big bunch of computers, networks and online services strapped together through a global, sprawling communications network. These computers talk to each other using an internationally accepted lingo, and anyone who connects to one of these and has the appropriate software can send e-mail, download files, browse the World Wide Web and chat with people from around the world.

ISDN (Integrated Services Digital Network) A special digital telephone line with a faster speed than ordinary analog telephone lines.

ISP (Internet Service Provider) A local or national company that connects your computer to the Internet (if your computer has a modem).

Joystick A stick used by hand for controlling the play of computer games.

Keyboard The input device for most PCs, used to type and enter commands.

Kilobyte One thousand twenty-four bytes. In the old days, when floppy drives had much smaller capacity, you used to hear a lot about 360 kilobyte floppies. Today, it's rare to hear kilobyte used around computer people.

Laptop See *notebook computer*.

Laser printers High-quality, usually monochrome, printers extremely popular with business PC users. These printers use a toner-based process. They produce sharper text and graphics than ink-jet printers, printing each page very quickly on any type of paper.

Load To transfer program instructions or data from disk to the computer's memory.

Megabyte (MB) A unit for measuring the storage capacity of a disk, the amount of memory in your computer or the size of a file. One megabyte is 1,048,576 bytes.

Megahertz (MHz) A measure of the speed with which the CPU, or microprocessor, can process information. The higher the number, the faster the computer. For microprocessors "hertz" is the number of times that a switch (called transistors by the chip crowd) can go from on to off or vice versa (also called "states" by the techies) in one second. Everything a microprocessor does is based on whether a transistor, or group of transistors working together, is on or off. The faster you can switch states the more decisions can be made in a second, which translates into more power for demanding things like multimedia.

Memory Special chips inside the PC that store data and files while you (or the computer) are working on them. (When you're through, the computer moves the files and data to a more permanent storage place like your hard disk.) In the old days, hard disks and floppies were thought of as memory. Today, the term generally refers to your PC's RAM (random access memory).

Microprocessor See *CPU*.

Microwave modem A new approach to accessing the Internet that combines the use of a special high-speed microwave PC receiver for incoming information and standard modems and phone lines to send outgoing requests for a Web page.

Modem The computer's "telephone." Traditional modems take the digital bits and bytes a PC can understand and converts the information into the analog form that regular telephone lines can handle. Today many forms of modems exist, including satellite modems, cable modems and microwave modems.

Monitor The "TV thing" that sits in front of you and displays whatever you're doing on the computer. Also called the display or screen.

Moore's Law A rule stated by Gordon Moore of Intel Corporation that every eighteen months or so the speed of the microprocessor (actually, the number of transistors) doubles.

Motherboard Part of the guts of your PC; a green circuit board about a foot square that the brain chip, graphics card, modem card, keyboard and floppy drives all plug into via some form of connector (internal or external).

Mouse A small, hand-held device you use to access commands and program features on the computer screen. You roll the mouse over the mouse pad (a smooth rubber mat) and point and click as the on-screen cursor points at the item you want.

Multimedia A combination of sound and advanced graphics found in today's educational and entertainment software. Multimedia "rich" programs include video, high-resolution digital pictures and audio elements.

Multitasking Performing two or more tasks on the computer at the same time, like downloading e-mail in one window while you're typing something in another one. The Windows operating system and the power of modern processors, such as the Intel Pentium II and Celeron processors, allow you to multitask between several applications.

Newbie A novice; a person who's new to Internet-related or other computer activities.

Newsgroups Services on the Internet where you post messages, read responses to your message (or other messages) and send or receive files between various people. The files you can send or receive can be text, computer programs, pictures and so on.

Notebook computer A portable computer that's smaller, more fragile and more expensive than regular desktop PCs. Notebooks can be powered by battery or power line to a electrical wall outlet, and most come with a built-in modem so you can hook up to a phone line and access the Internet. Also called a laptop computer.

Online Connected to the Internet or another computer via a communications link.

Operating system (OS) A software program, Microsoft's Windows being the most popular, that kicks into action before any other programs and controls all the parts of the computer.

Parallel port A port used typically to connect a printer into your computer. A parallel port sends data in parallel bits instead of one bit at a time, but it can only transport data reliably for fifteen to twenty feet.

PC Personal computer. At one time this term was used for IBM personal computers only, to distinguish them from Apple Macintosh and other non-IBM or IBM clone desktops. Today the term is loosely used to describe any desktop computer, specifically IBMs or compatible computers such as Packard Bell, Gateway, Dell, Compaq.

Pentium processor Intel's latest family of processors for PCs. The Pentium processor line was introduced in 1993.

Peripheral An external device you connect to your PC. A printer, a box modem, a monitor, a scanner, a digital camera, a mouse, or an external box hard drive or tape unit are all peripherals.

PICS (Platform for Internet Content Selection) An industry standard established by a group of twenty-two companies for software that works with your browser and helps block access to objectionable Web sites. The PICS standard is used by a variety of ratings schemes to filter out Web sites based on parameters you can set to match your family's values, your kids' ages and other factors.

Port A computer port is a thing that lets you connect something to your PC. There are internal and external ports. Inside your PC there are connectors for connecting the hard drive and display screens. External PC ports include a serial port for modems, digital cameras or scanners, a parallel port for printers or scanners, and connectors for the keyboard and mouse. Modern PCs also include a new high-speed Universal Serial Port that looks like a big, flat telephone jack.

Program An application or other piece of software.

Prompt A request from the computer for you to provide more information or a command.

Protocol A bunch of communications settings that computers use when they want to talk to each other. The rules and formats for communication established by a protocol can be thought of as an agreed-upon language two computers can use to communicate.

RAM (random access memory) A set of memory chips that serve as temporary storage for information from computer programs. See also *memory*.

RSACi (Recreational Software Advisory Council on the Internet) A Web site ratings system that rates content on Web sites by using categories such as violence. See also *ESRBI* and *SafeSurf*.

SafeSurf A Web site ratings system that applies a complex and comprehensive series of numeric codes to rate content on Web sites. See also *ESRBI* and *RSACi*.

Satellite modem A high-speed modem connected to a satellite dish that receives Internet data at speeds ranging up to 400,000 bits-per-second.

Scanner A device you can connect to your PC to scan text, photographs or graphic images and convert them into electronic images that you can then view on your screen, store on your PC or send to other PC users.

Screen saver A program that kicks in if the computer isn't used for a while and prevents stagnant images from permanently burning or damaging the screen. The Windows operating system comes with a variety of screen savers, and you can also buy your own or download free ones from the Internet.

Search engine A program that searches the Internet for you. You tell it what topic you want more information on, and it gives you a list of the Web documents it finds.

Serial port A port used to connect devices such as printers and modems into your computer. Serial communications are reliable over long distances and work by transferring bits of data one at a time (that's the serial part) rather than transferring several bits of data on a multilane highway at once, as a parallel port does. See also *parallel port*.

Server The computer your PC is connected to when you're using the Internet. (Your PC is the client.) When you send e-mail, your Internet Service Provider's e-mail server acts as an electronic post office and sends the e-mail to the correct address. At work your computer may be connected with other units in a Local Area Network. Here you'll also find computers that act as servers for the many individual PCs linked together on the network.

Shareware Programs you can download from the Internet and use for a free trial period before you decide whether to buy them.

Slot Receptacles on the big circuit board of your PC (called the motherboard) into which you can plug in extra items such as more memory, a modem card or even a card that will allow you to watch TV on your PC.

Snail mail Internet slang for the Postal Service, or any traditional postal service, known for its lack of speed compared to e-mail.

Software A comprehensive term for the programs that run on your computer, including the operating system (like Windows 98) and applications. See also *hardware*.

Sound card An add-on card or set of chips on the motherboard of the PC that processes and translates the various digital audio inputs of a program into the sounds you hear from your PC's speakers. Tip: a 64-bit sound card or built-in system will produce better sound than a 16-bit system.

Spreadsheet A program such as Microsoft *Excel* that lets you organize numerical and other information into grids and calculates numeric results for you. You might use a spreadsheet to set up a family budget.

Streaming video A technology for the Internet that makes it possible to deliver video continuously as opposed to the older method of downloading an entire video file to the receiving PC before it can be viewed. When you request a video or audio file from a Web site using streaming technology, the digital data starts to stream into your PC immediately, as opposed to the total download routine mentioned above. Just enough data is transmitted to get things going with the balance coming in waves or chunks as needed. The downside to streaming video is quality. The act of simultaneously receiving and displaying digital video is super demanding and tradeoffs are made in quality and smoothness.

Suite A collection of applications or programs.

Surfing the net Exploring Web pages on the Internet, often randomly.

System requirements The bare bones equipment you need to operate a software program on your PC.

TCP/IP (Transmission Control Protocol/Internet Protocol) A set of rules that controls the transfer of information over the Internet.

Toolbar Usually found at the top of a program window, this is a row of buttons you click to initiate a feature (such as cut or paste) or to open up a menu or dialogue box into which you enter commands.

Tower A PC box that stands up separately from the monitor, as opposed to traditional desktop horizontal PC boxes upon which the monitor is placed. We like the tower PCs because they usually give you more room to expand and they're much easier to work on (i.e., open up) than the horizontal models.

Universal Serial Bus (USB) A new high-speed external-peripherals connector that lets you hook up lots of different types of products. The idea behind the USB connector is to have one type of connector for all the external peripherals that hook up to a PC instead of an array of serial, parallel and other separate connectors. A USB connector looks a lot like an ordinary phone jack.

Upgrading Putting a new brain chip, more memory, a fancier graphics adapter, etc., into your PC so it runs faster and/or runs programs it was too wimpy to run before.

Upload To transfer data to another computer through either a modem and a telephone line or through a network connection.

URL (Uniform Resource Locator) The address or location of Web pages on the Internet. Pronounced "earl." www.intel.com is an example of an URL.

Usenet groups A set of worldwide newsgroups where you can share ideas and information with other people. Usenet groups are an older service on the Internet and don't require the use of a browser or the Web. They're also unmonitored in contrast to forums and newsgroups run by private Internet Service Providers such as America Online and CompuServe.

Virtual A fancy term for simulating something on a computer. Often used combined with reality, as in virtual reality.

Virus A destructive program that attaches itself to other files on the hard drive or floppy disk and may erase or make strange changes to them. Computer viruses come from copying a file from an infected floppy disk or downloading an infected file from an Internet site. When you execute the file you were trying to copy or download, you initiate the virus, and it may spread to other files. Virus protection software can help you detect and destroy viruses before they damage your PC.

Voice recognition program Software that makes it possible to run a PC by speaking to it, or that lets you dictate a letter or memo. IBM's *ViaVoice* and Dragon Systems *Naturally Speaking* are two examples.

Wallpaper Your desktop's background, ranging from a solid color that stays the same to designs that move around.

Web browser A software program that helps you view what's on the Internet by pointing and clicking on pictures and home pages. Netscape Communicator and Microsoft Internet Explorer are the leading Web browsers as of this writing.

Web filtering software A program that acts like an online watchdog, constantly monitoring and blocking access to adult sites and other Internet hot spots.

Web site A place where information lives on the World Wide Web; Web sites can be created by companies or by individuals.

Window A way of displaying information in different sections of the screen.

Word processor A program you use to create documents, i.e., you enter text by typing it on the keyboard, make changes to it till it's just the way you want it, format it (fix the fonts and spacing) so it looks cool, then save it, print it out or send it to someone else via an e-mail attachment.

World Wide Web (WWW; "the Web") A special feature of the Internet where you use a browser to navigate the information on the Internet. The Internet has been around for years, but it wasn't till the invention of the Web (including hyperlinks and browsers) that it became easy enough for regular folks to use. The Web lets you jump around the Internet and surf without having to know any kooky computer language. Also see *browser, hyperlink, Internet*.

Appendix

FAVORITE SOFTWARE, WEB SITES AND RESOURCES

FAVORITE SOFTWARE

Kid-friendly interface and computer control programs

Plus! For Kids for Windows 95 by Microsoft (age 5 and up)

Kid Desk Family Edition by Edmark (age 5 and up)

Art/creativity programs

Kid Pix Studio by Broderbund (ages 3–12)

Crayola Art Studio by Micrografx (age 5 and up)

Inspiration by Inspiration Software (age 12 and up)

T-shirt Maker & More by Hanes Printables (age 12 and up)

American Greetings Crafts by Mindscape (age 10 and up)

Desktop publishing

Microsoft Publisher 98 by Microsoft (age 12 and up)

Ultimate Writing & Creativity Center by The Learning Company (ages 6–10)

Greeting card software

Greetings Workshop by Microsoft (age 6 and up)

Print Artist by Sierra (age 10 and up)

Kid Cuts by Broderbund (an add-on to *Kid Pix Studio*) (ages 3–12)

American Greetings Create a Card by Mindscape (age 10 and up)

Educational

Math programs

Math Blaster series by Davidson Software

    Episode 1: In Search of Spot (ages 6–12)

    Episode 2: Secret of the Lost City (ages 8–12)

    Math Blaster Jr. (ages 4–7)

    Math Blaster Mystery: The Great Brain Robbery (age 10 and up)

Major League Math by Sanctuary Woods (ages 8–12)

Baseball Math by Sanctuary Woods (ages 8–12)

Math for the Real World by Davidson (age 10 and up)

Mighty Math series by Edmark

    Astro Algebra (ages 11–14)

    Calculating Crew (ages 8–10)

    Carnival Countdown (ages 5–7)

    Cosmic Geometry (ages 11–14)

    Number Heroes (ages 8–10)

    Zoo Zillions (ages 5–7)

Amazing Math Starring Marvel Super Heroes by Brighter Child Interactive (ages 8–14)

Math Heads by Theatrix (ages 9–13)

Millie's Math House by Edmark (ages 2–6)

James Discovers Math by Broderbund (ages 5–8)

Reading programs

Just Grandma and Me by Living Books (ages 2–5)

Reader Rabbit series by The Learning Company

    Reader Rabbit 1 (ages 4-6) and *Reader Rabbit 2* (ages 6–8)

    Reader Rabbit's Interactive Reading Journey Volume 1 (ages 5–8) and *Volume 2* (ages 4–7)

Arthur books (*Arthur's Teacher Trouble*) by Living Books (ages 3–7)

Dr. Seuss's ABC and *Green Eggs and Ham* by Living Books (ages 2–6)

Let's Go Read by Edmark (ages 4–6)

Ready to Read with Pooh by Disney Interactive (ages 3–6)

Sesame Street Elmo's Preschool by Creative Wonders (ages 2–5)

Reading Blaster 2000 by Davidson (ages 4–7)

The Great Reading Adventure by Kid's World (ages 5–9)

Richard Scarry's Best Reading Program Ever by Simon & Schuster
    Interactive (ages 3–6)

Science programs

Magic Schoolbus series by Microsoft (ages 6–10)

Thinkin' Things by Edmark
    Collection 1 (ages 3–8)
    Collection 2 (ages 6–12)
    Collection 3 (ages 7–13)

Super Solvers Gizmos & Gadgets! by The Learning Company (ages 7–12)

Multi-subject educational suites

My Personal Tutor series (Preschool: ages 2–5; Kindergarten: ages 4–6;
    first and second grade) by Microsoft

JumpStart series (Preschool: ages 2–5; Kindergarten: ages 4–6; first,
    second and third grade) by Davidson

Dr. Seuss Preschool (ages 2–5) and *Dr. Seuss Kindergarten* (ages 4–6)
    by Broderbund

Financial management

Money by Microsoft (age 12 and up)

Quicken by Intuit (age 12 and up)

Games

General games

Putt-Putt series by Humongous Entertainment (ages 3–8)

Adventures with Barbie Ocean Discovery by Mattel Media (ages 5–9)

Tomb Raider by Eidos Interactive (age 12 and up)

Simulation games

SimCity series by Maxis:
    SimCity 2000 (age 12 and up)
    The Streets of SimCity (ages 8–12)
    SimPark (ages 8–12)

SimTown (ages 8–12)

SimIsle (age 12 and up)

Oregon Trail III by The Learning Company (ages 10–16)

Amazon Trail II by The Learning Company (ages 10–16)

MayaQuest by The Learning Company (ages 10–16)

Action games (low violence, ages 8 and up)

Monster Truck Madness II by Microsoft

Need for Speed by Electronic Arts

Pod by UbiSoft

VR Sports Powerboat Racing by Interplay Productions

Test Drive Off-Road by Accolade

Redline Racer by UbiSoft

Jet Fighter II by Interplay Productions

SWIV by Interplay Productions

NHL Powerplay '98 by Virgin Interactive

VR Soccer by Interplay Productions

Hardball series by Accolade

Star Wars series by Lucasarts Entertainment Company

Action games with educational value

Flight Simulator 98 by Microsoft (age 10 and up)

Age of Empires II by Microsoft (age 10 and up)

Command & Conquer by Westwood Studios (age 8 and up)

Skill-building games

Chessmaster 5500 by Mindscape (age 9 and up)

The Incredible Machine by Sierra On-line (age 8 and up)

I Spy by Scholastic (ages 5–9)

Logic Quest by The Learning Company (ages 8–14)

Board/arcade games

Life by Hasbro Interactive (age 6 and up)

Monopoly by Hasbro Interactive (age 6 and up)

Sorry! by Hasbro Interactive (age 6 and up)

Frogger by Hasbro Interactive (age 6 and up)

Centipede by Hasbro Interactive (age 6 and up)

Girls' software

Purple Moon titles (ages 8–12)

Rockett's New School, Rockett's Tricky Decision, Rockett's Secret Invitation, Rockett's Adventure Maker, Rockett's Starfire Soccer Challenge, Secret Paths in the Forest and *Secret Paths to the Sea.*

The American Girls Premier by The Learning Company (age 8 and up)

Cosmopolitan Virtual Makeover by Sega Soft

Barbie Fashion Designer by Mattel Media (ages 5–9)

The Magic Schoolbus series by Microsoft (ages 6–10)

The Carmen Sandiego series by Broderbund

Where in the USA is Carmen Sandiego? (ages 8–12)

Where in the World is Carmen Sandiego? (ages 8–12)

Where in the World is Carmen Sandiego? Junior Detective Version (ages 5–8)

Myst by Broderbund (age 10 and up)

Creative Writer 2 by Microsoft (age 8 and up)

3D Movie Maker by Microsoft (age 10 and up)

Cyber safety

Cyber Patrol by The Learning Company (adult)

CYBERsitter by Solid Oak Software (adult)

Net Nanny by Net Nanny Software International (adult)

SurfWatch by SurfWatch Software (adult)

Presentation

PowerPoint by Microsoft (age 12 and up)

Reference

Grolier Multimedia Encyclopedia by Grolier Interactive (age 8 and up)

Encarta Encyclopedia Deluxe series by Microsoft (ages 10–17)

Encarta Virtual Globe by Microsoft (ages 10–17)

ABC World Reference: 3D ATLAS '98 by Creative Wonders (age 10 and up)

The Complete National Geographic by Mindscape (age 9 and up)

Knowledge Adventure: Random House Kids Encyclopedia by Random
   House (ages 7–12)

Skill building

Driving
   Driver's Education '98 by Sierra (age 8 and up)
Typing
   Mavis Beacon Teaches Typing by Mindscape (age 8 and up)
   Mario Teaches Typing by Interplay (ages 5–9)
   JumpStart Typing by Davidson (ages 7–10)

Spreadsheet

Lotus 123 by Lotus Development (age 12 and up)
Excel by Microsoft (age 12 and up)

Word processing

Word by Microsoft (age 8 and up)
Creative Writing Center and *Creative Writer* by Microsoft
   (age 8 and up)
The Amazing Writing Machine by Broderbund (ages 6–12)
The Ultimate Writing & Creativity Center by The Learning Company
   (ages 6–10)
Student Writing and Research Center by The Learning Company (age 9
   and up)

Travel planning

AAA Map'n'Go by Delorme (age 12 and up)
Trip Planner by Microsoft (age 12 and up)

Web Page Design and Creation

Hot Dog by Sausage Software (age 12 and up)
Front Page 98 by Microsoft (age 12 and up)
Web Workshop by Vividus (age 10 and up)

Genealogy Programs

Ultimate Family Tree by Palladium Interactive (age 12 and up)

Family Tree Maker by Broderbund (age 12 and up)

FAVORITE WEB SITES

PC Dads (www.intel.com/go/pcdads)

Best sites by category

The Mining Company (www.miningco.com)

College information

U.S. News & World Report's education site
(www.usnews.com/usnews/edu/home.htm)

College Funding Company (www.collegefundingco.com)

College and University information
(dir.yahoo.com/Education/Higher_Education/College_Entrance)

The Financial Aid Information Page (www.finaid.org)

FastWEB (www.fastweb.com)

SRN Express (www.rams.com/srn)

ExPAN Scholarship Search
(www.collegeboard.org/fundfinder/bin/fundfind01.pl)

The National College Resource Association (www.collegeresource.com)

Computer information

General

FamilyPC magazine (www.zdnet.com/familypc)

Smart Computing magazine (www.pcnovice.com)

Manufacturers

Dell Computers (www.dell.com/dfs/leasing)

Gateway (www.gateway.com)

PC donations

(www.wco.com/~dale/list.html)

Technical support

AnswerExpress 1-888-795-7357 (www.answerexpress.com)

The PC Crisis Line (www.pccrisis.com)1-800-828-4358

Used computers

American Computer Exchange (www.amcoex.com) 1-800-786-0717

Computer camps

American Computer Experience (www.computercamp.com)

Kids 'n Computers (calgary.shaw.wave.ca/~knc)

Kids' Camps (www.kidscamps.com)

Educational websites

For homework help

The Research Paper (www.researchpaper.com)

Study Web (www.studyweb.com)

B.J. Pinchbeck's Homework Helper (tristate.pgh.net/~pinch13)

Homework Helpers (w3.trib.com/%7Edont/hwhelp.html)

Kids' Web (www.npac.syr.edu/textbook/kidsweb)

Yahooligan's School Bell
   (www.yahooligans.com/School_Bell/Homework_Answers)

For home schooling help

Train-up-a-child (www.techplus.com/ncm/TUAC.html)

MultiMag Homeschool Magazines on the WWW
   (multimag.com/home)

National Homeschool Association (www.n-h-a.org)

The Homeschool Zone (www.caro.net/~joespa)

Homeschoolers' Curriculum Swap (theswap.com)

Knowledge Adventure (www.knowledgeadventure.com/home)

Educational material clearinghouse

ERIC (the Educational Resources Information Center)
   (www.aspensys.com/eric)

Family Web sites

Yooligans (www.yahooligans.com)

Disney (family.disney.com)

Edmark (www.edmark.com)

Parents Soup (www.parentsoup.com)

Financial management

The Young Investor Web Site (www.younginvestor.com or younginvestor.com/pick.shtml)

Free e-mail

Juno (www.juno.com)

Girls/women's Web sites

iVillage.com (www.village.com)

Women Online (www.women.com)

Expect the Best from a Girl and That's What You'll Get (www.academic.org)

Club Girl Tech (www.girltech.com)

New Moon (www.newmoon.org)

Purple Moon (www.purple-moon.com)

Online safety

National Center for Missing and Exploited Children Web site (www.missingkids.com) 1-800-843-5678

E-mail blocker shareware
www.zdnet.com

Filtering software sites

Cyber Patrol from The Learning Company (www.cyberpatrol.com)

CYBERsitter from Solid Oak Software (www.solidoak.com/cysitter.htm)

Net Nanny from Net Nanny Software International, Inc. (www.netnanny.com)

SurfWatch Software from SurfWatch Software
(www.surfwatch.com/home)

Kid safety

www.missingkids.com (National Center for Missing and Exploited
Children)

www.uab.edu/pedinfo/Control.html (List of cyber safety software
programs)

www.safesurf.com (The "original Internet rating system")

www.cyberangels.org (Internet safety organization)

www.safekids.com (Child safety on the info highway)

www.larrysworld.com/articles/parentright.htm (See article: "Rights of
Parents in the Digital Age")

www.zdnet.com/zdnn/content/zdnn/1201/249786.html (See article:
"Few Parents Use Filtering Software")

www.larrysworld.com/articles/kidspriv.htm (See article: "Marketers Are
a Bigger Threat to Your Kids Than Porno")

www.zdnet.com/zdnn/content/zdnn/1201/249834.html (See article:
"*FamilyPC* Details Findings of 'Net Parent' Survey")

Web ratings

RSACi (www.rsac.org)

SafeSurf (www.safesurf.com)

ESRBI (www.esrb.org)

Shopping

Auction

First Auction (www.firstauction.com)

eBay (www.ebay.com)

Software ratings

ESRB Web site (www.esrb.org)

Software reviews

SuperKids Educational Software Review   (www.superkids.com)

The Review Zone   (www.TheReviewZone.com)

The Games Domain   (www.gamesdomain.com)

FamilyPC magazine (www.zdnet.com/familypc)

Travel planning

Citysearch.com (citysearch.com)

Microsoft Expedia (expedia.msn.com/forums/theme)

City.net (city.net)

MapQuest (www.mapquest.com)

Travel Industry Association of America (www.tia.org)

Preview Travel (destinations.previewtravel.com)

The Mining Co. (travelwithkids.miningco.com)

    (camping.miningco.com)

Disney (family.disney.com)

Web publishing tips

Intel Web site (www.intel.com)

PC RESOURCE MATERIALS

Computer books

Dummies series of books from IDG Books Worldwide

Internet for Dummies

PCs for Dummies

PCs for Kids and Parents

The Little PC Book (Peachpit Press)

Complete Idiot's Guide to PCs (QUE/McMillan Publishing)

How to Use Your Computer (ZD Press)

Computer magazines

FamilyPC

EasyComputing

Smart Computing

Computer Life

Magazines, books, and newsletters with software reviews

FamilyPC magazine

Smart Computing magazine

EasyComputing magazine

Great Software for Kids & Parents (IDG Books)

The Computer Museum's Guide to the Best Software for Kids
(HarperCollins Perennial)

The FamilyPC, Guide to Homework (co-published by Hyperion and
FamilyPC)

Children's Software (a quarterly newsletter jointly created by the
Department of Communication, Technology and Computing in
Education at Teachers College, Columbia University)

Game review magazines

Computer Gaming World

PC Gamer

Donated PC—collection and distribution

Computer Bank Charity (206) 365-4657

The Detwiler Foundation (619) 456-9045

Nonprofit Computing, Inc., New York (212) 759-2368

Internet directories for kids

300 Incredible Things for Kids on the Internet
by Ken Leebow (VIP)

Animal Lover's Guide to the Internet by Bonnie Shields
(K & B Products)

Cybersurfer: The Owl Internet Guide for Kids by Nyla Ahmad, Martha
Newbigging (Owl Communications)

Internet Directory for Kids & Parents (1st Ed) by Barbara Moran (IDG
Books Worldwide)

Internet for Kids (Teacher Created Materials)

Kids on the Internet: A Beginners Guide by Kim Mitchell (Instructional
Fair)

Kids Rule the Net: The Only Guide to the Internet by Kids by Michael Wolff (Wolff New Media)

Online Kids: A Young Surfer's Guide to Cyberspace by Preston Gralla (John Wiley & Sons)

The Internet Kids & Family Yellow Pages (2nd Ed) by Jean Armour Polly (Osborne McGraw-Hill)

Index

I

J

K

L